WITHDRAWN

Cultural Work and Higher Education

Cultural Work and Higher Education

Edited by

Daniel Ashton
Bath Spa University, UK

and

Caitriona Noonan
University of South Wales, UK

First published 2013 by
PALGRAVE MACMILLAN

Palgrave Macmillan in the UK is an imprint of Macmillan Publishers Limited,
registered in England, company number 785998, of Houndmills, Basingstoke,
Hampshire RG21 6XS.

Palgrave Macmillan in the US is a division of St Martin's Press LLC,
175 Fifth Avenue, New York, NY 10010.

Palgrave Macmillan is the global academic imprint of the above companies
and has companies and representatives throughout the world.

Palgrave® and Macmillan® are registered trademarks in the United States,
the United Kingdom, Europe and other countries.

ISBN 978–1–137–01393–4

This book is printed on paper suitable for recycling and made from fully
managed and sustained forest sources. Logging, pulping and manufacturing
processes are expected to conform to the environmental regulations of the
country of origin.

A catalogue record for this book is available from the British Library.

A catalog record for this book is available from the Library of Congress.

Contents

Tables

Contributors

Kim Allen is Research Fellow in the Education and Social Research Institute (ESRI) at Manchester Metropolitan University, UK. Before that she was Senior Research Fellow at the Institute for Policy Studies in Education (IPSE) at London Metropolitan University, UK. A feminist and sociologist of education, Kim's research focuses broadly on inequalities of social class and gender within educational spaces, with a particular focus on young people's career aspirations and transitions into the creative industries. Kim is co-investigator on the Economic and Social Research (ESRC) funded project 'Celebrity Culture and Young People's Classed and Gendered Aspirations' (http://www.celebyouth.org/).

Daniel Ashton is Senior Lecturer at Bath Spa University, UK and teaches on the media communications and creative media practice degree courses. His research addresses the links between cultural work and higher education in relation to identity, employability and cultural workforce issues. His work appears in: *Convergence*; *Journal of Cultural Economy*; *Journal of Education and Work*; *Information Technology and People*; *Media Education Research Journal*; and *Art, Design and Communication in Higher Education*. He is also on the editorial boards of *Digital Culture & Education* and *Media Education Research Journal*.

Richard Berger is Associate Professor at the Centre for Excellence in Media Practice (CEMP), Bournemouth University, UK. He is also editor of the *Media Education Research Journal*. Richard's main research interests are in literary adaptation, pedagogy and literacy.

David Lee is Lecturer in Documentary in the Institute of Communications Studies at the University of Leeds, UK. David's research focuses on creative labour, copyright, cultural production, television studies and cultural policy. He is currently a co-investigator on two major research grants: the ESRC-funded study 'Communicating Copyright: An Exploration of Copyright Discourses in the Digital Age' and the AHRC-funded project 'Cultural Policy under the Labour Government, from 1997 to 2010'. Before academia, David worked in television production, policy research and consultancy. This included working at the BBC within current affairs and documentary production, on programme strands such as *Newsnight, Panorama* and *The Money Programme.*

Karen Littleton is Professor of Psychology in Education at the Open University, UK, where she directs the Centre for Research in Education and Educational Technology. Karen's research focuses on the significance of talk for learning, development and creativity. Her previous publications include *Collaborative Creativity* (with Dorothy Miell) and *Contemporary Identities of Creativity and Creative Work* (with Stephanie Taylor).

Susan Luckman is Associate Professor and Associate Head of School at the School of Communication, International Studies and Languages, University of South Australia, Australia. She was a foundation member of the ARC Cultural Research Network. She is the author of *Locating Cultural Work: The Politics and Poetics of Rural, Regional and Remote Creativity*; co-editor of an anthology on creative music cultures and the global economy (*Sonic Synergies*, 2008); author of numerous book chapters, peer-reviewed journal articles and government reports on creative cultures and industries.

Annette Naudin is Senior Lecturer in Creative and Media Enterprise and is an Enterprise Education Fellow of the National Centre for Graduate Entrepreneurship. Annette developed her entrepreneurial experience by setting up and running her own successful creative business, but she is now firmly set on an academic career and is undertaking a PhD at the Centre for Cultural Policy Studies, University of Warwick, UK, exploring cultural entrepreneurship.

Caitriona Noonan is Lecturer in Media, Culture and Communication at the Cardiff School of Creative and Cultural Industries, University of South Wales, UK. Her research interests include cultural policy decision-making, the concept of the 'creative city', and production cultures and professional identity. Her work has appeared in the *International Journal of Cultural Policy, Media History* and the *European Journal of Cultural Studies*. She is also on the editorial board of the *Media Education Research Journal*.

Kate Oakley is Professor of Cultural Policy at the University of Leeds, UK and Visiting Professor at the University of the Arts London. Her research interests include the politics of cultural policy, work in the cultural industries and regional development. She came into academia following careers as a journalist, market researcher and civil servant, and she worked for a long time as an independent consultant and policy analyst.

Emma Pollard is Senior Research Fellow at the Institute for Employment Studies, UK and leads their research on higher education. She has been researching education and employment policy and practice for many years, using both quantitative and qualitative methodologies, and has been involved in and led a wide range of projects for educational establishments, policy bodies and employers. Her key research interests include student choices and decisions about undergraduate and postgraduate study, diversity in students' higher education experiences, graduate transitions to the labour market and their early careers, and the workings of higher education.

Anamik Saha is Lecturer in Communications Studies at the Institute of Communications Studies, University of Leeds, UK. He completed his PhD in sociology at Goldsmiths, University of London. His research interests are in 'race' and the cultural industries, and in particular, the politics of British Asian cultural production.

Stephanie Taylor is Senior Lecturer in Psychology in the Faculty of Social Sciences at the Open University, UK. Her research employs a narrative-discursive approach to explore identification and a complex, divided subject. Her books include *Narratives of Identity and Place* (2010) and *What Is Discourse Analysis?* (forthcoming). She is co-editor, with Mark Banks and Rosalind Gill, of the collection *Theorizing Cultural Work*.

Jonathan Wardle is Director of Curriculum at the National Film and Television School, UK. Jon's main research interests are in digital media and learning and practical learning.

Marketa Zezulkova is a doctoral researcher at CEMP, Bournemouth University, UK. Her particular research interests are in media literacies and philosophy of education.

Cultural Work and Higher Education

Daniel Ashton and Caitriona Noonan

Over the last few decades, policy-makers have been busy in the fields of cultural industries and higher education (HE), as both undergo significant changes in an era of globalization, economic instability and austerity agendas. However, there has been a marked difference in the ways in which both these spheres have responded to the opportunities and challenges that they currently face. Despite ambiguities in their definition (Galloway and Dunlop, 2007), the cultural industries, or more accurately their partial political successor, the creative industries, have emerged as one of the most celebrated sectors of the UK economy (Confederation of British Industry, 2010). With strong, albeit controversial (Garnham, 2005; Tremblay, 2011), growth figures reported, these industries have been reframed and endorsed as part of a new knowledge economy for a digital society.[1] As a result, the sector is often framed as a panacea to numerous and often disparate financial and social ills, including economic development, urban regeneration and remedying social inequalities. At this moment, HE in the UK seems to lie on the other end of the spectrum of political taste. If cultural and creative industries are associated with and characterized by neoliberal values and ideals of flexibility, enterprise, competition and modernity, HE is often criticized for being old-fashioned, bureaucratic and in need of reform so as to bring it up to speed with the needs of a globalized economy. Focusing primarily on the UK, but attentive to global debates, this volume critically explores the relationship between cultural work and HE and provides an opportunity to reflect upon the changing forms and functions of HE and how it is being called upon to contribute to the development of cultural workers at a time of significant change.

Like never before, HE is facing a major interrogation of its role and the fundamental values which underpin it, along with threats to the

1

financial viability of some of its institutions. Many in the academy have reflected on this battleground (Bailey and Freedman, 2011; Zelizer, 2011; Collini, 2012), with responses to this challenge varying. Some argue that this is a necessary part of the evolution of any institution as it responds to increased competition and a reduction of public funding, and as it attempts to counter those who label it elitist, self-indulgent and paternalistic. On the other hand, there are those who argue that the continued autonomy of institutions is worth maintaining and that universities continue to fulfil an essential societal role through their range of research, teaching and ancillary activities.[2] As a result of this uncertain ground, one of the main shifts within the academy concerns the ways in which its functions are increasingly being fused with the drive for economic growth. Such privileging of economic goals proves particularly uncomfortable for many – especially those within the arts and humanities, where the metrics to calculate value are largely subjective and out of step with the current market-led approach to measuring performance (see Brown et al., 2012).

It is against this background that this volume critically interrogates the complex entanglement of the cultural sector and HE – a relationship defined at times by collaboration and at other times by collision. The intersections between cultural work and HE are hugely significant and enacted at a macro level through government policy interventions and employer-led demands for 'industry-ready talent', and at a micro-level in the work placements, professional accreditation, critically reflective modules and creative practice simulations which have increasingly become part of the everyday curriculum and research agendas of departments and institutions aligned with these sectors. Furthermore, this intersection is realized through a complex series of relationships with industry and other external stakeholders which are likely to become more embedded and normalized in the future. Therefore, this volume and its contributors ask, 'as the cultural and creative industries and HE become more entwined, what are the rewards of such a merger and, crucially, what is at stake?'

Culture: Industry, work, life

There has been a sizeable academic interest in the cultural and creative industries, partly in response to the various government-led programmes which have attempted to provide a strategic plan for the industry in the UK. Scholarly attention has included the historic origins of this intervention and its current limitations (Garnham,

2005; Schlesinger, 2007), and the geographical and symbolic space these industries occupy (Landry, 2000; Florida, 2002; Pratt, 2004). For Hesmondhalgh (2008, p. 563), however, 'serious attention to cultural work represents something of a gap in the analysis of creative and cultural industries'. While the nature of 'work' performed within these sectors has in recent years come under some scrutiny from academics (Banks, 2007; Banks and Hesmondhalgh, 2009; Oakley, 2009; Hesmondhalgh and Baker, 2011) and professional groupings (Saundry et al., 2007), training and education rarely occupy a central interest. Specifically, the relationship between HE and work in the sector has not been critically interrogated in terms of how HE may reproduce problematic aspects of various industry work practices, values and identities.

In establishing the scope for this volume, there are a number of uncertainties around the application of labels and terminology. Many discussions of the cultural and creative industries begin with an account of the conceptual ambiguities and inconsistency of terminology which surround these labels. Both Galloway and Dunlop (2007) and Hesmondhalgh (2008) chart the etymology of these terms, in particular how the radical ambitions for the UK's cultural industries in the 1980s were eventually subsumed by the conformist and largely market-driven agenda of the New Labour political party which came to power in 1997.[3] In particular, critics argue that the economic rationale continues to loom large over any questions on the public value of culture (Garnham, 2005; Galloway and Dunlop, 2007; Hesmondhalgh, 2008). There is no clear consensus in the debates and policy frameworks that attempt to define and locate the cultural and creative industries. Confusion occurs over the way these terms are applied interchangeably and, as Miller (2009) addresses, rhetorically deployed and positioned. For Banks and O'Connor (2009, p. 366), there are various rhetorical slippages, as they can be understood as a 'distinctive economic grouping, a framework for conjoining certain types of intellectual or artistic labour, or simply a shapeless policy construct'. Similarly, for Galloway and Dunlop (2007, p. 29), 'creative industry' has proved difficult to define coherently as 'once the layers are discarded at heart it appears an amorphous entity, with no specific cultural content at all'. Taking a global perspective, Cunningham (2009) identifies several variations on the cultural and creative industries theme as it has travelled around the world, and points to the varying emphases and outcomes across the USA, Europe, Asia, China, Australasia and the global South (see also Keane, 2009 on China; and Power, 2009 on Nordic and Scandinavian countries). These conceptual ambiguities have implications for theory, industry and policy analysis as specific agendas, interventions and stakeholders negotiate for ideological control. In this introduction, we note the importance of being attentive to different 'theoretical lineages and policy contexts' (Hesmondhalgh, 2008, p. 552) of the terms 'cultural' and 'creative industries' but employ both in recognition of the ambiguities and the different usages across contributors. As Hesmondhalgh (2008, p. 552) suggests, 'for all the considerable difficulties of scope and definition they raise, it is clear that both concepts refer to a domain that no serious cultural analysis can afford to ignore: how cultural goods are produced and disseminated in modern economies and societies'. The following now turns to processes of cultural production.

This volume employs the phrase 'cultural work' for its title. Following Banks (2007, p. 3), this refers to 'the act of labour within the industrialized process of cultural production'. As Hesmondhalgh and Baker (2011, p. 9) point out, in elaborating on their choice of 'creative labour' compared to Banks' 'cultural work', these terms raise problems of boundary and definition.[4] Furthermore, for those studying cultural work, a fundamental tension arises when we ask, what counts as cultural work? One obvious starting point to make sense of this may be the Department of Culture, Media and Sport's (DCMS) (2001) *Mapping Document* and the 13 sectors therein: advertising; architecture; art and antiques; computer games; crafts; design; designer fashion; film and video; music; performing arts; publishing; software; and TV and radio. However, in their discussion of the research design deployed in their study, Hesmondhalgh and Baker (2011, p. 10) argue against the treatment of the cultural and creative industries as an 'undifferentiated mass'. Elsewhere, Caldwell (2009, p. 200) notes that ' "the" industry is comprised of numerous, sometimes conflicted and competing socio-professional communities'. In any of these sectors, workers will have very different experiences of working conditions, practices and associated professional identities (e.g. freelance and permanent employment; public service versus profit orientated; different genres of output), and quite often move flexibly between these contexts. Attempts to reach a coherent definition of the sector are complicated further when we take into account how workers outside these sectors, but in 'creative roles' (e.g. marketing, advertising and communication) and so-called 'embedded creatives' (Higgs and Cunningham, 2008) working in fields such as healthcare, might feature within investigations and theorizations of cultural work given that they are likely to encounter a very different set of occupational challenges.

Further to these obstacles in defining cultural work, 'co-creative' (Banks and Deuze, 2009) processes through which consumers participate in the process of making and circulating media content also present challenges for identifying a discrete sector of 'workers', as the 'line between paid and unpaid work, between "professionals" and "amateurs" is often blurred' (Hesmondhalgh and Baker, 2011, p. 13). Within the context of participatory culture (Delwiche and Henderson, 2012) and 'web 2.0' (Gauntlett, 2011), conceptualizations of cultural work are unsettled by practices of those 'people formerly known as the audiences' (Rosen, 2006). Through their practices of production (e.g. producing videos for uploading onto sites like YouTube), the boundaries of cultural production and understanding of who cultural producers are become extended and reconfigured. These activities are framed by some as the 'devaluation' of cultural work, while others argue that they exist within and contribute to creative communities and professional identities (Hesmondhalgh, 2010). Irrespective of the view taken, these actions stretch and disrupt further our understanding of cultural production and complicate attempts to critically engage with cultural work as an object of study.

Moving past these conceptual deliberations for a moment, the work performed in the cultural and creative industries can be seen as emblematic of the conditions of modern labour. The celebratory framing of creative and cultural work as 'good work', as defined by creative freedom, autonomy, self-fulfilment and economic rewards, often masks more problematic and inequitable conditions that characterize the sector: long hours, low pay, limited benefits and 'self-exploitation'. Hesmondhalgh (2008, p. 563) points to Towse's (1992) summary of the modus operandi of the artistic labour market, including: its reliance on self-employed and freelance workers; the precarious and temporal nature of work contracts; the potentially exploitative nature of the work, such as long working hours and low pay, where career prospects are uncertain; and the inequity of the earnings and employment opportunities according to social class, gender and ethnicity (see Creative Skillset, 2009a). Despite some attempts to address these issues at both industry and policy level (e.g. in diversity policies and strategies for access) there is clearly some way to go and many of these problematic features have been taken up and scrutinized elsewhere. For example, both McRobbie (2002) and Gill (2002) examine the gendered aspects of these working conditions, challenging the myth of the industry as 'cool, creative and egalitarian' (Gill, 2002). These authors usefully broaden the study of the cultural worker and their experiences of both 'good' and 'bad' work, offering an important critique of the valorization of cultural work which features heavily in policy for the cultural and creative industries.

Meaningful engagement with the conditions of work becomes even more important as the creative and cultural workforce appears to be growing and its appeal spreading.[5] The *Creative Graduates Creative Futures* (Ball et al., 2010; see also Pollard, this volume) report on the career patterns of graduates in art, design and crafts identifies that the cultural and creative industries are heavily reliant on HE graduates, with this group now making up 73 per cent of the workforce, compared to 66 per cent in 2003 (Creative Skillset, 2009b). In the UK, since 1999/2000 there have been above-average increases in enrolments in 'mass communications' and 'creative arts and design' (UK Universities, 2010). Media studies as a subject shows 'an increase of 150 per cent between 1999/2000 and 2008/2009' and 'creative arts and design also continue to show a significant increase (64 per cent overall)' (UK Universities, 2010, p. 27). However, the legitimacy of this expansion also raises concerns. Drawing on data collected from the Higher Education Statistics Agency, Comunian et al. (2011) demonstrate that 'Bohemian graduates' (i.e. those in artistic or creative subjects) face an uncertain and challenging labour market and that there are both 'winners and losers' following graduation. They conclude that the growth of creative disciplines in HE has 'expanded the provision of those skills without real corresponding opportunities' (p. 305). The result is oversupply, and the cycle of lower economic prospects and precarious working conditions continue. All of this structural data suggests, therefore, that there is an acute need to move discussions of cultural work forward and to do this not only in terms of the quantity of jobs but also in terms of the quality and conditions of the work encountered. It also reiterates the role and impact of HE in the creative ecology and how its agenda could feed some of the structural issues encountered by workers.

Work and education within cultural policy

The cultural policy landscape in the UK is very complex, being conditioned by and composed of multi-level, multi-actor and multi-sectoral interventions across a number of ministries including the Treasury, the Department of Business, Innovation and Skills (BIS), the Department of Culture, Media and Sport (DCMS) and the Department for Education (DfE) – with official thinking among these groups 'circulat[ing] in a dominant culture of largely uncritical acceptance' (Schlesinger, 2007, p. 377). 'Creativity', in particular, has established itself as a hegemonic term in this elaborate framework of policy ideas (Schlesinger, 2007). Discourses of 'talent' and 'creativity' resonate strongly in many of the documents in this field and have a long lineage within the policy agenda (Black, 2006). Paradoxically, while they are now more visible and banal they are also applied more instrumentally and narrowly with official rhetoric often conceiving of creativity predominantly in terms of economic gain.

Notions of creative talent – and the imperative for education to foster this – can be traced to early New Labour strategies, with the Secretary of State for Culture, Media and Sport at the time, Chris Smith, stating in the *Creative Industries Mapping Document*, 'I want to see us putting creativity at the heart of education, encouraging our children to develop their innate talents' (cited in Department of Culture, Media and Sport, 2001, p. 3). Building on this, the DCMS strategy *Creative Britain* (2008) can be seen as a further blueprint for how to develop this talent and how it may be put to work in the creative economy. It is an approach Banks (2007, p. 81) connects with management literature that locates creativity as a form of human capital:

> [I]n business and management discourse the idea that creativity is a product of individual 'inner conditions' is pervasive, and continues to stimulate a whole range of behaviouristic interventions designed to make employees harness their creative potential for productive ends.

The *Creative Britain* report was explicit in its view of the intersections between HE and the working contexts of these industries. In the 'Foreword by the Prime Minister' to *Creative Britain,* former Prime Minister, Gordon Brown (DCMS, 2008, p. 1) highlights the (then) government's priority 'to help more people discover and develop their talents and to use those talents to build a dynamic and vibrant society, providing entertainment alongside opportunity'. Brown (DCMS, 2008, p. 7) goes on to signal the approach to helping this creative talent 'flourish', and states that, 'having unlocked creativity, the vital stage is to ensure that young people have real opportunities to develop, and that they can see clearly the directions in which their talent can take them'. While personal fulfilment is part of this, the key message is that these talents should be market orientated. Therefore, the education system becomes an important partner in the discovery of talents and subsequently directs these to become commercially exploitable resources (Thornham and O'Sullivan, 2004; Ashton, 2011a).

For Banks and Hesmondhalgh (2009, p. 426) the positioning of the cultural industries under the 'creative economy' canopy in the *Creative Britain* report indicates a policy direction in which cultural labour and employment are conceived in terms of 'a concerted drive to develop workplace skills, stimulate business-orientated education and improve competitive advantage across the creative industry sector'. Such discursive and political framing of the creative economy and its relationship to education is significant. As Banks and Hesmondhalgh (2009, p. 427) suggest, the move to ensure that higher education institutions (HEIs) prioritize 'economically valuable skills' and meet the 'needs of employers' has placed under threat 'the role of further and higher education in providing a relatively informal context for creative diversity and for experimental cultural production'.

Student *professionals* at the heart of the system

The last decade has also signalled a series of major changes in the function and form of HE, particularly in the UK as it undergoes a period of self-reflection and introspection (Collini, 2012). Changes to funding structures, the possibilities afforded by new technologies, a changing student body as a result of Widening Participation agendas, and the introduction of management intervention in the form of metrics and the language of business have all resulted in considerable changes to the way HE is conceived of and delivered. Instrumental attitudes to education, threats to academic freedoms and the explosion of official and unofficial emphasis on employability are features that increasingly characterize HE provision both in the UK and beyond.

The historical coupling of education and work-related policy can be traced back to the Robbins Report (1963), which recommended the expansion of HE in the UK and identified 'instruction in skills for employment' as one of the central purposes of HE. This view was subsequently developed by the Dearing Review (1997) and the 'Life-long Learning' agenda which expressed that, alongside contributions to society and personal fulfilment, individuals should be well equipped for work and that HE must play a significant role in delivering this.

It is against this background that we can trace the development of media studies as an 'unruly' (Geraghty, 2002) academic discipline in the UK. According to Durant (1991, p. 416), 'media studies programmes (like programmes in virtually all other academic fields) are composites, having forged apparently distinct identities out of a range of often contradictory materials in an over determined history'. In relation to media studies, the composite materials were drawn from three pre-existing fields: English studies, sociology and vocational media training. As a result, one of the main difficulties for the discipline of media studies has been its negotiation of reflective theory and creative practice, leading to much ongoing public criticism of the discipline focusing on the supposed 'unemployability' of media studies graduates providing further context in which other critiques around standards and value can take place (Thornham and O'Sullivan, 2004). As policy around creative industries has grown a concurrent shift has occurred in HE structures and provision with media studies and creative industries education increasingly fused together. However, the increased emphasis in curriculum development and content on students' transition into the cultural and creative industries can represent a further tension in programmes which aim for a critical and reflective space. Indeed for Miller (2008, foreword in Bolas, 2009, p. xi), 'media studies [...] has become something akin to a handservant of government and money via the popular uptake of the "creative industries", complete with a utopic faith in media access that denies the power and malevolence of corporate control and valorizes the folksy myths of entrepreneurship'. Addressing this criticism is a pressing issue for the discipline and debating whether there is space for both is something which is considered by the contributors to this volume.

Today, across all disciplines there is marked investment in HE in the UK in orientating and facilitating teaching and learning so that graduates can 'hit the ground running' in the labour market, and to foster future flexible workers. Most recently, the prioritizing of economic discourses in HE policy was manifest in the government-commissioned Browne Review (2010) and its changes to HE funding and student finance. Some argue this has signalled the surrender of HE to the logic of the market (Collini, 2012), in which the purpose of HE is framed as delivering solely for the economy.

In June 2011, the Department of Business, Innovation and Skills (BIS) released its *Students at the Heart of the System* white paper which stated the government's intention to 'create the conditions to encourage greater collaboration between HEIs and employers to ensure that students gain the knowledge and skills they need to embark on rewarding careers' (BIS, 2011, p. 33). This strategy is further evidence of the ever-increasing overlap between work and HE. As Knight and Yorke (2003, p. 3) highlight, 'in the UK higher education institutions (HEIs) are now charged with promoting graduate employability'. Today, as a result of the above policy foundations, there is an assumption within university management, curriculum development and teaching that transferable employment skills are – and should be – central to the concerns of HE staff, an assumption which is firmly embedded and increasingly difficult to move against (Thornham and O'Sullivan, 2004, p. 722).[6] A further development of this employability agenda has been the move away from a focus on developing general employability to more sector-specific skills; as Willis (2010) argues in her work on creative professionals, 'professionalism' is held out as a benchmark to which students can aspire and orientate themselves (see also, Brennan, 2008). Despite research data highlighting an oversupply of creative graduates (Comunian et al., 2011), HEIs are increasingly monitored in relation to 'enhancing employability' with graduate labour market outcomes gathered through instruments such as the Destinations and Leavers from Higher Education (DLHE) survey and data included in the Key Information Set (see Higher Education Funding Council for England, n.d.).[7] Strategies to enhance employability include the introduction of work placements and simulations, research collaborations with industry, and bringing practitioners into the design and delivery of the curriculum. Employability literature has consistently emphasized the importance of work placements and internships for gaining insights and securing employment post-graduation. For example:

> Internships are today an essential part of the career ladder in many professions. They are part and parcel of a modern, flexible economy and are useful both for interns and for employers. Indeed, many professional employers put a great deal of time and effort into their internships. Where once they were an informal means of gaining practical insight into a particular career, today internships are a rung on the ladder to success.
>
> (The Panel on Fair Access to the Professions, 2009)

Yet, despite these opportunities to professionalize, concerns remain that HE is not delivering for the creative economy. For example, Creative Skillset (2009b), the skills council responsible for the creative sector, has warned that despite an oversupply of willing graduates competing for jobs in the sector, the industry is reporting that HE is failing to deliver the right kinds of skills needed. Reports from various skills councils indicate serious skills shortages in areas such as digital technology and multi-platform capability, broadcast engineering, business and commercial know-how, visual effects and craft-orientated jobs (see Creative & Cultural Skills and Creative Skillset, 2011). As Guile (2010, p. 470) notes, 'despite universities' close links with this sector, studying for a C&C-related [creative and cultural] degree rarely provides an expectation or understanding of what is required in vocational contexts'. Again, the pressure is placed on the HE sector to remedy this, for example, through ensuring a 'greater uptake of Skillset-backed courses and accreditation services, such as Skillset Academies [...] strongly supported by employers' (Creative Skillset, 2009b).

Structure of this volume

This volume aims to critically explore some of these intersections between HE and the cultural and creative industries. Building on the literature and policy shifts discussed above, this book is positioned at the nexus between HE and cultural work and is intended as a way of stretching our critical engagement with formal educational spaces and practices as they impact on cultural work identities and practices. The volume critically reflects on, and contributes to, some of the current debates on the nature of cultural work and cultural worker identities relating to issues such as instability, precariousness and exclusion. Some of the contributors analyse the role that HE plays in the (re)production of the social and cultural capital of workers and how this enables or constrains access to the sector for some groups. Other contributors reflect on HE as a space for students to think critically about the occupational characteristics and working conditions of the sector and their future working contexts, echoing Henry Giroux's (2000) call for critical pedagogy within the broader education system today. In relation to the focus of this volume, we return to Banks and Hesmondhalgh's (2009, p. 427) statement that HE is a 'place where the values of autonomy [...] might be allowed to prosper' and ask how this autonomy and critical engagement might be sustained – and constrained – in an era of significant change for HE, its values and institutions. This volume therefore provokes its readers to think about how academics and students working within the fields of arts, design, creative production and media studies might engage critically with the themes and concerns outlined in this volume. Attending to the everyday practices of teaching and learning, chapters in this book investigate whether the academy is – or might be – a site in which a meaningful engagement with the questions of 'good' and 'bad' cultural work can be nurtured. For some, HE becomes a site where some of the structural challenges within the cultural and creative industries relating to access and equality can not only be highlighted but also partially resolved.

This volume aims to present a series of critical perspectives rooted in empirical research that can offer insights into the experiences of students as 'cultural workers in-the-making' (Ashton, 2010, 2011b, 2013). As outlined previously, any contribution to this field will be conditioned by the conceptual ambiguity and uncertainty which threatens both the cultural and creative industries and HE. For that reason, the volume is deliberately interdisciplinary, drawing on the work of scholars in media and cultural studies, psychology, sociology and labour studies. This highlights the various approaches that are possible within this field and provides an opportunity for cross-disciplinary dialogue. The collection also addresses the experiences of staff, students and practitioners across a wide range of institutions: contributions come from universities and independent research institutes, and from across the HE sector.[8] While the focus is predominantly on the UK experience, research is also drawn from outside of the UK, where education along with economic and political interventions may differ depending on the structure of governance in that country, nation or region. For the purposes of this collection, and to challenge the view of the cultural and creative industries as a homogenous mass, we have also drawn on empirical research from a variety of industrial experiences (including television, film, advertising, digital gaming and art and design), and attend to a range of occupational levels (e.g. those established within the industry, recent graduates and students aspiring to a creative career). This adds to the richness of the volume as it attempts to combine a number of distinct but complementary perspectives. Importantly, many of the chapters ground their theoretical arguments in the actual voices and experiences of students/young workers as they seek to enter and work in the cultural and creative industries. This breadth and variety allow us to see the complex interplay of policy, values and practice in this ever-changing field.

This volume is divided into four inter-related sections: The dynamics of cultural work; cultural and creative industries and the curriculum; identities and transitions; and the politics of access. 'The Dynamics of Cultural Work' sets the scene for the volume, combining questions of policy and lived experience. For Oakley (2009), the announcement of formal apprenticeships suggests that the DCMS is, for the first time, explicitly considering issues of working within the cultural and creative sectors, not just as part of its skills policy or small business support, but as part of a broader focus on the cultural labour market itself. In her contribution to this volume, Oakley suggests that the dramatic changes in the role and funding of HE in recent years have seen the relationship between HE and cultural industries workplaces become 'more formal, more measured and more calculating'. Oakley's opening contribution identifies a number of key questions around critical engagement between academic research on cultural labour markets, the teaching of students and future directions in vocational education. Oakley identifies forms of critical engagement in relation to the growth of internships and the number of campaigning organizations raising awareness of working conditions and pay. For Oakley, this 'frenzy of activity suggests a policy environment that could in fact be responsive to labour market concerns', and HE is specifically identified as place in which such critical conversations can begin.

Pollard's empirical research provides a valuable large-scale snapshot of cultural work as experienced by creative graduates today. Presenting quantitative and qualitative data from the largest study of the early career patterns of graduates in art, design, crafts and media subjects from HEIs across the UK, this chapter captures the experience of 3,500 creative graduates as they reflect on their HE experience, their transition from university, how their working lives have developed since graduating, and their imagined working futures. Like Comunian et al. (2011), the data presented here signals the complexities of how students might, or might not, 'make their way' as cultural workers. In combining this data on student experiences and identity positions with careful analysis of labour markets, this chapter usefully contextualizes later chapters in this volume and provides further detail not generated in annual graduate destinations statistics.

The second section of this volume examines 'Cultural and Creative Industries and the Curriculum', and its contributors study the global mobility of workers, work-based learning, work placements and discourses of entrepreneurship as they feature in the contemporary HE landscape. In the first chapter of this section, Luckman draws links between the preparation of students within the university classroom and cultural workforce mobility. Luckman investigates notions of mobility and questions the desirability of the 'flexible' 24-hour hot-desking life that characterizes much 'frequent flier' cultural work. In examining how international students can prepare (and be prepared) for this globalized world of work, Luckman argues that international student recruitment facilitates students' immersion with other cultures, thus fostering students' understanding of the intercultural dimensions of cultural work.

Industry-orientated teaching experiences are addressed in Berger, Wardle and Zezulkova's chapter on work placements. This chapter draws on interviews with students and course leaders about their expectations and experiences of work placements and suggests how engagement with professional work contexts can be the 'foundation of an entire curriculum'. While recognizing that critical attention must be paid to the design and implementation of work placements, Berger et al. see these activities as a vital aspect of the vocational mandate of HE, supporting students as they enter an uncertain labour market characterized by 'portfolio working'. The shift from seeing work placements as industry-specific to having a wider pedagogic value is outlined with reference to the institutional resources and forms of reflections that should be supported by both teaching staff and employers. The possibilities afforded by moving away from a narrow employer-led, instrumental work placement agenda are raised here, and the authors form a dialogue with equality issues as raised by Lee and Allen in later chapters.

Following Oakley and Luckman's earlier discussion of the prevalence of self-employment and freelancing in the sector, Chapter 6 turns to the diverse entry routes and approaches into cultural work which characterize the sector. Based on a recognition that entrepreneurship and skills for self-employment are increasingly important in UK media courses (ADM-HEA and NESTA, 2007), Naudin presents a broad overview of entrepreneurship and a critique of its dominant discourses. Social entrepreneurship is introduced as an emerging discipline and, drawing on interviews with graduates and students, Naudin addresses the challenges and opportunities entrepreneurship offers creative industries students. Engaging with earlier chapters exploring professionalism, Naudin moves away from ready-made templates of enterprise education to offer a contextualized account for emphasizing lived experience which enables students to negotiate their professional development according to personal needs, skills and aspirations.

Complementing Pollard's earlier chapter, the third section of this volume, on 'Identities and Transitions', focuses on the experiences and aspirations of students as they enter HE, graduate and develop cultural work career trajectories. Firstly, Noonan considers students' choice to go to university in relation to work-life biographies. Drawing on qualitative research with first year media undergraduates, Noonan traces how students understand the nature of cultural work and conceptualize it in terms of their emerging professional identities. She considers wider factors such as place and institutional cultures in shaping students' views of their future within the industry. One of the main challenges identified by Noonan is how, as researchers and teachers, we balance a duty to foster students' enthusiasm for their futures as cultural workers with a critical understanding of some of the uncomfortable realities of work in the industry, as discussed earlier in this introduction.

The accounts of the complexities of working patterns and career choices presented in section one is a productive lead into Taylor and Littleton's chapter which discusses findings from research with cultural workers at the transition point between study and work. Taylor and Littleton explore the formation of creative identities and work through theorizations of the contemporary cultural worker. Drawing on interviews with students and alumni of London art colleges, Taylor and Littleton discuss recurrent images, constructions and conflicts within the creative identities of the cultural workers interviewed as part of their sample. Noting the under-representation of certain categories in the cultural and creative industries, and with a specific focus on the experiences of women creatives, Taylor and Littleton use theory from social, narrative and discursive psychology to explore the concept of 'deficient identities' and the repair work performed by cultural workers. They address the motivations and personal dimensions of cultural work and the investment in the personal aspects of cultural work as it compares to industry needs.

In the final chapter in this section, Ashton turns to the place of cultural industries practitioners working within HE and the contribution those with industry knowledge and expertise make to students' learning experiences. Empirical research with 'teacher-practitioners' from a range of industry sectors and disciplinary fields is drawn on to explore practitioner pathways into HE. Ashton draws on practitioners' career stories to identify common motivations around working conditions, security and quality of life in seeking employment within HE, and examines how industry practitioners shape the HE contexts through which students engage with industry. HE is understood as offering the time and space to investigate and explore possible interventions into the nature of cultural work, and Ashton closes by considering how teacher-practitioners can help students make sense of their emerging identities as cultural workers and critically reflect on their future cultural work environments.

Central to many of the chapters are the challenges of cultural labour markets, including unpaid work and insecurity, and the tensions of self-actualization and self-discipline. In pursuing these issues further, the final section addresses the 'Politics of Access' and presents critical reflections and interventions on the role and responsibilities of HE. Lee explores the role of networks and associations for cultural workers within the creative economy. Based on extensive field research into the British independent television industry and attentive to findings from other creative sectors, this chapter examines the implications of the shift towards a network culture and issues of social class exclusion associated with the dependency on who, rather than what, you know as the basis for securing employment. With reference to internships and work placements, Lee addresses how these networking practices – as both dependent on access to cultural and social capital and a site for capital accumulation – are embedded in HE practice and pedagogy. Lee assesses HE's position in either challenging or being complicit with reproducing such exclusions.

The next two chapters address questions of access to cultural work in relation to race and gender. Saha explores social and cultural barriers to entry in terms of how they impact upon representations of minorities in the media. Arguing against a policy discourse that assumes that improving minority representation in the cultural industries is simply a matter of increasing the numbers of non-white workers, Saha argues that the difficulties that minority cultural producers encounter are a result of the cultural and creative industries' shift towards deregulation and marketization, and that minority representation can only improve following deeper structural changes to the cultural and creative industries as a whole. For Saha, HE can provide a critical space in which future media practitioners from minority backgrounds can learn about and engage with issues of difference, and identifies the university as providing the requisite resources and safe environment in which to carry out such self-reflective work.

Responding to the gender imbalance in the sector – where women represent less than two-fifths of the cultural workforce – Allen draws together critical work on gender in the cultural industries (e.g. Gill, 2002; McRobbie, 2002) and literature on post-feminism and neoliberalism with empirical data from a qualitative study into student work placements in the cultural sector to interrogate how HE practices might contribute to this underrepresentation of women. She argues that dominant constructions of the 'creative' worker and normative workplace practices, encountered by female students in formative experiences of cultural work, reinforce gender-based inequalities within the cultural sector. In connection with earlier chapters on work placements, workplace identity and exclusion, Allen argues that these young women's gendered subjectivities were produced within their work placement experiences and examines how they negotiated gendered practices of exclusion. In closing, Allen turns our attention to the complexities of 'speaking the unspeakable' and breaking silences around discriminatory experiences in the cultural sector. Stressing the responsibility of HE practitioners to provide a space in which inequalities can be named, practical recommendations are introduced as part of her call for HE to challenge, rather than reproduce, inequalities in cultural work.

Attentive to David Buckingham's criticism that 'books on Media Education read rather like teachers' manifestos, which take learning entirely for granted' (1986, p. 81), the final chapter of this book reflects on some of the common themes and concerns of contributors and signposts some emerging agendas for scholarship and research. We recognize that the suggestions made are easy to propose in theory, but difficult to achieve in practice; however, we feel that such a reflection is needed if the sector and HE more widely are to successfully navigate their current paths.

Moving beyond a view in which HE is positioned as responding to employer demands and equipping students as 'industry-ready' talent, this volume raises questions about the nature of cultural work. These questions have emerged in conversation with some of the extant literature on cultural work and HE policy referenced in this introduction, and explores how HE may provide openings for understanding cultural work *and* presenting different ways of working, different identity dispositions and different social concerns. Raising questions of working practices and conditions echoes the educational critique of vocationalism as outlined by Ryan (2003, p. 15): 'it is faulted both for a general lack of moral and political perspectives and – a contemporary twist – for an uncritical acceptance of work as currently organized, with all its hierarchy and inequality'. In identifying and mapping the multiple connections between HE and working in the creative and cultural industries, contributions across this volume highlight moral and political questions that cover the role and responsibilities of universities, HE practitioners and students and the future of cultural work.

Notes

1. According to economic estimates (DCMS, 2011) in 2009, the creative industries accounted for 2.89 per cent of gross value added (GVA) in the UK, 10.6 per cent of the UK's exports and employed 1.5 million people either directly or in a creative role in another industry (5.14 per cent of UK employment).
2. An example of this counter perspective is the Council for the Defence of British Universities (CDBU), which was launched in November 2012 following a conference in London the previous year titled 'Universities Under Attack'. The CDBU's manifesto calls for universities to be free to pursue research 'without regard to its immediate economic benefit' and stresses 'the principle of institutional autonomy' (www.cdbu.org.uk). The council's initial 65-strong

membership includes 16 peers from the House of Lords plus a number of prominent figures from outside the academy.
3. For a critical discussion of New Labour policy on the creative/cultural industries see Banks and Hesmondhalgh (2009) and Comunian et al. (2011).
4. Again, in recognizing the different backgrounds and orientations of contributors no prescriptions were made on usage in this volume.
5. In employment terms between 2008 and 2009 there was a small increase in the workforce (up from 1.44 million to 1.5 million employed) (DCMS, 2011). There has also been a small increase in the number of creative enterprises in the UK (4.9 per cent to 5.1 per cent) (DCMS, 2011).
6. While these reports are specific to the UK, and England within that, similar ideologies exist elsewhere across Europe with such policies often being global in scope (Smith et al., 2008).
7. The Destination of Leavers from Higher Education survey 'collects information on what leavers from higher education programmes are doing six months after qualifying from their HE course (employed, engaged in further study and so on)'. Key Information Sets (KIS) are 'comparable sets of information about full or part time undergraduate courses and are designed to meet the information needs of prospective students' (see Higher Education Funding Council for England, n.d.).
8. In 1992, polytechnics were reclassified as universities almost doubling the number of universities in the UK. A number of other HE colleges were also granted their university charter in the 2000s (see Collini, 2012 for a discussion of this development). This group is often referred to as the 'new university' sector. See Marr and Forsyth (2011) for a history of UK universities.

References

ADM-HEA and NESTA (2007) *Creating Entrepreneurship: Entrepreneurship Education for the Creative Industries* (London: ADM-HEA and NESTA).
Ashton, D. (2010) 'You Just End Up Feeling More Professional': Media Production and Industry-Ready Personhood, *Networks* 10: 14–19.
Ashton, D. (2011a) Pathways to Creativity: Self-Learning and Customising in/for the Creative Economy, *Journal of Cultural Economy* 4(2): 189–203.
Ashton, D. (2011b) Media Work and the Creative Industries: Identity Work, Professionalism and Employability, *Education and Training* 53(6): 546–560.
Ashton. D. (2013) Cultural Workers in-the-Making, *European Journal of Cultural Studies*. DOI: 10.1177/1367549413484308.
Bailey, M. and Freedman, D. (2011) *The Assault on Universities* (Cambridge: Pluto Press).
Ball, L., Pollard, E. and Stanley, N. (2010) *Creative Graduates Creative Futures* (Brighton: Creative Graduates Creative Futures Higher Education Partnership and the Institute for Employment Studies).
Banks, J. and Deuze, M. (2009) Co-Creative Labour, *International Journal of Cultural Studies* 12(5): 419–431.
Banks, M. (2007) *The Politics of Cultural Work* (Basingstoke: Palgrave Macmillan).

Banks, M. and Hesmondhalgh, D. (2009) Looking for Work in Creative Industries Policy, *International Journal of Cultural Policy* 15(4): 415–430.

Banks, M. and O'Connor, J. (2009) Introduction: After the Creative Industries, *International Journal of Cultural Policy* 15(4): 365–374.

Black, L. (2006) 'Making Britain a Gayer and More Cultivated Country': Wilson, Lee and the Creative Industries in the 1960s, *Contemporary British History* 20(3): 323–342.

Bolas, T. (2009) *Screen Education: From Film Appreciation to Media Studies* (London: Intellect).

Brennan, J. (2008) *The Flexible Professional in the Knowledge Society – New Demands on Higher Education in Europe* (Report to HEFCE by Centre for Higher Education Research and Information, The Open University). [Online] Available from: http://www.hefce.ac.uk/data/year/2008/theflexibleprofessional intheknowledgesocietyreflex-newdemandsonhighereducationineurope/

Brown, P., Lauder, H. and Ashton, D. (2012) *The Global Auction* (Oxford: Oxford University Press).

Browne, J. (2010) *Independent Review of Higher Education Funding and Student Finance* (London: Department for Business, Innovation and Skills).

Buckingham, D. (1986) Against Demystification: A Response to Teaching the Media, *Screen* 27(5): 80–95.

Caldwell, J.T. (2009) Cultures of Production: Studying Industry's Deep Texts, Reflexive Rituals, and Managed Self-Discourses, in Perren, A. and Holt, J. (eds) *Media Industries* (Oxford: Wiley Blackwell): 199–212.

Collini, S. (2012) *What Are Universities for?* (London: Penguin).

Comunian, R., Faggian, A. and Jewell, S. (2011) Winning and Losing in the Creative Industries: An Analysis of Creative Graduate's Career Opportunities Across Creative Disciplines, *Cultural Trends* 20(3–4): 291–308.

Confederation of British Industry (2010) *Creating Growth: A Blueprint for the Creative Industries* [Online] Available from: http://www.cbi.org.uk/media/943560/2010.07-cbi-blueprint-for-creative-industries.pdf [Accessed 11 July 2012].

Creative Skillset (2009a) *Employment Census 2009* [Online] Available from: http://www.creativeskillset.org/uploads/pdf/asset_14487.pdf?5 [Accessed 5 July 2012].

Creative Skillset (2009b) *Strategic Skills Assessment for the Creative Media Industry* [Online] Available from: http://www.creativeskillset.org/uploads/pdf/asset_14582.pdf [Accessed 5 July 2012].

Creative & Cultural Skills and Creative Skillset (2011) *Sector Skills Assessment for the Creative Industries of the UK* [Online] Available from: http://www.creativeskillset.org/uploads/pdf/asset_16295.pdf?4 [Accessed 14 November 2012].

Cunningham, S. (2009) Trojan Horse or Rorschach blot? Creative Industries Discourse Around the World, *International Journal of Cultural Studies* 15(4): 375–386.

Dearing, R. (1997) *National Committee of Inquiry into Higher Education* (London: Department for Education & Employment).

Delwiche, A. and Henderson, J.J. (2012) Introduction: What Is Participatory Culture?, in Delwiche, A. and Henderson, J.J. (eds.) *The Participatory Cultures Handbook* (London: Routledge): 3–9.

Department for Business, Innovation and Skills (2011) *Students at the Heart of the System* (London: BIS).

Department of Culture, Media and Sport (2001) *Creative Industries Mapping Document* (London: DCMS).

Department of Culture, Media and Sport (2008) *Creative Britain* (London: DCMS).

Department of Culture, Media and Sport (2011) *Creative Industries Economic Estimates: Full Statistical Release* [Online] http://www.culture.gov.uk/images/research/Creative-Industries-Economic-Estimates-Report-2011-update.pdf [Accessed 4 July 2012].

Durant, A. (1991) Noises Offscreen: Could a Crisis of Confidence Be Good for Media Studies? *Screen* 32(4): 407–428.

Florida, R. (2002) *The Rise of the Creative Class: And How it's Transforming Work, Leisure, Community and Everyday Life* (New York: BasicBooks).

Garnham, N. (2005) From Cultural to Creative Industries: An Analysis of the Implications of the 'Creative Industries' Approach to Arts and Media Policy Making in the UK, *International Journal of Cultural Policy* 11(1): 15–29.

Galloway, S. and Dunlop, S. (2007) A Critique of Definitions of the Cultural and Creative Industries Public Policy, *International Journal of Cultural Policy* 13(1): 17–31.

Gauntlett, D. (2011) *Making Is Connecting* (Cambridge: Polity).

Geraghty, C. (2002) 'Doing Media Studies': Reflections on an Unruly Discipline, *Art, Design & Communication in Higher Education* 1(1): 25–36.

Gill, R. (2002) Cool, Creative and Egalitarian? Exploring Gender in Project-Based New Media Work in Europe, *Information, Communication & Society* 5(1): 70–78.

Giroux, H. (2000) Cultural Politics and the Crisis of the University, *CultureMachine* 2 [Online] Available from: http://www.culturemachine.net/index.php/cm/article/viewArticle/309/294 [Accessed 16 June 2011].

Guile, D. (2010) Learning to Work in the Creative and Cultural Sector: News Spaces, Pedagogies and Expertise, *Journal of Education Policy* 25(4): 465–484.

Hesmondhalgh, D. (2008) Cultural and Creative Industries, in Bennett, T. and Frow, J. (eds) *The SAGE Handbook of Cultural Analysis* (London: SAGE): 552–569.

Hesmondhalgh, D. (2010) User-Generated Content, Free Labour and the Cultural Industries, *Ephemera: Theory & Politics in Organization* 10(3/4): 267–284.

Hesmondhalgh, D. and Baker, S. (2011) *Creative Labour: Media Work in Three Cultural Industries* (London: Routledge).

Higgs, P. and Cunningham, S. (2008) Embedded Creatives – Revealing the Extent and Contribution of Creative Professionals Working Throughout the Economy, *International Forum on the Creative Economy* 17–18 March 2008.

Higher Education Funding Council for England (n.d.) What we do – Learning and Teaching in Higher Education [Online] Available from: https://www.hefce.ac.uk/whatwedo/lt/ [Accessed 6 November 2012].

Keane, M. (2009) Creative Industries in China: Four Perspectives on Social Transformation, *International Journal of Cultural Policy* 15(4): 431–444.

Knight, P.T. and Yorke, M. (2003) Employability and Good Learning in Higher Education, *Teaching in Higher Education* 8(1): 3–16.

Landry, C. (2000) *The Creative City: A Toolkit for Urban Innovators* (London: Earthscan).

Marr, L. and Forsyth, R. (2011) *Identity Crisis: Working in Higher Education in the 21st Century* (Stoke on Trent: Trentham Books).

McRobbie, A. (2002) Fashion Culture: Creative Work, Female Individualization, *Feminist Review* 71(1): 52–62.

Miller, T. (2009) From Creative to Cultural Industries: Not All Industries Are Cultural, and No Industries Are Creative, *Cultural Studies* 23(1): 88–99.

Oakley, K (2009) '*Art Works*' – *Cultural Labour Markets: A Literature Review* (London: Creativity, Culture and Education).

Power, D. (2009) Culture, Creativity and Experience in Nordic and Scandinavian Cultural Policy, *International Journal of Cultural Policy* 15(4): 445–460.

Pratt, A. C. (2004) The Cultural Economy: A Call for Spatialised 'Production of Culture' Perspectives, *International Journal of Cultural Studies* 7(1): 117–128.

Robbins, C. (1963) *Committee on Higher Education* (London: HMSO).

Rosen, J. (2006) The People Formerly Known as the Audience, *Press Think* [Online] Available from: http://archive.pressthink.org/2006/06/27/ppl_frmr.html [Accessed 5 November 2012].

Saundry, R., Stuart, M. and Antcliff, V. (2007) Broadcasting Discontent – Freelancers, Trade Unions and the Internet, *New Technology, Work & Employment* 22(2): 178–191.

Schlesinger, P. (2007) Creativity: From Discourse to Doctrine? *Screen* 48(3): 399–387.

Smith, D., Comunian, R. and Taylor, C.F. (2008) Universities in the Cultural Economy: Bridging Innovation in Arts and humanities and the Creative Industries. *International Conference on Cultural Policy Research*, 9–12 July 2012.

Ryan, P. (2003) Evaluating Vocationalism, *European Journal of Education* 38(2): 147–162.

The Panel on Fair Access to the Professions (2009) *Unleashing Aspiration: The Final Report of the Panel on Fair Access to the Professions* (London: The Cabinet Office).

Thornham, S. and O'Sullivan, T. (2004) Chasing the Real: 'Employability' and the Media Studies Curriculum, *Media Culture Society* 26(5): 717–736.

Towse, R. (1992) The Labour Market for Artists, *Richerce Economiche* 46: 55–74.

Tremblay, G. (2011) Creative Statistics to Support Creative Economy Politics, *Media Culture & Society* 33(2): 289–298.

Universities UK (2010) *Patterns of Higher Education Institutions in the UK* Tenth Report. [Online] Available from: http://www.universitiesuk.ac.uk/Publications/Documents/PatternsOfHigherEducationInstitutionsInTheUK.pdf [Accessed 14 November 2012].

Willis, J. (2010) How Do Students in the Creative Arts Become Creative Professionals?, in Jackson, N. (ed.) *Learning to be Professional Through a Higher Education e-book* (2009–Available from: http://learningtobeprofessional.pbworks.com/w/page/15914981/Learning%20to%20be%20Professional%20through%20a%20Higher%20Education%20e-Book [Accessed 20 August 2012].

Zelizer, B. (ed.) (2011) *Making the University Matter* (London: Routledge).

Part I
The Dynamics of Cultural Work

1

Making Workers: Higher Education and the Cultural Industries Workplace

Kate Oakley

Introduction

The last 30 years or so have seen a rapid evolution in the relationship between higher education (HE) and the cultural industries. While HE has always been vital to the production of fine artists, designers and musicians, among others, the links between HE and the cultural workplace have often been as much social as vocational. As Frith and Horne (1987) pointed out and many studies have testified since, the experience of going away to college, full student grants, and the chance for a period of cultural and personal experimentation, were all more significant in terms of producing cultural workers than the provision of particular courses at universities. As late as 2000 or so, the role of universities as incubators of the cultural industries could be seen *primarily* as a by-product of their teaching, an aspect of their role in the incubation of certain aspects of youth culture, rather than the implementation of public policy.

This is not to say that policy has hitherto played no role. Any historical account of the collaborations between HE and cultural organizations in the UK would need to go back to the mid-19th century and the 1836 report of the Select Committee on Arts and Manufactures (Selwood, 1999). Its (now) familiar concern was to improve UK competition with European exports after the passing of free trade agreements. Some 170 years later, and the rhetoric hasn't changed that much. Government expectations of what universities should deliver still includes contributing to economic prosperity, nurturing skills development and offering professional training. But the global growth of the cultural and creative industries, both as a policy construct and as a sector of the economy (Cunningham, 2006), and the dramatic changes in the role and funding of HE, have seen this relationship become more formal, more directed and more calculating.

The growth in the number of degree courses in the creative arts and related areas has been paralleled by an increase in work-related learning in various forms; student work placements, internships, incubation and knowledge exchange programmes have all multiplied. In part, this reflects the fact that some sectors of the cultural industries, particularly the smaller firms who have been the subject of so much policy attention, display a suspicion of vocational qualifications and a preference for experiential learning in their recruits, a preference that HE increasingly seeks to satisfy (Guile, 2006). In this case, the argument is that the best way to prepare students for work in the cultural industries is to provide them with a mix of knowledge, skill and judgement, together with the networks of contacts:

> [T]his cultural capital is not just about the formal knowledge transmitted by education, it is about a way of acting, a way of understanding, a way of conceiving one's self-identity.
>
> (Raffo et al., 2000, p. 218)

Many academics now find themselves in closer contact with cultural labour markets, and are increasingly being asked to act as intermediaries between them and HE in a variety of ways that go beyond teaching. Yet as awareness of the problems of cultural labour markets becomes more evident, it is increasingly difficult to avoid asking questions. A growing body of evidence, about the nature of work in the creative industries and who gets it, the geographic distribution of such jobs, not to mention the deflation of the bubble of expectations about the growth in the creative industries themselves (DCMS, 2011), has challenged many of these assumptions.

Despite the meritocratic rhetoric, the cultural sectors in the UK, as elsewhere, are stratified by social class, ethnicity and gender (Skillset, 2010); characterized by long working hours, high levels of casualization and insecurity and the preponderance of unpaid work (Oakley, 2011). While many of the HE initiatives undertaken under a 'creative industries' rubric (broadly in the 2000 to 2008 period) were primarily focused on involving HE more explicitly in economic development, part of what one might consider a neoliberalizing of the university (Ross, 2009), there was nonetheless often an implicit assumption that work in the creative industries was 'good work'.

Such schemes were never egalitarian in emphasis, but they did reflect the goal of 'widening participation', as the New Labour government's policy for increasing the number of working-class students in HE was known (Dann et al., 2009). This, it was felt, was aided by the participation in such schemes of post-1992 universities, arts schools and other HE institutions (HEIs) outside the so-called 'research intensive' universities (the assumption being that such institutions had a more mixed social intake). Similarly, the idea of the 'creative city' and the use of the creative industries as a tool of regional development meant that HEIs across the country could become involved; not just those in London and the South East, the heartland of the UK's creative industry employment.

The aim of this chapter is to consider the relationship between HE and the cultural industries, particularly in the light of recent policy directives and the 'problematizing' of certain aspects of the cultural labour market. The focus of the chapter is primarily on the UK. While the growth of the cultural industries is an acknowledged global phenomenon (UNCTAD, 2010; Luckman this volume), as is what Nelson calls the 'corporate' university (Nelson and Watt, 1999), the particular expectations that students have about university and the practices of HE often differ. Despite the rhetoric about globalization, the development of the cultural industries is embedded within particular places, forms of industrial organization and social norms.

My argument is that in the UK the experience of full student grants and the practice of leaving home to study as an undergraduate created a particular kind of milieu in which cultural industries often thrived (Leadbeater and Oakley, 1999). Moreover, the assumptions underlying that system are often invoked by policy-makers and others (e.g. Universities UK, 2010), at the same time as the system itself is systematically being dismantled.

Changes to student funding and the introduction of fees have helped produce a more calculating relationship between students, HE and the labour market, one in which assumptions about the student experience, common even 20 years ago, no longer apply. Living away from home as an undergraduate is becoming less common, and is less likely to be the case for working-class than for middle-class students (Holdsworth and Patiniotis, 2005). In response, and as part of a concerted effort to try and replicate such conditions in a different era, universities have become more involved with formal or semi-formal collaborations and knowledge exchange programmes with the cultural sectors. The stated aim of these is often redistributive; to try and help overcome the acknowledged disadvantages, faced by female graduates, or those from working-class or ethnic minority backgrounds in trying to gain work in the cultural sectors. However, as with other creative industry initiatives (Oakley, 2013), by ignoring many of the longer-term structural problems of cultural work, particularly low pay and insecure working conditions, such schemes often end up replicating the exclusionary nature of labour markets themselves (Allen et al., 2010, 2012; Allen, this volume).

The challenge therefore is to consider what forms of critical engagement the academy needs to develop, both including and beyond the pedagogical issues. What is the role of critical engagement in the teaching of practice, the monitoring of work placements, the job fairs and the knowledge transfer projects? How does research on cultural labour markets inform debates about 'employability' or the practice of incubator schemes? And how does this fit into a wider debate about 'good work' at what, in many Western countries, is a time of rising unemployment?

Higher education and the knowledge economy

Despite the inability to establish a stable terminology (other cognate terms such as information economy, digital economy and creative economy still persist), the notion of a knowledge economy has been central, not only to economic policy, but to education and even social policy in the UK and other developed economies (Amin, 1994; Thompson, 2002; Bevir, 2005). There are subtle differences between these notions, but what they have in common is that they can be seen as a response to the post-war crisis in Fordist production and the Keynesian welfare state (Jessop, 2002). In place of Keynes comes Schumpeter and the centrality of innovation to economic growth. The cultural industries fit neatly into any such notion, with their dependence on new ideas and highly skilled labour, and indeed the riskiness and precariousness of employment and institutions can easily be repackaged as beneficial to 'creative destruction' (Cunningham, 2006).

In the case of the UK, this has been reflected in a series of government policy papers, beginning with the then Department of Trade and Industry's competitiveness white paper, *Our competitive future, building the knowledge-driven economy* (DTI, 1998), which was released shortly after New Labour came into office and established the tone of their economic policy thinking. This was followed by a series of reviews and policy papers aimed at addressing the relationship between HE and the economy, including the Lambert Review (HM Treasury, 2003), the Leitch Review of Skills (Leitch, 2006), and the Browne Review (Department of Business, Innovation and Skills, 2010), designed, as Stefan Collini noted:

> [T]o make 'contributing to economic growth' the overriding goal of a whole swathe of social, cultural and intellectual activities which had previously been understood and valued in other terms.
>
> (Collini, 2011, p. 9)

The Wilson Review of a few months later did its best to crystallize these fears with its reference to universities as, 'an integral part of the supply chain to business' (Wilson, 2012, p. 2). Even for those who claimed to be, or indeed were, unconcerned about the instrumentality of education policy in this period, here were genuine questions about how effective such initiatives could be, given the characteristics of cultural labour markets themselves.

Among these concerns was the idea that the models of so-called 'knowledge transfer' and collaboration which were being put in practice were drawn largely from science and technology, and did not adequately reflect the workings of the cultural sector (Crossick, 2006). The desire to reproduce the success of high technology regions such as Silicon Valley led to an initial over-emphasis on formal knowledge transfer activities and an initial concentration on 'spin-off and start-up' firms (Hague and Oakley, 2001). Despite the exceptional, rather than replicable nature of these examples, science and technology has remained the model for many knowledge transfer initiatives in a way that crucially underestimates the importance of the existing, often dense, sets of relationships between practice and education, production and consumption in the cultural sectors, and may over-estimate the ability of often very small organizations to collaborate with (relatively) large HEIs.

As a host of work in economic geography has demonstrated, the importance of HE within particular economies (much of this work has been done at the regional level) is largely determined by demand-side factors: the kind of businesses out there to employ people, rather than the role of the university *per se* (Cohen and Levinthal, 1990; Charles and Benneworth, 2001; Charles, 2003). Beyond the degree courses offered by universities, the wider milieu they create is often more important in the development of local cultural industries than the provision of particular skills. Universities employ highly educated professionals who are often willing to pay for high levels of both public and private cultural amenities; in their student populations, they provide a large and ready audience for cheap, often experimental music, art, film and so on (Leadbeater and Oakley, 1999), and they house substantial cultural assets of their own including art galleries, museums, theatres and film clubs (Luger and Goldstein, 1997).

As Lee notes (in this volume) the research suggests that this wider milieu does not just support individual consumption practices, important though that is, but enables small firms and freelancers to be more productive by giving them somewhere to tune into industry 'noise': rumours, impressions, recommendations, trade folklore and strategic information. Economic geographers have more recently been joined by writers on innovation in stressing the importance of public space and public institutions in creating 'interpretive spaces' where 'conversations' can take place in an atmosphere of trust and relative openness (Castells and Himanen, 2002; Verganti, 2003; Lester and Piore, 2004). Similarly, the relationship between consumption and production is a relationship long-attested to in the cultural sectors; where the producers and consumers are not just close but are often the same person (Frith and Horne, 1987).

In a sense, therefore, many of the activities badged as knowledge transfer, knowledge exchange or industry linkage are attempts to replicate processes (the teacher – practitioner in an art school, for example (Ashton, this volume), the social relationships between university 'ents' officers and up-and-coming bands) that were once a by-product of the normal existence of a university.

However, in current circumstances, where undergraduates are more likely to live at home (Higher Education Funding Council for England (HEFCE), 2009) and more likely to be doing paid work in their free time, these assumptions cannot simply be maintained.[1] New relationships between HE and the 'real world' are deemed necessary. But forging a relationship between HE and the workforce in the cultural sectors faces not only misunderstanding and difficulties in implementation but also resistance, and not just on the part of the academy.

'No course can re-create the experience of working' – meeting resistance

Although cultural labour markets have above-average representation of graduate labour, there is no simple coupling of qualification with employment trajectories. There are, of course, areas, from acting to museum curating, where formal training in a specific discipline is strongly linked to employment. But it is equally likely to be the case that a general humanities or social science degree, coupled with interest in consumption or personal practice, is what leads to a career in the cultural sectors. Such anomalies lie behind many of the misunderstandings of HE and the labour market's relationship, from the seemingly endless debate about the 'relevance' of media studies (it does not get you a job in the media, apparently) to the idea that the most important thing that a town or city lacking a vibrant cultural sector needs is an institution of higher learning, preferably with some vocational degrees.

Concomitant with the growth of cultural and creative industries as a sector of the economy, therefore, has been a growth in vocational education for these sectors.[2] In part this simply reflects a broadening and changing of media and cultural forms; fine art, music and design education have been part of higher and further education for some time, other newer forms are simply following in this line. But it also represents an increasingly vocational slant in post-compulsory education in general, and a formalization of what were once largely informal, tacit knowledge bases.

At the same time, employers themselves in the cultural industries have often shown equivocation about the relevance of formal vocational education (Guile, 2006). While a demand for 'better quality' specialist courses and more industry relevance continues in the more high-tech sectors of the industries such as video games (Livingston and Hope, 2010), the wider cultural industries remain the haunt of what one might call the 'educated, but not specifically trained' workforce.

According to Skillset, the publicly supported industry body charged with supporting skills and training in the UK, the television industry, is characterized as follows:

> Of those members of the TV workforce who hold an undergraduate degree or diploma 35 per cent have a qualification in Media Studies or a related subject (varying from 42% in Cable and Satellite TV, to 34% in Independent Production and 33% in Terrestrial TV). The vast majority (68%) hold a qualification in some other subject. In the wider Creative Media workforce a smaller proportion hold a Media Studies or related degree (28%).
>
> (Skillset, 2011, p. 11)

Many employers have not been 'trained' in the crafts they practice. They may have studied something else at college, were self-taught, or have failed in a variety of jobs and careers before they found their niche

(Towse, 1996). This has produced a culture of scepticism among employers and reliance instead on demonstrated experience or on what might be called the 'guru' method, whereby people's credentials are established by the quality of those they have worked with, rather than by paper qualifications.

More worryingly, this stress on learning-by-working also serves to legitimize the often long-term unpaid work that people undertake in order to enter the field. 'Paying your dues', demonstrating your commitment, mastering the attitudes and codes of behaviour that such jobs are said to require, are all ways in which the industry seeks to maintain its image as diverse and open, while operating exclusionary recruitment and retention practices (Gill, 2010; see Noonan this volume for student testimony on 'paying their dues').

For some commentators, this shift in public policy towards experiential learning opened up an opportunity for universities from which they, and students, could benefit (Guile, 2006; Guile and Okumoto, 2009). This argument is not simply that qualifications alone rarely provide access to cultural labour markets, but that the lack of diversity – socially, ethnically and in terms of gender – that such labour markets display, could most effectively be tackled by experiential learning schemes. Greenbank and Hepworth (2008), for example, argue that working-class students in particular are disadvantaging themselves in the labour market by concentrating on getting a 'good degree' rather than gaining labour market experience, as they are unaware that employers value experience as much, if not more, than degree results. Furthermore, they argue that mentoring schemes, work placements and internships, should be publicly supported and, in that way, rather than allowing them to operate simply though exclusive social networks, they could be 'opened up'; an argument that public policy-makers seems to be pursuing (Wilson, 2012).

However, research that looks specifically at the effect of work placements (Özbilgin and Tatli, 2006; Allen et al., 2010, 2012) reveals that such schemes often founder in their attempts to promote diversity of ethnicity, gender, class or disability. It found a general reluctance to acknowledge problems of inequality, both within host institutions and universities, when it comes to discussing work placements and that such schemes did little to help students identify, or even discuss, issues of inequality. Individuals are encouraged to 'fit in' and not complain when they experience feelings of exclusion. The rhetoric of openness and meritocracy is stubbornly adhered to; anyone who cannot succeed in such situations is viewed as unfit to enter the industries. Indeed:

[T]he discursive construction of the ideal work placement student and potential creative worker – with a currency on flexibility, enterprise and self-sufficiency – privileges whiteness, middle classness, masculinity and able-bodiedness.

(Allen et al., 2012, p. 6)

Equally problematic are the assumptions about what lies on the other side of such schemes; in other words, what are the characteristics of such labour markets? Many such schemes ask few questions about the conditions of work within the cultural industries themselves. These include the difficulties that working-class graduates have maintaining a career in fields which are often low paid, where they are paid at all. They face the need to accept unpaid work, not only as the price of entry, but also when shifting track or retraining (Randle and Culkin, 2009), not to mention the difficulties of sustaining long working hours and freelance careers once workers have families, mortgages and the like (Skillset, 2010).

Much of this was ignored by educators and policy-makers whose concern was often to secure representation of particular groups within the cultural labour market and were therefore resistant to hearing that the price of such representation was often high for the individuals involved (Allen et al., 2012; Oakley, 2013). It is important, I think, not to characterize this as an example of bad faith, or indifference, but to use it to understand the nature of the kind of conflicts produced by the changing landscape of HE and the changing expectations of students (McRobbie, 2011). Such dilemmas are sharpened when they come into contact with clear examples of exploitation, such as the case of unpaid internships.

This case is instructive for a discussion of HE's responsibility towards cultural labour, not because internships *per se* are initiated by HE (though many students will be undertaking them while studying), but because they demonstrate both the possibilities and limitations of a policy approach to improve working conditions.

Public policy and the issue of internships

Concern with the labour market itself – questions of representation and participation, let alone working hours, benefits, training, job security, health and safety and so on – almost never featured in the many hundreds of documents devoted to developing the creative industries. This lack of interest was in marked contrast to the growing volume of academic and other research in sociology (Miege, 1979; Ryan, 1992), cultural economics (Throsby, 1994), economic geography (Jarvis and Pratt, 2006), cultural studies (McRobbie, 1998; Ross, 2003; Miller et al., 2004) and so on.

As Banks and Hesmondhalgh (2009) have noted, public policy has tended to gloss over the problems of cultural labour markets, in part at least, because of the assumption that such work is inherently good. In addition, as argued above, much public policy work and the efforts of educators in both formal and informal education has been concerned with trying to ensure that questions of representation are attended to; that young people from disadvantaged backgrounds get into the cultural industries. The last thing such people want to hear is that work in the cultural industries itself is a problem, and as such they are often implicated in the silence that surrounds these issues. The image of the cultural industries as a desirable place to work is one that matters not only to boosterists and city marketers but also to community arts activists and teachers. The alternative seems to be to abandon the cultural sectors to those who are financially well protected enough to be able to cope with them, with all the implications that has not just for social justice, but for culture.

However, in the last few years, the problems of cultural work and the increasingly unrepresentative nature of the labour market, have become so apparent that policy-makers have been forced to pay some attention. The spur to action, however, was not a debate about labour markets *per se*, but concern with declining social mobility.

Creative Britain (DCMS, 2008), in some ways the 'last hurrah' of the New Labour creative industries period, had dipped its toe in the debate about cultural labour markets in the UK and had referenced the particular issue of unpaid internships as a barrier. Rather than regulate labour markets themselves, a notion that would have been anathema to New Labour, the suggestion was to create a parallel stream of entry – paid apprenticeships – which would use public money to create opportunities to work in the cultural sector largely for non-graduates and those deemed disadvantaged. But the relatively heavy bureaucracy of the system of paid apprenticeships that was proposed, and the fact that the New Labour government was rapidly running out of steam and more importantly money as the financial crisis bit, meant that implementation of *Creative Britain* was essentially abandoned.

The internships issue however continued to resonate, not particularly within the context of cultural work, but as part of a wider public conversation about (lack of) social mobility. Increasing inequality, not just in the UK, but in many developed (and developing) economies, and the relationship between this and declining social mobility had become an important political issue, albeit belatedly (Wilkinson and Pickett, 2009; Dorling, 2010).

The Panel on Fair Access to the Professions (Cabinet Office, 2009) was set up by the Prime Minister, Gordon Brown to see, 'what more could be done to ensure fair access to careers in key professions' (2009, p. 3). The use of 'more' here is interesting given how much had been done to undermine any chance of 'fair' access to the professions; defined in this report as law and medicine, management and business services (including finance), creative industries and the public sector professions. Indeed, the evidence presented was fairly sobering; while some 7 per cent of the UK population is privately educated at school, 75 per cent of judges, 70 per cent of finance directors, almost 50 per cent of top civil servants and 32 per cent of MPs were privately schooled.

Some of the starker data related to the cultural sectors, or at least to the media. While the average journalist born in 1958 came from a family with an income 5.5 per cent above the average, those born in 1970 came from families with an income 42.4 per cent above average.[3]

The role of social networks and extracurricular activities in helping young people enter the professions was again attested to, as was the importance of internships, presented, in this case rather benignly, as a way of picking up 'soft skills and confidence' (Cabinet Office, 2009, p. 40).

Public policy think tanks also became active in this area. The Social Market Foundation (SMF), an organization with hitherto little published interest in the creative industries, published *Disconnected,* a dismayingly complacent report on social mobility and the creative industries (SMF, 2010). A rather more critical line was taken by the Institute for Public Policy Research (IPPR) in its report *Why Interns Need a Fair Wage* (Lawton and Potter, 2010). In what seems to have become the generally accepted position (Wilson, 2012), it argued that unpaid internships essentially excluded from the labour market those from low-income families who could not afford the periods of unpaid work deemed necessary to gaining experiential knowledge. The issue also had geographical implications as many internships in the cultural industries would be undertaken in London and the South East of the UK where living costs are highest, effectively barring those from outside the region, or those who could not live with family or friends for nothing.

The injustice of unpaid internships, together with fact that in many cases they could be found to be illegal, meant that internships became a sort of lightning rod for wider problems.[4] The issue entered the political bloodstream in a way that many other injustices of labour markets had failed to do. A variety of campaigning organizations (Intern Aware, Graduate Fog, the Carrotworks Collective and The Precarious Workers Brigade, among others) acted to raise awareness and maintain a critical voice, while social enterprises and voluntary organizations such as Internocracy and New Deal of the Mind developed paid internships to counter what they saw as the core problem.

The case of Keri Hudson, who, with the help of the National Union of Journalists took her former employer to an employment tribunal in order to claim 'back pay' from her period as an unpaid intern, suggested that the law could, on occasion, have teeth in this area (Malik, 2011). Meanwhile, the UK's Deputy Prime Minister sought to identify himself with the issue, launching the government's social mobility strategy with the defiantly meritocratic, rather than egalitarian, statement that: 'The true test of fairness is distribution of opportunities' (Cabinet Office, 2011, p. 3). There was nothing in the strategy about the links between inequality and lack of mobility or any attempt to regulate pay or working conditions, though minimum wage legislation was to be enforced against employers using unpaid interns as workers.

Public bodies, such as the Arts Council, also entered the fray, largely seeking to clarify the current legal position on internships, provide guidance to employers on 'good practice' and make interns aware of their rights along with providing sources of information and guidance (ACE, 2011).

Such a frenzy of activity suggests a policy environment that could in fact be responsive to labour market concerns. More likely, however, the issue of internships has particular characteristics that make such apparent responsiveness possible. Firstly, as minimum wage legislation already covered the majority of those asked to work as interns, there was no need to introduce primary legislation. Secondly, the issue could easily be reframed as a meritocratic one – denial of opportunity – rather than an issue of inequality of outcome. As such it suited the politics of the current Coalition government, as well as it did the former New Labour government. This is not to suggest that an effective policy on unpaid internships would not have beneficial outcomes in terms of diversifying the labour market; nor that the removal of unpaid internships, if that is indeed what happens, is not the remedy of an injustice. It is more that such an outcome leaves unresolved equally troublesome issues of work in the cultural industries and beyond.

'You can make a killing, but you can't make a living': The cultural industries workplace

Debates about *quality* of work, as opposed to quantity or representativeness, have been absent from some of the more policy-focused discussion about work for what now seems like decades. In cultural labour markets such debates are particularly problematic, not least because even in the 'good times', when unemployment in the rest of the economy is not on the rise, there is a large reserve army of labour waiting to enter such sectors. This means that while there is pressure from below – as the campaign on unpaid internships demonstrates – it is often counteracted by the sheer number of people wishing to enter these labour markets at whatever cost.

In addition, even those undertaking critical work in the area have to contend with the frequent expressions of pleasure and commitment that cultural workers make. Gill, in her study of new media workers in the UK and the Netherlands, speaks of the 'extraordinary passion and enthusiasm' (2007, p. 12) that people have for their work and the many different elements of this passion: the sense of autonomy and opportunity, the playful and pleasurable nature of the work and the opportunity for community and political activism.

Alongside this, however, and often in the same research, the psychological costs of such work, experienced in manifold ways, is revealed. Some commentators relate this to particular structural changes in media markets. Ursell (2000) argued that decentralization in the TV market went along with the de-recognition of unions and collective wage bargaining, a process which made television companies more like other firms in the cultural sectors and that 'average earnings have dropped, and working terms and conditions have deteriorated' (Ursell, 2000, p. 805).

de Peuter and Dyer-Witheford examine the 'forced workaholism' of video game development (de Peuter and Dyer-Witheford, 2005) and the divisions of labour based on age, gender and parenthood. Meanwhile, Gill (2007) found that in new media freelancers in particular worked an average of 65 hours per week and that the lack of pension, insurance and paid holidays meant that many feared becoming older or regarded having children as something that they would not be able to combine with their working lives. Other writers similarly found that it was not uncommon to find freelancers in fashion, web design or TV working excessive hours, taking no holidays and pushing themselves to physical and psychological limits, not only because of looming externally imposed deadlines, but in some cases because of their own passion for their work (Ursell, 2000; Banks, 2007). My own research suggests that such characteristics can also be found in the visual and fine arts, even though such work abuts on the publicly funded sectors, which are sometimes seen as a refuge of more supportive working conditions (Oakley, 2008).

Public policy bodies have been slow to pick up on such research, but in 2010, Skillset (now known as 'Creative Skillset') published a report which drew attention to the rate at which women were leaving the media industries; an issue which could not help but reflect the conditions of work within them (Skillset, 2010). The report revealed that while the TV industry in general was reporting a decline in employment figures, between 2006 and 2009 nearly 5,000 women left the industry compared with 750 men. Women's insecure employment status accounted for some of this: women were more likely to work as freelancers than men and women freelancers worked longer hours than their male counterparts. Women earned on average less than men and nearly half said they had worked unpaid at some point in their careers. As a result of what Skillset called a 'gender drain' women were underrepresented in older age groups – while 64 per cent of women workers in the economy overall are over 35, in the screen industries this falls to 50 per cent. For Skillset the issue is a loss of talent and gender balance in the industry; for the individuals involved, loss of sleep, health, money and security are presumably equally important.

Unlike internships, however, there is no obvious policy 'fix' that can reduce the need for a prolonged debate about the need to ameliorate working conditions as a *sine qua non* of improving the diversity and representativeness of cultural labour markets. McRobbie sees hope in the growth of radical social enterprise and new forms of co-operative in the cultural sectors and beyond (McRobbie, 2011). Others see the salience of well-being in public policy as a possible avenue for renewed attention to working conditions (Davies, 2011). Even for those pessimistic about the possibility of improving work in an era of growing unemployment, the growth of campaigning organizations of students and young cultural workers should, at the least, be seen as a positive extension of the space for debate.

Conclusions

This chapter has argued that policy changes in recent decades have altered the relationship between UK academia and the cultural sector in ways that have yet to be fully acknowledged. The experience of full-time undergraduate education in which students live away from home, receive full student grants and enjoy a relatively hands-off approach to future career development have been replaced in many cases by a more instrumental relationship in which previous assumptions no longer hold.

Many of those who enter these industries successfully may have degree-level qualifications, but it is still the case that many of these degrees will be in 'unrelated' fields, and prospective cultural workers will have learned their skills through personal practice and engagement. This personal practice and informal engagement was facilitated – for many students, not just those studying 'creative subjects' – by a university system in a way that it now finds very difficult to do. At the same time, pressure from below (students who want work experience) and above (the monitoring and measurement of 'impact') has encouraged the development of a panoply of interventions, such as student work placements, internships and incubation (see Allen, this volume).

The question is, can this space be opened up, not only for a more critical engagement, but as a space to develop practical interventions that can improve the quality of working life? In many ways it seems an unpromising time to do so.

As Allen et al. (2012) argue, staff involved in such schemes often express a strong commitment to increasing the diversity of the cultural workforce and to combating discrimination. However, too often, working with the sector can simply mean reflecting its own self-image, absorbing its 'cool, creative and egalitarian' rhetoric (Gill, 2002) and providing too little space for acknowledgement of its inequalities.

The increasing pressure on academic staff to work with 'industry', and indeed the need to involve external employers in work-based learning, can curb the willingness of academic staff to be critical. In some cases the provision of courses has become dependent on external income (Oakley, 2010), and in all cases measures of industry engagement are used as measures of academic effectiveness. Furthermore, the casualization of academic labour markets, with the extension of short-term contracts and the very real threat of redundancy in some cases, is likely to produce a workforce fearful for their own future, and unwilling to be seen as disruptive or critical (Ross, 2009).

The difficulty of speaking out about issues of inequality can be experienced even within the relatively safe confines of the classroom. The student body itself reflects the same structural inequalities and is sometimes resistant to the characterization of itself as particularly 'advantaged'. The argument that taking unpaid work is not just self-exploitation, but by creating a market for unpaid work, is helping to exploit others, tends to be met with a mixture of mystification and defensiveness.

But HE remains a crucial site for such conversations and the responsibility not to avoid them is pressing. While caution about industry involvement is warranted, there are also employers and industry bodies who are concerned about levels of exploitation in the cultural industries. If the growth of social enterprise and co-operatives in the cultural industries is to become a reality, educational engagement with such institutions is vital, as it is with trade unions and activist organizations. Debates about what constitutes 'good work' should form an increasingly significant element of vocational education, helping to recover a debate lost to mainstream economic thought (Spencer, 2009).

The demands of policy-makers and students for a more instrumental HE is widely lamented, and rightly so. But the informality of the links between HE and the cultural sectors helped inculcate the culture of exploitative work we see today. This changed relationship is unlikely to lead to a more progressive outcome in terms of work. But by putting the question of work centre stage in HE, it could at least open up an opportunity for critical engagement around the issue of work which desperately needs to be grasped.

Notes

1. In 1984/85 about 8 per cent of first-year undergraduates were living at home, by 2006 it was around 20 per cent (HEFCE, 2009).
2. Creative arts and design (including music and drama), together with media and communications subjects have seen above-average increase in enrolments in the years 1998–2008 (Universities UK, 2009).
3. This data looks at people's professional occupation at age 33 and examines the family background they grew up in (specifically their family's income at age 16). It compares two cohorts – those born in 1958 (from the National Child Development Survey) and those born in 1970 (from the British Cohort Survey) (Cabinet Office, 2009).
4. Under UK law, if an intern can be established as a worker, they are entitled to National Minimum Wage (NMW). Workers can be defined as individuals engaged under a contract (written, oral, express or implied) to personally carry out any work or services.

References

ACE (2011) *Internships in the Arts: A Guide for Arts Organizations* (London: Arts Council and CCSkills).

Amin, A. (1994) *Post-Fordism* (Oxford: Blackwell).

Allen, K., Quinn, J., Hollingworth, S. and Rose, A. (2010) *Work Placements in the Arts and Cultural Sector. A Report for the Equality Challenge Unit* (London: ECU).

Allen, K., Quinn, J., Hollingworth, S. and Rose, A. (2012) Doing Diversity and Evading Equality: The Case of Student Work Placements in the Creative Sector, in Taylor, Y. (ed.) *Educational Diversity: The Subject of Difference and Different Subjects* (Basingstoke: Palgrave Macmillan): 180–200.

Banks, M. (2007) *The Politics of Cultural Work* (Basingstoke: Palgrave Macmillan).

Banks, M. and Hesmondhalgh, D. (2009) Looking for Work in Creative Industries Policy, *International Journal of Cultural Policy* 15(4): 415–430.

Bevir, M. (2005) *New Labour: A Critique* (London: Routledge).

Braun, E. and Lavanga, M. (2007) *An International Comparative Quickscan into National Policies for Creative Industries* (Euricur: Rotterdam).

Browne, J. (2010) *Independent Review of Higher Education Funding and Student Finance* (London: Department for Business, Innovation and Skills).

Cabinet Office (2009) *Final Report of the Panel on Fair Access to the Professions* (London: Cabinet Office).

Cabinet Office (2011) *Opening Doors, Breaking Barriers: A Strategy for Social Mobility* (London: Cabinet Office).

Castells, M. and Himanen, P. (2002) *The Information Society and the Welfare State, the Finnish Model* (Helsinki: Sitra).

Charles, D. (2003) Universities and Territorial Development: Reshaping the Regional Role of UK Universities, *Local Economy* 18(1): 7–20.

Charles, D. and Benneworth, P. (2001) *The Regional Mission: The Regional Contribution of Higher Education: National Report* (London: Universities UK).

CIC Skillset (2012) *Report to Creative Industries Council* (London: Creative Industries Council Skillset Skills Group).

Cohen, W. and Levinthal, D. (1990) Absorptive Capacity: A New Perspective on Learning and Innovation, *Administrative Science Quarterly* 35(1): 128–152.

Collini, S. (2011) From Robbins to McKinsey, *London Review of Books* 33(16): 9–14.

Cox, Sir G. (2005) *Cox Review of Creativity in Business: Building on the UK's Strengths*, http://www.hm-treasury.gov.uk./independent_reviews/cox_review/coxreview_index.cfm, date accessed 6 November 2008.

Crossick, G. (2006) *Knowledge Transfer Without Widgets: The Challenge of the Creative Economy*, http://www.london.ac.uk/fileadmin/documents/about/vicechancellor/Knowledge_transfer_without_widgets.pdf, date accessed 21 January 2012.

Cunningham, S. (2006) *What Price a Creative Economy?* (Sydney: Platform Papers No 9).

Dann, L., Ware, N. and Cass, K. (2009) *Tacking Exclusion in the Creative Industries: An Enterprise-Led Approach* (London: NALN).

Davies, W. (2011) *Happiness and Production*, http://www.opendemocracy.net/ourkingdom/william-davies/happiness-and-production, date accessed 21 March 2012.

Department of Business, Innovation and Skills (BIS) (2011) *Higher Education: Students at the Heart of the System* (London: Department of Business, Innovation and Skills).

Department of Culture, Media and Sport (DCMS) (2008) *Creative Britain* (London: Department of Culture, Media and Sport).

Department of Culture, Media and Sport (DCMS) (2011) *Creative Industry Economic Estimates* (London: DCMS).

Department for Trade and Industry (DTI) (1998) *Our Competitive Future, Building the Knowledge-Driven Economy.* Government White Paper (London: Department for Trade and Industry).

Dorling, D. (2010) *Injustice: Why Social Inequality Persists* (Bristol: Policy Press).

Frith, S. and Horne, H. (1987) *Art into Pop* (London: Methuen).

Gill, R. (2002) Cool, Creative and Egalitarian? Exploring Gender in Project-Based New Media Work in Euro, *Information, Communication & Society*, 5(1): 70–78.

Gill, R. (2007) *Techobohemians or the New Cybertariat? New Media Work in Amsterdam a Decade After the Web* (Amsterdam: Institute of Network Cultures).

Gill, R. (2010) Life Is a Pitch: Managing the Self in new Media Work, in Dueze, M. (ed.) *Managing Media Work* (London: Sage): 249–262.

Greenbank, P. and Hepworth, S. (2008) *Working Class Students and the Career Decision Making Process – A Qualitative Study* (London: HECSU).

Guile, D. (2006) Access, Learning and Development in the Creative and Cultural Sectors: From 'Creative Apprenticeship' to 'Being Apprenticed', *Journal of Education and Work* 19(5): 433–453.

Guile, D. and Okumoto, K. (2009) They Give You Tools and They Give You a Lot, But It Is Up to You to Use Them': The Creation of Performing Artists Through an Integrated Learning and Teaching Curriculum, *Studies in the Education of Adults* 41(1): 21–38.

Hague, D. and Oakley, K. (2001) *Spin-Offs and Start-Ups in UK Universities* (London: Universities UK).

Higher Education Funding Council of England (HEFCE) (2009) *Patterns in Higher Education: Living at Home,* http://www.hefce.ac.uk/media/hefce/content/pubs/2009/200920/09_20.pdf, date accessed 24 July 2012.

HM Treasury (2003) *Lambert Review of Business-University Collaboration* (London: HM Treasury).

Holdsworth, C. and Patiniotis, J. (2005) Seize That Chance! Leaving Home and Transitions to Higher Education, *Journal of Youth Studies* 8(1): 81–95.

Jarvis, H. and Pratt, A. C. (2006) Bringing it All Back Home: The Extensification and 'Overflowing' of Work. The Case of San Francisco's New Media Households, *Geoforum* 37: 331–339.

Jessop, B. (2002) *The Future of the Capitalist State* (Cambridge: Polity Press).

Leadbeater, C. and Oakley, K. (1999) *The Independents Britain's New Cultural Entrepreneurs* (London: Demos).

Leitch, S. (2006) *Prosperity for all in the Global Economy* (London: HM Treasury).

Lester, R. and Piore, M. (2004) *Innovation: The Missing Dimension* (Cambridge Massachusetts: Harvard University Press).

Lawton, K. and Potter, D. (2010) *Why Interns Need a Fair Wage,* http://www.ippr.org/publication/55/1788/why-interns-need-a-fair-wage, date accessed 21 July 2012.

Livingstone, I. and Hope, A. (2010) *Next Gen* (London: NESTA).

Luger, M. and Goldstein, H. (1997) What Is the Role of Public Universities in Regional Economic Development? in Bingham, R.D. and Meir, R. (eds.) *Dilemmas of Urban Economic Development*: *Issues in Theory and Practice* (London: Sage): 55–72.

Malik, S. (2011) Unpaid Website Intern Celebrates Court Victory, *The Guardian*, Monday 23 May: 7.

McRobbie, A. (1998) *British Fashion Design: Rag Trade or Image Industry?* (London and New York: Routledge).

McRobbie, A. (2011) Re-Thinking Creative Economy as Radical Social Enterprise, *Variant* 41, http://www.variant.org.uk/41texts/amcrobbie41.html, date accessed 21 July 2012.

Miege, B. (1979) The Cultural Commodity, *Media, Culture and Society* 1: 297–311.

Miller, T., Govil, N., McMurria, J. and Maxwell, R. R. (2004) *Global Hollywood* (London: BFI Publishing).

Nelson, C. and Watt, S. (1999) *Academic Keywords: A Devil's Dictionary for Higher Education* (London: Routledge).

Oakley, K. (2006) Include us Out – Economic Development and Social Policy in the Creative Industries, *Cultural Trends* 14(4): 283–302.

Oakley, K. (2008) From Bohemia to Britart – Art Students over 50 years, *Cultural Trends* 18(4): 281–294.

Oakley, K. (2010) *The Impact of Business Engagement on Learning and Working.* Unpublished Report for University of the Arts (London: UAL).

Oakley, K. (2011) In its Own Image: New Labour and the Cultural Workforce, *Cultural Trends* 20(3–4): 281–289.

Oakley, K. (2013) Absentee workers: representation and participation in the cultural industries, in Banks, M., Gill, R. & Taylor, S. (eds.) *Theorizing Cultural Work, Labour, Continuity and Change in the Cultural and Creative Industries.* (London: Routledge): 56–67

Özbilgin, M. and Tatli, A. (2006) *Scoping of London Based Higher Education Institute Work Placement Practices within the Creative and Cultural Industries* (London: LCACE).

de Peuter, G. and Dyer-Witheford, N. (2005) A Playful Multitude? Mobilising and Counter-Mobilising Immaterial Game Labour, *Fibreculture Journal*, 5, http://journal.fibreculture.org/issue5/depeuter_dyerwitheford.html, date accessed 13 September 2006.

Raffo, C., O'Connor, J., Lovatt, A. and Banks, M. (2000) Attitudes to Formal Business Training and Learning Among Entrepreneurs in the Cultural Industries: Situated Business Learning Through 'Doing with Others', *Journal of Education and Work* 13(2): 215–230.

Randle, K. and Culkin, N. (2009) Getting in and Getting on in Hollywood: Freelance Careers in an Uncertain Industry, in McKinlay, A. and Smith, C. (eds.) *Creative Labour* (Basingstoke: Palgrave Macmillan): 93–115.

Ross, A. (2003) *No-Collar, The Humane Workplace and Its Hidden Costs* (New York: Basic Books).

Ross, A. (2009) *Nice Work If you Can Get It* (New York: New York University Press).

Ryan, B. (1992) *Making Capital from Culture* (Berlin: Walter de Gruyter).

Selwood, S. (1999) *The Applied Art museum's Commercial Role: Intervening in the 'Creative Economy'*, unpublished paper presented to the conference, Museums of Applied Art Re-Appraised, A&A, London.

Skillset (2010) *Women in the Creative Media Industries* (London: Skillset).

Skillset (2011) *TV Labour Market Intelligence Digest* (London: Skillset).

Social Market Foundation (SMF) (2010) *Disconnected: Social Mobility and the Creative Industries* (London: Social Market Foundation).

Spencer, D.A. (2009) The 'Work as Bad' Thesis in Economics: Origins Evolution and Challenges, *Labor History* 50(1): 39–57.

Thompson, N. (2002) *Left in the Wilderness: The Political Economy of British Democratic Socialism Since 1979* (Chesham: Acumen).

Throsby, D. (1994) A Work-Preference Model of Artist Behaviour, in Peacock, A.T. and Rizzo, I. (eds.) *Cultural Economics and Cultural Policies* (Boston: Kluwer): 60–87.

Towse, R. (1996) Economics of Training Artists, in Ginsberg, V.A. and Menger, P.M. (eds.) *Economics of the Arts: Selected Essays* (Amsterdam: Elsevier): 22–40.

UNCTAD (2010) *Creative Economy Report 2010* (Geneva: UNCTAD).

Universities UK (2009) *Universities UK Patterns of Higher Education Institutions in the UK: Ninth report* (London: Universities UK).

Universities UK (2010) *Creating Prosperity: The Role of Higher Education in Driving the UK's Creative Economy* (London: Universities UK).

Ursell, G. (2000) Television Production: Issues of Exploitation, Commodification and Subjectivity in UK Television Labour Markets, *Media, Culture and Society* 22(6): 805–827.

Verganti, R. (2003) Design as Brokering of Languages: The Role of Designers in the Innovation Strategies of Italian Firms, *Design Management Journal* 3: 34–42.

Wilkinson, R. and Pickett, K. (2009) *The Spirit Level: Why More Equal Societies Almost Always do Better* (London: Allen Lane).

Wilson, T. (2012) *A Review of Business-University Collaboration*, www.wilsonreview.co.uk, date accessed 26 June 2012.

2
Making Your Way: Empirical Evidence from a Survey of 3,500 Graduates

Emma Pollard

A unique study of creative graduates

The Creative Graduates Creative Futures (CGCF) project provides a unique insight into the experiences of creative graduates from across the UK, the value and benefits of a creative education and how this experience shapes working lives. It is the largest longitudinal study that has focused solely on creative graduates. The research was specifically designed to capture the realities and complexities of their lives, the totality of their experiences and contributions to the labour market, and the challenges faced and successes achieved in their early careers. These are aspects that are not adequately captured for creative graduates in annual graduate destinations statistics, as these statistics do not allow time for creative graduates to fully make the transition into work, and do not provide detail on graduates' individual journeys.

Moving beyond destination statistics to inform curriculum and choices

The CGCF research therefore explores experiences further into careers, takes account of all work activities and looks at wider measures of success. It also examines in some detail graduates' reflections on their higher education (HE) experience. The research builds upon and updates the seminal study, *Destinations and Reflections* (Blackwell and Harvey, 1999), which was undertaken in the late 1990s. *Destinations and Reflections* was a landmark in British cultural enquiry and, via in-depth analysis of graduates' career experiences, demonstrated synergy between HE and growth in the creative industries, creative graduates' generic

45

capacity for roles within and also beyond the creative industries and their multi-tracking approach to working, which involves a combination of work activities and development activities.

The CGCF study was initiated by the University of the Arts London who, with the support of the Council for Higher Education in Art and Design (CHEAD), drew together an innovative partnership of 26 UK higher education institutions (HEIs) to guide and fund the research.[1] The institutions wanted more detailed intelligence to inform curriculum design, effective learning and teaching and careers guidance. This intelligence would also help prospective and current students make the most of their time at university and college, inform them of the range of opportunities open to them and help them in developing career plans. In addition, the research would provide evidence to policy-makers of the enduring contribution of creative graduates in practice-based subjects to the creative and cultural industries, to other sectors of the economy and to society as a whole.

Understanding complex careers

All partners felt the research was timely as there have been significant changes since the *Destinations and Reflections* study. The creative industries have continued to grow and are a recognized priority sector for the economy (HM Treasury, 2011) as they have the potential to create wealth and jobs and maintain the UK position in the global economy. HE has expanded and diversified, and demand for creative courses has surpassed that of many other subjects (Ball et al., 2010). However, progression from a university education to work, particularly in an economic downturn, is neither smooth nor predictable; and notions of what we understand to be a graduate level job and a linear career path are being challenged. Graduates of all subjects are now more likely to work in smaller enterprises, in more precarious work and to face the prospect of unemployment. It is now more important than ever to understand the issues and challenges faced by 21st century graduates, the complexities of their working lives and their experiences of the workings of the creative sector in order to inform HE, industry and government strategies for nurturing creative talent.

The institutions provided funding for the research and drew together a sample of almost 27,000 of their graduates from practice-based programmes in art, design, craft and media, who had completed their studies in 2001–2002, 2002–2003 and 2003–2004.[2,3] Practice-based subjects (from animation to visual communication) were the focus of the research as these subjects have experiential learning at the heart of their pedagogy and the knowledge created is rooted in the creative process.[4]

Graduates were surveyed via postal and/or online questionnaire in late 2008 and 3,478 eligible responses were received.[5] They were surveyed again via email one year later in late 2009 (as the recession began to take hold in the UK); and, finally, in March 2010, 40 graduates took part in in-depth interviews to capture their detailed career stories.[6]

Looking back on the value of the higher education experience

Creative graduates reflected upon their creative education and provided feedback on the learning activities and experiences they had engaged in, and which they found most useful in developing their careers. Overall they found their courses to be exciting and stimulating, opening them up to new experiences, encouraging free and creative thought and nurturing an enjoyment in learning which they carried through into their working lives. The practice-based, flexible and self-directed nature of their courses offered them a unique opportunity for personal exploration, self-discovery and development. Personal and Professional Development (PPD), although a relatively recent curriculum element, was widely experienced by creative graduates and was recognized as the most useful element in most disciplines. PPD typically includes students' own assessment of their learning progress and skills developed, career planning, and taught elements relating to professional practice. Graduates reflected on how creative practice and active or experiential learning was at the heart of their courses, and how they had opportunities to apply learning in different contexts through external and live projects, industry-linked initiatives, shows and exhibitions, competitions and placements.

Preparing for life beyond higher education through work placements

Placements were particularly valued, and two in five creative graduates (42%) had undertaken a work placement either as a course requirement or outside of the curriculum. Placements were regarded as important to career development, helping to prepare creative graduates for the transition to work, providing an insight into working practices and enabling them to build contacts in industry. Generally, longer placements and those organized by graduates themselves were felt to be most useful, and feedback suggests that these self-initiated placements may be more closely aligned with graduates' immediate interests.

There was almost universal support for placements. Graduates who did not gain placement experience during their course felt they had

missed out, felt let down by their HEIs and criticized their institutions
and courses for their lack of support for acquiring placements. Those
who had participated in work placements felt strongly that placement opportunities should be more widespread, longer and some even
suggested they should be made a compulsory element of creative
courses. However, formal placements and other work-related experience
are unlikely to grow as creative industries are dominated by micro-
businesses with arguably limited capacity to provide such experiences,
particularly as the economy as a whole is contracting.[7]

Formal placement activity was higher among younger graduates and
those studying fashion design, 3-D design and other visual and inter-
disciplinary arts courses. This pattern may reflect a greater perceived
need for formal work experience to be built into specific courses or targeted at specific students, and the availability of dedicated HEI resources
to support this activity. However, it is likely to reflect the greater availability of placement opportunities in some creative sectors, particularly
sectors with larger employers and thus the capacity to take on students; and, perhaps more cynically, the networks of HEI staff and their
inclinations to use these to help students:

> There wasn't enough work placement places or enough people from
> the world of work. They were just interested in taking the students
> who were top of the class rather than helping those in the middle.
> No good having excellent degrees when not enough companies are
> willing to train or take on those without 2 yrs experience. I have 2:1
> but not the experience.

> The work placements were useful but the tutors were influential over
> who went where.

Learning with and from others while establishing networks of practice

A creative education enabled graduates to work alongside and learn from
others, which was also highly valued. The vast majority of graduates
had team-working and peer and self-evaluation built into their courses
(86% and 89%, respectively). A substantial group (43%) also had opportunities to collaborate with others from different disciplines, and this
reflects moves within creative education to promote inter-disciplinarity
across creative subjects and beyond, with some institutions encouraging
and facilitating links with business, engineering and scientific disciplines. Creative graduates talked of the importance of their peers, and

how the feedback and criticism of others had informed their practice and developed their self-confidence, and how this had been particularly helpful for presenting and defending their work in commercial settings:

> Letting go of the work and seeing it in the bigger picture, particularly how handing over some responsibility to others and allowing their views to be heard can make the work better.

The input and support of not only academic staff but of experienced technicians and visiting professionals was also appreciated by creative graduates of all disciplines, which suggests that these wider inputs into curriculum development and delivery should be acknowledged, supported and encouraged (see Ashton, this volume, for a discussion of how industry professionals reflect on cultural workforce issues). A high proportion of creative graduates (84%) had teaching input from industry professionals and teacher-practitioners providing them with a professional and commercial context to their creative activity, and these tutors appeared to greatly influence graduates' experiences:[8]

> I feel I benefited most from the outside tutors who came in to teach and critique us than from the design course staff at that time. They were my main inspiration and, if it hadn't been for their confidence and encouragement in my ideas, I would not have pursued an artistic career.

Graduates felt that building relationships with peers, tutors and industry professionals while in HE was fundamental and provided the foundations for finding work, for the creation of work opportunities and maintaining confidence and motivation through networks of support:

> The most valuable part of my undergraduate study is the people I met whilst studying. You realise you have a network of potential collaborators and contacts who end up being spread around the country, and sometimes world. With these people there is a bond and loyalty which is invaluable in working life.

Building self-confidence, skills for innovation and personal effectiveness

Graduates also considered the skills they had developed, how they had changed during their time at university or college and how this had helped them in their working lives. A creative education is about providing an environment that enables an individual to develop as a creative, while developing workplace skills and attributes, and skills for business and self-employment. During their time in HE, graduates felt they had gained confidence in themselves and their work, learned how to speak to others about their work and knew more about themselves.

Generally, creative graduates felt satisfied with the level of skills development they had experienced on their courses. They considered the skills most developed during their creative education were creative and intellectual skills fundamental to creative practice and creative careers, such as: creativity and innovation, visual skills and presentation of self and work. Other well-developed areas were research skills, critical thinking, collaborating with others and making/design skills. These are the skills that have been linked with innovation (Oakley et al., 2008), the high-level skills needed to support growth in the creative industries and skills in demand across the economy (UUK, 2010).[9]

Personal effectiveness skills were felt to be developed to some degree during studies and these included: flexibility/adaptability, self-management, problem solving, self-confidence, initiative/risk taking, project management and written communication. In terms of career importance, creative graduates felt that self-confidence and self-management were critical attributes to acquire and improve.

Room for course improvement: Better industry insight and advice

Overall, just over half (52%) of creative graduates felt their courses had prepared them fairly or very well for the world of work. However, graduates felt that some skill areas were less well developed during their time in HE, and did level several criticisms at their courses. There were graduates who felt their courses lacked opportunities for learning specialist/technical IT skills as well as more general office-based software applications. These individuals felt that greater access to the facilities and particularly the software used in the creative industries would have prepared them better for working to industry standards. Another key area of course criticism centred around a desire for a better insight into industry and the pressures and challenges they would face, and creative graduates felt there was limited attention paid to developing skills in understanding client needs, which were felt to be highly important to career development. There were also calls for greater focus on preparing for self-employment and on developing entrepreneurial skills during HE. With hindsight, graduates felt that the following would have been useful: practical information on tax returns and copyright, budget management, how to price and sell their work and general information about working freelance and engaging with contract working. They also wanted to develop skills in marketing and self-promotion, influencing skills and negotiating, and skills around how to find work and meet the needs of clients. Graduates also called for more advice and guidance while in HE particularly on career options and pathways after graduating and how to find and apply for jobs. Some graduates stayed in contact with their university or college after graduating and were able to access support in these key areas which helped them to make a successful transition from HE into the world of work.

Making the transition from university into complex patterns of work

Setting the scene

After graduating from university and college, creative graduates engage in a range of work and development activities and the research set out to capture this variety and to explore progression over time. The term 'activity' was used to ensure that the focus was not placed on jobs alone, but instead encompassed all endeavours that involved active preparation for future employment, including the development of creative practice, further learning, voluntary work, unpaid work and self-employment; as well as full- and part-time paid employment. The survey captured data on the experience of different types of activity throughout graduates' early careers and also a snapshot of activity to see what graduates were doing at one point in time (September to December 2008).

Virtually all creative graduates had experienced employment of some kind since graduating, whether in creative roles or industries or wider roles and sectors; and most were in work at the time of the survey. The majority were in permanent work or had held a permanent job (and the likelihood of permanent work increased over time in the labour market), although working on short-term contracts and part-time work was common. Indeed, compared to the position of creative graduates in their early careers captured ten years ago in the *Destinations and Reflections* research, graduates now have a higher propensity to be involved in part-time work and to be on fixed-term or temporary contracts, which indicates a shift towards less stable working patterns. This reflects the contract economy in the creative industries, where many creative graduates gain work. However, this is also perhaps a feature of the contemporary workplace in all sectors, with companies using short-term contracts to maintain a flexible workforce and reduce overheads in an increasingly competitive environment.

However, some of the most striking findings when exploring career progression and labour market activity were: the prevalence of self-employment, the extent of portfolio working, the importance of unpaid work (at least in early careers), the need for continued development and, overall, how these factors help creative graduates achieve and maintain creative work.

The importance of self-employment: A positive career move or back-up plan?

The research found that self-employment was common, with 45 per cent of creative graduates working on a commission or freelance basis, and 25 per cent running their own business at some point in their early careers. Four to six years after graduating, this remained a frequent feature of creative graduates' careers. Indeed, the proportion of graduates working freelance, and particularly running their own businesses was found to have increased substantially over the last decade since the *Destinations and Reflections* research.

Self-employment clearly has a central role in the working lives of creative graduates and they are considerably more likely to be self-employed than graduates from other disciplines. Comparing destinations at six months, creative graduates were four times more likely to be self-employed after graduation than graduates as a whole.[10] Self-employment could therefore act as a career entry strategy, a way for creative graduates to gain experience and prove themselves, particularly in the absence of paid employment. However, graduates looking back on their careers noted that it could be difficult to set up as a freelancer immediately after graduation without experience, contacts and cash flow:

> Becoming a freelancer straight out of university would be really difficult – you need to work with people for a number of years to get an idea of how the industry works.

> To begin with finances were the biggest challenge. To really get to grips with what I was doing I needed to put in as much time as possible to produce lots of work for the collection. But I didn't have any idea of what might sell or when I would make any money from it. It took a good 4 months before I started getting any real money in. I joined the New Deal scheme for people wanting to set up their own business or become self-employed. This gave me lots of help with finding out about tax, accounts, budgets and business plans. It also

gave me valuable financial support whilst I was starting out. By the time the scheme ended I was able to fully support myself and have been stable ever since.

Self-employment became more common among creative graduates as careers progressed, and as time passed self-employment became an accepted aspect of working lives. Looking to the future, 62 per cent of creative graduates anticipated being self-employed, including 44 per cent who expressed an interest in running their own business. Feedback from creative graduates indicated that, for many, career progression was often characterized by gravitation towards self-employment from (or alongside) salaried careers. They note that making the move required confidence and contacts, in addition to determination and considerable persistence to seek new work and new clients.

A key question is whether becoming self-employed, working freelance or setting up in business is a free choice for creative graduates or an imposed pattern of working in the absence of other opportunities that becomes accepted as 'the norm'. This is worthy of further research as the CGCF study suggests that this is not clear cut; for some graduates the feedback indicated that self-employment was their 'Plan B':

> The first year was a bit depressing I have to say. After having graduating I started applying everywhere I knew there was a knitwear line within fashion companies, but never managed to get the job I wanted – knitwear designer. I did not want to give up on my dream of being a knitwear designer so it occurred to me that the only way of living my dream was to start producing some knitwear of my own and seeing whether people might have been interested. So, it turned out they were and I started selling through friends that way.

Self-employment tends to be part-time work, can be financially insecure and involve a high degree of uncertainty, and can be somewhat isolating as most self-employed creative graduates work alone. In the CGCF study, those who were self-employed or working freelance, often sought the company of others by sharing a studio or by engaging in other forms of work. Indeed, one graduate had this advice to pass on to those considering self-employment:

> If they are becoming self-employed straight after art college then it is good to keep contact with others in their field. Joining networks and associations also allows them to keep up to date with what is

happening. I found it very useful having the extra 2 years of being in the supportive environment of college but finding a studio where other artists work can also keep you from going mad working on your own.

For others, self-employment enabled them to work in a creative occupation and in the creative industries, and wanting to 'work for oneself' was at least a fairly important factor in the career decisions of more than half (57%) of the graduates surveyed. Here, feedback showed that self-employment gave creative graduates freedom and flexibility; provided them with access to, and more of a say in, the direction and outcomes of creative projects; helped them to achieve a better life/work balance; and allowed them to work with different companies without making a long-term commitment while building relationships with new people:

> I didn't like living in London and wanted to be more 'hands-on' creative and work for myself. Started [company name] two years ago and haven't looked back. I love working on and away from the computer and driving myself to come up with ideas and products as well as marketing techniques. I keep doing regular weeks of freelance design to keep my skills current, meet people and keep my options open.

Portfolio working is an established working pattern

The research demonstrated that creative graduates tend to be involved in multiple work and/or development activities simultaneously; this is often termed 'portfolio working'. At the time of the survey, four to six years into their careers, approximately half (48%) of working creative graduates were involved in more than one job or work activity and so were 'portfolio working': 30 per cent had two activities, 13 per cent had three activities and 5 per cent had at least four activities. These graduates were typically mixing different types of activities and combining a full-time job or work-related activity with one or more part-time jobs/activities. Most commonly creative graduates were combining paid employment with self-employment, but could also be in voluntarily work or developing their creative practice. In addition, work was often combined with formal learning at MA level.

The likelihood of portfolio working did not change significantly across the graduating cohorts in the study, indicating that portfolio working was just as prevalent early on in careers as it was mid career – it was not a phase of development but a recognized and sought-after pattern of life. Creative graduates also anticipated continuing with portfolio working over the next phase of their careers, with 66 per cent expecting to be doing a range of jobs and activities. Feedback from graduates suggested four key drivers for portfolio working:

- creativity – to focus on creativity and to control its direction;
- the contract economy – to adapt to the opportunities available;
- personal development – to gain new experiences and develop new skills; and
- contacts – to respond to work opportunities from network contacts and form collaborations to meet market needs.

Juggling multiple activities brought creative graduates personal fulfilment, provided the context for personal and professional development, and provided a model for generating work and income. However, graduates were concerned about the lack of career and salary progression, the limited opportunities to develop leadership and managerial skills, and anticipated a serious effect on later careers as incomes might not progress in line with financial commitments, lifestyle changes and family needs. This raises the question as to how far into one's life is portfolio work sustainable or satisfying?

Unpaid work to establish a foothold

A substantial group (42%) of creative graduates had undertaken some form of voluntary or unpaid work during their early careers, and voluntary work is a recognized strategy for finding paid work in the creative industries (see also this volume: Oakley; Berger et al.). It is becoming a more common recruitment method for employers, allowing them to 'try before they buy'. Internships of this kind allow creative graduates to gain insights into different sectors, acquire valuable post-graduation work experience, build contacts and 'get a foot in the door'. However, feedback from graduates indicated that these periods without pay could be too long (up to one year or more), might only be accessible to those from more advantaged backgrounds who have other means of financial support and might not lead directly to more permanent work. Further into their careers, approximately one in ten creative graduates were working unpaid but this was rarely their only or their main activity. Generally, they combined it with other paid work, which could be creative or non-creative, but their unpaid/voluntary work tended to be related to their creative practice, allowing them to develop their interests and more personally driven work. As one graduate noted:

> I do a variety of creative things in my spare time but choose not to work in the art world because I'm not interested in working to other people's specifications.

Examples of voluntary work included working with disabled students, working in the community arts sector, acting as a chair of trustees and volunteering in a gallery.

Continued creative practice and further training and development

The research demonstrated that creative graduates are lifelong learners, with further learning and development playing a central role in their portfolio of activities and their career decisions. Being able to make full use of their knowledge and skills, and being able to continue to improve these were the most important career drivers for creative graduates (over and above considerations of income and creative practice). The majority (72%) of graduates had engaged in either some form of formal or informal learning since graduating including postgraduate study (most commonly masters level courses or courses leading to teaching qualifications), and short skills-based courses generally in a creative arts subject or one involving business skills. However, learning could also involve developing their creative practice/portfolio, doing studio work or self-directed study. A substantial group (39%) were still engaged in learning activities at the time of the survey, and 82 per cent anticipated undertaking some training and learning new skills in the next few years. These proportions are higher than were found ten years ago in the *Destinations and Reflections* research, and imply that graduates are now placing more importance during their early careers on continuing their development, refreshing their practice and producing new work.

Engaging in learning tended to be self-initiated and self-funded and graduates were inventive in finding ways and opportunities to learn and develop. One graduate (an art worker for a pharmaceutical company) noted:

> I am learning to do things myself and to continually keep on learning to progress and move forwards. I am self-teaching myself in some relevant design packages.

Continuing their professional development was considered to be a critical factor in achieving and maintaining career success, in enhancing their practice and exploring new areas of application, to respond to changes in tastes and technologies and to develop their businesses and prepare for future roles:

> I am interested in learning more about photography and Photoshop to allow me to take better photographs of my own work to use for publicity and to approach galleries with. At the moment I use a professional photographer to do this but this is expensive and not always possible as work is sometimes only finished just before it needs to be sent away. I am also keen to learn CAD as I feel that this would help with designing and production of new work in line with the new technologies now available.

> I'd like to do a course of some description in digital design. So far I have stuck to print based projects as that's where my skills lie but ultimately everything is moving in the digital direction so it would be a huge bonus if I had that skill as well.

Working in creative roles and in creative industries (and beyond)

Creative graduates do have complex working patterns, combining varied work and development opportunities simultaneously to provide multiple income streams, but much of their work is either creative in nature and/or takes place in the creative industries. In their early careers, 73 per cent of all creative graduates reported they had had experience of working in the creative industries and the same proportion said they had worked in an area directly related to their degree. Generally, this was paid rather than unpaid work. Some four to six years after graduating, the vast majority continued to engage in work and employment that was creative and closely related to their field of expertise or course of study. Over three quarters (78%) of creative graduates were in creative occupations, across a very wide range of job roles; and 77 per cent of creative graduates worked for at least part of their time in the creative sector. The proportion of creative graduates in creative roles and creative sectors is higher than that found in the *Destinations and Reflections* study. Looking across all their work and development activities, most creative graduates felt that the work they did related significantly to art, craft, design and media (79%), that they could be creative in their work (77%), and that their work was directly related to their degree subject (68%).

Yet not all of the work undertaken by creative graduates was considered to be creative. Looking across all activities, a quarter (25%) of creative graduates were in a non-creative role, but they were often doing so alongside more creative activities. For some this non-creative work was a strategy for moving into a more creative role with the same employer, while for others it was a decision to keep their creative practice as a separate interest outside of work. Only a small minority (13%) were not working in a creative role in any of their activities, and instead were working in a diverse range of roles, for example, working as civil servants, senior managers, bank clerks and police constables.[11] Similarly, not all activities of creative graduates took place in the creative industries, and key sectors (outside of the creative industries) were: not-for-profit/charities sector, often involving work in support, advocacy and management roles; the public sector including health and social work and work with national and local government; retailing, manufacturing and engineering; and the education sector.

Teaching is an important career destination

Teaching is traditionally seen as a popular career destination for creative graduates, and the research confirmed the importance of teaching to creative careers. One third (33%) of creative graduates had indeed had some experience of teaching since graduating. This was generally paid and was related to art, design, craft and/or media. The proportion with teaching experience was larger than that found in the *Destinations and Reflections* study. At the time of the survey 18 per cent were working as teachers, and half combined teaching with other work or self-employment. Creative graduates were teaching at all levels (primary, secondary, further, adult and community education settings) with one key exception – very few creative graduates entered an academic career, fewer than 1 per cent indicated that they were teaching at HE level.

Routes into teaching were varied, but many graduates gravitated towards teaching as their careers progressed from fine art and design practice and from work in community settings. Women, those who were older, those who graduated with a higher class of degree or those who had studied fine art or arts and crafts disciplines were more likely to have worked as a teacher. These patterns may follow career motivations but are likely to reflect the greater challenges in finding stable paid work in some sub-sectors of the creative industries. Indeed, teaching often acted as a balancing career for makers and creative practitioners and a way for them to achieve a stable income, particularly in a difficult economic climate:

I tried to be self-employed but didn't enjoy producing art work to sell. I looked at and shadowed an occupational therapist but decided it wasn't for me. I worked as a support assistant in a Special Needs School for two years. Then did the G.T.T.P. in a year. I'm now teaching full time and just started a distance learning Masters in Education through Birmingham University.

I decided to study a PGCE primary as it was difficult to find any creative work (sculpture) apart from commission work and I wanted to have the option to supply teach as well as do my art work. After studying I've been working full time as a primary teacher.

I have taught in secondary schools for 6 years and am now in my second year at FE level, leading a Level 3 course.... Now, I am rethinking my own skills and wanting to develop myself personally so would like to combine my teaching with my own projects.

Understanding how careers have developed

Higher education fuels creative ambitions

By the time they graduated, creative graduates were clear about their career intentions and they overwhelmingly aspired to creative careers, with their specific goals tending to align with their subject discipline. This suggests that their time in HE had served to fuel rather than diminish their creative ambitions. A wide range of ambitions were reported in the survey. Most were very specific about their intentions and some even spelled out the route they intended to take. The most commonly cited goals were to work 'successfully' as artists, designers and makers. Approximately one in ten were interested in following a general creative career – wanting work that would allow them to be creative and use the knowledge and skills they had gained.

After the first few months in the labour market, approximately one third (36%) of creative graduates reassessed these goals. For those revising their ambitions, goals and aspirations tended to remain centred on creative practice, with graduates refocusing their goals or career pathways away from those they had envisaged for themselves while in HE. However, there was some indication of a move away from creative occupations, in these cases the most common change was from a solely creative career to one involving teaching their practice (although they were unclear about where this would take place).

Early labour market challenges can lead to compromise

Feedback from graduates indicated that their early experiences in the first year or so after leaving university or college could be challenging, often involving periods of unemployment, compromise and re-evaluation. Many returned to their family home to save money and think about their plans, and for some it took time to find out what they wanted to do and what they wanted from a career. Graduates spoke of the importance of testing out different types of work, often as a portfolio of activities, to gain insights into different sectors and areas of work. This helped them to determine and refine their career direction. They spoke of using slack periods, when they were unable to find paid work, to gain experience or develop new skills by working unpaid or volunteering and engaging in formal and informal learning. They also reported generating income from paid work of all kinds, often continuing with the part-time jobs they had had as students, in order to maintain their practice and to support themselves until something more aligned to their aspirations became available.

Barriers to career progression were mostly financial

Career entry could be difficult and finance was recognized as the major barrier to creative careers. Creative graduates described how a lack of finance impacted upon their abilities to learn new workplace, technical or IT skills and to build relevant experience and networks. They spoke of not being able to afford to undertake further study due to the fees involved or the loss of earnings that would result from taking time out to study. They also spoke about not feeling able to move from relatively well-paid jobs to risky or unpaid jobs that could provide them with useful experiences and contacts:

> I would love to return to college to complete a post-grad. I'd also be interested in several short courses, not least art management and business skills. However, as cost is an issue and I don't have enough work coming in, this is a catch 22. Which is neither pleasant or optimistic!

> I have always considered doing an MA to further my career, but feel that maybe I might just end up taking a step back when I came out.

> I am considering moving into the design for social care sector and have been thinking about taking an Open University course in sociology to create a foundation for this. However, it's not something that is financially viable for me at the moment. Possibly it's something

that my company might have helped to fund, but as there are redundancies and a pay freeze, it wont be one of their priorities.

Need for self-belief and support networks

Personal factors were also felt to impact on career development. Graduates felt they had to

- have confidence and self-belief in the face of not being able to find work;
- be persistent, determined and resourceful to cope with the lack of full-time employment and high levels of competition; and
- be open to new opportunities, adaptable and pro-active in order to find opportunities, paid employment and settle into creative careers in an industry which relies on informal recruitment methods.

Creative graduates also recognized the importance of the support they received from their family, friends and contacts and networks in developing their careers. Networks were particularly important as, in the main, graduates found work early on through personal contacts and networking, and from their placement experiences or unpaid work, rather than through responding to job adverts. Creative graduates acknowledged the importance of building and maintaining networks not just for finding work and developing opportunities, but also for providing opportunities to discuss their work with others and seek the critical feedback they felt they needed to progress (see Lee, this volume, for a discussion of the implications of 'network culture').

Achieving success

Despite the initial turbulence, several years after graduating creative graduates were satisfied with their careers and positive about the future. Most were in employment, the majority were in creative roles undertaking work related to their degree subject; and felt they were in or were close to achieving their ideal careers. Graduates were generally positive about their work situation, with 77 per cent reporting that they were satisfied with their work, which was a much higher proportion than that recorded in the *Destinations and Reflections* study. They also felt they could be creative in their work (77%), that they had substantial autonomy and independence in their work (66%), and that they had career opportunities open to them (69%).

Creativity, being able to pursue and maintain their creative practice, was clearly an important motivating factor for creative graduates and central to their career satisfaction. Looking to the future, this remained central to their plans but creative graduates anticipated some element of change as their careers developed. They expected to undertake further personal development (as noted earlier), and they also assumed some form of promotion, with 79 per cent anticipating that they would be doing a higher level job in the same career within the next five years. At this stage relatively few anticipated a change of career direction or to be doing something completely different over the next few years.

The qualitative feedback from creative graduates demonstrated that they set high standards for themselves and were keen to progress in their working lives, develop new work and new ideas, and learn new skills. They recognized that they have some way to go yet but did expect their careers to continue to progress and there was evidence of movement to more senior roles over time. They spoke of wanting to improve income levels, gain greater experience, take on more responsibility, facilitate creativity in others, and to have more say in the direction and outcomes of creative projects and in the way their work is organized. The ultimate goals were to be able to sustain a living from their creative practice, to achieve financial success, and to gain recognition of themselves and their work by their peers and those who 'matter' in the sector.

Conclusions

The responses to the surveys and interviews provide a picture of the complexity of working patterns. Creative graduates described how their careers had developed and the totality of their activities in the labour market including: full- and part-time work, self-employment, unpaid work, continued creative practice and further training and development; work in the creative industries and in creative roles, and work in wider roles and areas of the economy. The research clearly shows that creative graduates place a high value on their HE experiences and the experiential and reflective learning approaches and opportunities provided by the creative curriculum, although they would have liked a stronger connection with the professional world to prepare them for the transition to work. It shows how graduates in art, design, craft and media subjects are driven by a desire to continue with their creative practice and the vast majority engage in work and employment that is creative and closely related to their field of expertise or course of study. Creative graduates are resourceful and adaptable and take a multi-tracking approach to working, often combining a variety of work activities with personal development. As such they are well-equipped to deal with the challenges of creative working and for contemporary life and work in a difficult economic climate, while maintaining a life/work balance and experiencing considerable personal and work satisfaction.

Reflecting on their experiences, creative graduates have advice to pass on to current students to help them make the most of their time at university and college and prepare for the transition to work. They encourage students to make the most of the people, resources and facilities available to them while in HE and after graduation. Their specific recommendations are

- To build a good professional network, starting by keeping in contact with tutors, peers and placement employers as this will be helpful for finding work, creating opportunities and maintaining confidence and motivation.
- To take every opportunity to learn while in HE, opportunities to learn excellent making, technical, IT and business skills; and also academic skills such as critical appreciation, research skills, contextual studies and academic writing; and to take an active role in their own learning and to keep a focus on longer-term goals.
- To gain as much work experience as possible while studying in order to gain credibility, build a reputation, learn how to run a business and open up opportunities for the future.
- To maintain their creative practice and link this to long-term career aspirations, and to continue to build their portfolio to reflect ongoing work and continued development, whether working in creative industries and creative roles or wider roles and areas of the economy.
- To be flexible, open to advice, prepared to juggle a range of activities and to relocate to where the work is, to be patient and persistent and to recognize that it takes time to achieve one's goals:

Be prepared that even though you have studied hard, achieved good grades, volunteered and undertaken work placements, it still might not be enough to get you where you want to be. You have to persevere and hope that in time you will get where you hoped even if you have to go a long way round, taking different jobs, to get there!

Don't think you are going to wear a beret and live in Paris making enough money from selling one-off pieces that make your lecturers proud! Don't be too precious about your ideals... all of the jobs will lead somewhere even if they seem a little dull to begin with!

Don't get hooked on the idea or fantasy of what you want to be as it might not make you happy, instead use your time to find out more about yourself and re-evaluate.

The research findings also raise issues and challenges for the creative HE sector and its institutions in preparing creative graduates for the realities of their working lives:

- How can HEIs nurture the self-confidence required for creative careers while also building resilience?
- How can HEIs positively influence the availability, accessibility and visibility of work placements or work experience opportunities for students and graduates of all backgrounds in an industry dominated by micro-businesses? Will new/alternative forms of work-related learning or employer engagement need to be developed?
- Working freelance and running a business is a common and sought after career path for creative graduates so how do HEIs signal the value of business and enterprise skills and encourage take-up of the activities that support development in these areas to current students?
- How can HEIs support students and graduates to make useful contacts and maintain networks, contacts that will help them to continue to develop their work, help them find work and help to combat the isolation of working freelance?
- Creative graduates have a strong appetite for further learning and personal and professional development throughout their careers, so what further development opportunities can HEIs provide to graduates and how might these be tailored to career stage?
- The inputs of visiting lecturers and technicians are clearly valued by students, so how can HEIs prepare the next generation of teacher-practitioners?

Author's note

The Author would like to acknowledge the significant contribution of Linda Ball, Nick Stanley, Joy Oakley and Will Hunt to this chapter, as co-authors and contributors to the original CGCF research outputs. The full findings of the CGCF study can be found in the three published reports, all of which can be accessed from the research website www.creativegraduates.com

Notes

1. Partner institutions: Bath Spa University, University of Bolton, Arts University College at Bournemouth, University for the Creative Arts, Coventry

University, Duncan of Jordanstone College of Art and Design, Dundee University, Edinburgh College of Art, Glasgow School of Art, University of Gloucestershire, Glyndwr University, University of Hertfordshire, University of Huddersfield, Leeds College of Art and Design, Liverpool John Moores University, University of the Arts London (lead partner), Loughborough University School of Art and Design, Manchester Metropolitan University, Middlesex University, University of Northampton, Norwich University College of the Arts, Nottingham Trent University, Plymouth College of Art, University of Portsmouth, Swansea Metropolitan University, University of the West of England, and York St John University. Note, these were the names of the institutions at the time of the research. This represented 41 per cent of CHEAD membership, and included both multi-disciplinary institutions and specialist arts colleges. Partner institutions were spread across the UK (with the exception of Northern Ireland).

2. The final starting sample was 26,806; and included graduates who had been classed as home students (originally from the UK, prior to starting their course), other EU students and overseas students.
3. Subjects were further classified as: graphic design; visual communication and typography; fashion and textiles design; fine art; 3-D design, media production, photography, interactive and electronic design; applied arts and crafts; and other visual and inter-disciplinary arts.
4. For a full list of eligible courses see Appendix 1 to the main report Creative Graduates Creative Futures (2010) available at http://www.employment-studies.co.uk/pdflibrary/471apx1.pdf.
5. This represents a response rate of 14 per cent. The distribution of the responding group was compared to that of the target population on a number of key (measurable characteristics). No significant bias was found and the responding sample was deemed to be representative and no weighting strategy was required.
6. A full description of the data collection methodology and analysis is contained in the research reports: Creative Graduates Creative Futures (2010), and Creative Career Stories (2010).
7. Eighty-seven per cent of creative businesses have fewer than ten workers (CC Skills, 2009).
8. This corresponds with the conclusions of the work by the Art, Design and Media subject Centre of the Higher Education Academy exploring links between creative industries and creative HE: 'Perhaps the most effective engagement in shaping the students' experience and curriculums towards relevance for creative industries is the employment of teacher practitioners' (Clews and Mallinder, 2010, p. 8).
9. These include: willingness to change, try new things or take risks; and reflective thinking, aesthetic inquiry, critical thinking, analytical skills, communication skills and teamwork.
10. Calculated by comparing the destinations of the 2003 graduate cohort, using Destinations of Leavers from Higher Education survey (2004, Table 3) and focusing on the destinations of all UK domiciled leavers for 2002/2003 who obtained first degrees through full-time study by subject of study.
11. Teaching is included here as a creative role, as almost all the teaching activity described involved teaching creative subjects.

References

Blackwell, A. and Harvey, L. (1999) *Destinations and Reflections: Careers of British Art, Craft and Design Graduates* (Birmingham: Centre for Research into Quality, University of Central England).

Ball, L., Pollard, E. and Stanley, N. (2010) *Creative Graduates Creative Futures* (Brighton: Creative Graduates Creative Futures Higher Education Partnership and the Institute for Employment Studies).

Ball, L., Pollard, E. and Stanley, N. and Oakley, J. (2010) *Creative Career Stories* (Brighton: Creative Graduates Creative Futures Higher Education Partnership and the Institute for Employment Studies).

Clews, D. and Mallinder, S. (2010) *Looking Out: Effective Engagement with Creative and Cultural Enterprise* (Brighton: Art Design Media Subject Centre, University of Brighton).

CC Skills (2009) *Creative and Cultural Industry Impact and Footprint* (London: Creative and Cultural Skills).

HM Treasury (2011) *The Plan for Growth* (London: HM Treasury).

Hunt, W., Ball, L. and Pollard, E. (2010) *Crafting Futures: A Study of the Early Careers of Crafts Graduates from UK Higher Education Institutions* (London: Crafts Council).

Oakley, K., Sperry, B., Pratt, A. and Bakshi, H. (eds) (2008) *The Art of Innovation: How Fine Arts Graduates Contribute to Innovation* (London: NESA Research Report).

Universities UK (2010) *Creating Prosperity: The Role of Higher Education in Driving the UK's Creative Economy* (London: Universities UK).

Part II

Cultural and Creative Industries and the Curriculum

3
Precariously Mobile: Tensions between the Local and the Global in Higher Education Approaches to Cultural Work

Susan Luckman

As noted by Oakley in a previous chapter, a key issue underpinning the growth of cultural work and creative industries training in higher education (HE) is the surplus of creative workers being produced. As is well established in the writing on cultural work (cf. Hesmondhalgh, 2002), this excess of willing talent has led to even higher barriers to entry for in-demand careers and a concurrent potential for exploitative work practices. Further, much of the rhetoric around cultural work follows that of other 'sexy' professions and talks up the need for, and desirability of, a cosmopolitan subjectivity and a physical global mobility as a precondition for gaining access to cultural work. Most famously, this is evident in the work of economist Richard Florida and his writings on the creative class; indeed it is explicit in the title of his 2007 book *The Flight of the Creative Class: The New Global Competition for Talent*. This situation is at once exacerbated by the Global Financial Crisis (GFC), which may necessitate a willingness to move further away and/or to places not previously favoured in order to gain employment. Another significant driver of demand for mobility – both inward and, especially, outward – is the concurrent growth of the emerging economies of Asia, especially China and India, which are working to further develop their service and knowledge economy sectors, alongside their existing expertise and manufacturing strengths. All this is, of course, further enabled by the potential of global digital technology to allow increased vocational workplace flexibility. While the frequent flier lifestyle may well be a dream come true for many, the veracity of this particular image of the idealized cultural worker presents a number of challenges for educators as we prepare graduates for the realities of cultural work. Ultimately, place still profoundly matters in cultural employment not only in terms of the benefits, but even down to the differential practicalities of the particular HE, arts and cultural, as well as economic policies governing the development of the creative sector in any given location (for example, see Noonan, this volume, for a discussion of this in the context of Cardiff, UK).

Thus, this chapter explores the tensions in preparing HE students for the world of cultural work around the local and the global. A number of issues coalesce here. Firstly, given much policy discourse and practical advice around cultural work presumes national, if not global, mobility on the part of creative workers, what are the challenges facing us for realistically preparing students for this, both personally and vocationally? Secondly, Anglosphere universities in particular are increasingly looking to train both local and international students for increased business dealings with Asia and/or are looking to Asian students and campuses as a growth market for fee-paying students. Given the unique place of cultural work as an intellectual property-generating sector which strongly intersects with issues of culture and identity as well as global flows of finance, how is this being incorporated into curricula and pedagogy, if at all? In particular, and drawing strongly on the Australian experience of cultural policy development and a mature international education market focussed on attracting undergraduate students from South East Asia, the chapter will consider how international student mobility intersects with the 'local' of host institutions. Given the networking and sociality presumed in discourses of cultural work mobility, it argues for greater attention to intercultural skills in the team-based skills development practices of the cultural work HE curricula. In so doing, and in order to negotiate the complexity of collaboration in a highly individualized yet networked employment environment, it further suggests that perhaps the kind of relationship one needs to cultivate is best described as 'co-opetition', a mix of co-operation and competition.

Context: Creative industries policy globally

Cultural, and more explicitly creative industries discourse has itself been something of a highly mobile feast, albeit one heavily concentrated, until recently, within the English-speaking world. It was the UK government, especially under Prime Minister Tony Blair in the heady days immediately after the 'Cool Britannia' moment of the late 1990s and into the noughties, which has most strongly championed the economic, social and cultural significance of cultural industries. The full flowering of the UK's creative industries agenda has especially been achieved through the DCMS (Department of Culture, Media and Sport), as well as via the targeted development and expansion of an already strong HE sector. But this kind of government-driven approach to the nexus between creativity and the affordances of digital technology was already manifest elsewhere, such as in the slightly earlier Australian government policy statement *Creative Nation: Commonwealth Cultural Policy*. Released in the dying days of the Australian Labor Party government of Paul Keating, the Department of Communication and the Arts' 1994 *Creative Nation* document was a predictor for how a culture-driven economy was an ideal model for approaching 'the information revolution and the new media not with fear and loathing, but with imagination and wit. We have to see the extraordinary opportunities for enjoyment and creativity it contains' (Department of Communication and the Arts, 1994). Moving beyond a traditional cultural emphasis on the arts and formal cultural institutions, in language now familiar to us, it firmly established this cultural policy as 'also an economic policy':

> Culture creates wealth....Culture employs....Culture adds value, it makes an essential contribution to innovation, marketing and design. It is a badge of our industry. The level of our creativity substantially determines our ability to adapt to new economic imperatives. It is a valuable export in itself and an essential accompaniment to the export of other commodities. It attracts tourists and students. It is essential to our economic success.
>
> (Department of Communication and the Arts, 1994, no page)

With Keating keen to locate Australia economically, if not culturally, as a nation located in Asia, the early 1990s in Australia were also a time of exponential growth in the provision of international education by Australian universities – offshore but, especially, onshore – a trend which has continued to the present day.[1] The release of *Creative Nation* likewise occurred at a time when cultural policy in Australia had a strong academic presence in the form of the Key Centre for

Media and Cultural Policy Research, based in Brisbane, Queensland and which brought together scholars from across the city's universities. More than any other place in Australia, Queensland has championed creative industries, largely arising from the research and policy work now being driven by the Queensland Institute of Technology's creative industries faculty. Scholars operating out of the faculty and its research centres are themselves the embodiment of global flows of cultural workers and creative industries policy development for not only are they key players domestically but also in the mapping and understanding of cultural industries in the UK (Higgs et al., 2008) and in Asia, notably China (Hartley and Keane, 2006; Keane, 2006a, 2006b, 2007a, 2007b, 2009a, 2009b, 2010; Keane and Hartley, 2006; O'Connor and Gu, 2006; O'Connor, 2009).

I offer this background here in order to demonstrate the global flow of ideas, as well as people. The Keating government's *Creative Nation* document was influential in the subsequent Blair government's DCMS framework for the development of Britain's creative industries. The election in Australia of the conservative Howard Liberal government in March 1996 signalled an end to the kind of approaches advocated in *Creative Nation*; however, the election in May 1997 of Tony Blair's Labour Party in the UK saw, in its championing of creative industries as a policy development framework, the full realization of the post-'subsidised arts' approach to intellectual property-driven cultural *qua* economic development nascent in *Creative Nation*. As even some of its strongest proponents concede, creative industries as a discourse has been particularly attractive to, and hence influential in, governmental policy circles on account of its hardwiring of creativity to innovation and economic growth within knowledge economies (Cunningham, 2009). For this reason too, it has appealed to both university leaders and undergraduate students increasingly focused upon vocational outcomes from degrees in the arts and humanities.

Presumed mobility in the face of precariousness

The melding of work and play has frequently been lauded as the great reward for workers lying at the heart of cultural work in the creative industries (Tapscott, 1996; Leadbeater and Oakley, 1999; Florida, 2003; Leadbeater and Miller, 2004; Tapscott and Williams, 2007). There has also been a presumption of individual mobility in pursuit of the idealized creative work lifestyle which sees a blurring between work and play, and which is further predicated on a strong link between one's occupation and social identity. Reaching its zenith in Richard Florida's work on the creative class (Florida, 2003, 2005, 2007), much policy discourse and practical advice around cultural work has as a focus national, if not global, mobility on the part of creative workers. But even Florida is somewhat alert to the personal issues at stake here:

> Creative people are indeed the chief currency of the emerging economic age. And these people tend to be mobile and change jobs frequently. But the upshot is complex. First, it's certainly not true that all leverage and bargaining power devolves to the free-agent worker – more likely, the balance of power shifts back and forth with supply and demand for particular talents. The free agent assumes more risk and responsibility along with more freedom. While the system looks lovely during good times, these risks and their consequences can be quite dire when the economy turns down. Furthermore, people are complex. Their motivations are many and varied, and not all creative people want to be self-employed or job-hopping free agents. The one consistent quality I detect among creative people is that they seek opportunities to exercise their creativity. If they can find these opportunities by becoming free agents they will do so, and if they can find them by joining a firm and staying with it for a good while, they will do that.
>
> (Florida, 2003, p. 28)

At the most celebratory end of the discourse, Florida's 'creative class', like other professionally mobile members of the global knowledge economy, are employment-centred exemplars of Zygmunt Bauman's metaphoric figure of the 'tourist'; those whose mobility is predicated upon choice, at least perceived choice. They 'keep the game short' and are wary of long-term commitments; they 'refuse to be "fixed" one way or the other', nor to 'get tied to one place, however pleasurable the present stopover may feel' (Bauman, 1997, p. 89). The tourist life is one of 'situational control', 'the ability to choose where and with what parts of the world to "interface" and when to switch off the connection' (Bauman, 1997, p. 91). This figure he sets in opposition, at the other end of a continuum, to another broad category of globally mobile people whose experience and motivations are very different, and whose mobility stories are all too frequently overlooked or ignored in the emphasis on the idealized world of 'tourist' level globalization: 'vagabonds'. For vagabonds, 'to be free means *not to have* to wander around'; the vagabond longs for a 'home and to be allowed to stay inside'; the 'vagabonds are the waste of the world which has dedicated itself to tourists' services' (Bauman, 1997, p. 92):

> The tourists stay or move at their heart's desire. They abandon the site when new untried opportunities beckon elsewhere. The vagabonds, however, know that they won't stay for long, however strongly they wish to, since nowhere they stop are they welcome: if tourists move because they find the world irresistibly *attractive*, the vagabonds move because they find the world unbearably inhospitable.... The tourists travel because they *want to*, the vagabonds – because they have *no other choice*.'
>
> (Bauman, 1997, pp. 92–93)

Bauman's taxonomy raises the important question in this context (with Florida's creative class the yardstick of policy discussions), what exactly do we mean by mobility in the cultural work context? The discursive hype, not to mention student dreams, presume an idealized privileged professional 'tourist' mobility which evokes an image of ease, cosmopolitanism and access. But we need to challenge the universal accuracy and desirability of this peripatetic picture.

An iconic exemplar of this unassuming international professional lifestyle is that of US-based talent scout Jason Siner. At a time when smart phones, tablet devices and lightweight laptops among other mobile digital technologies are being lauded as bringing about the death of the traditional office in favour of more locationally flexible and low-cost professional practices such as taking advantage of free Wi-Fi and quality coffee at cafes on the run (Burke, 2011), Jason's *modus operandi* means that his caffeinated, peripatetic hot desking is transnational. In a 2011 article reporting on a global commercial survey of 600 executives of large corporations on their perceptions of future office space needs and working patterns (undertaken by Regus, a company supplying flexible office spaces internationally to cater for globally mobile business travellers), Jason is the humanizing embodiment of the idealized 'remote worker' operating in an increasingly 'agile working environment' (Burke, 2011). Jason is a cultural worker. Interviewed in fashionably cool inner-city Glebe in Sydney at the appropriately named 'Well Connected Café', he speaks of how he keeps overheads down while travelling for work by conducting meetings in public spaces, such as cafes. Though staying in a hotel from which he could also operate, as he 'pushes aside his Macbook and iPad' he demonstrates a valuably gender-aware explanation of one of the clear advantages informal and public locations such as cafes have over the private space of the hotel room: '[as a talent agent] it would be a bit slimey meeting 18-year-old actresses in my hotel room, so I just move between cafes and everyone feels comfortable' (Burke, 2011).

While his own preferences around where he would prefer to work are not explicitly articulated in the article, the apparent ease with which Jason moves between cafes implies that he may too be one of the people identified in the survey as preferring to work in a 'third place', neither the traditional office nor the home but another, often public, location (Burke, 2011). Such work locations may be chosen for other reasons even when one is at 'home': good coffee, free Wi-Fi, or to cover the fact that one's global micro-enterprise is conducted from the kitchen counter. It may also be sought out as a means of overcoming the worst isolations of working from home (Felstead and Jewson, 2000), or, perhaps, as one means by which to attempt to maintain work–home boundaries, while simultaneously keeping overheads down and locational flexibility maximized. Jason, like many other employed cultural workers, is a tourist; the employees who left home for the dormitories of Foxconn and who make our workstyle-enabling iProducts are, in Bauman's terms, the enabling 'vagabonds'. But even at the 'high-flying' end of creative work such as that iconically presented by in-demand Silicon Valley programmers, not all is rosy in the peripatetic, creative work fast lane. The commercial pressures of the GFC mean that iconic knowledge economy employers are allegedly seeking out their own ways to contain the costs associated with employing globally mobile tech talent. In reports which emerged from an anti-trust hearing in the US, it is alleged that Google, Intel, Adobe Systems, Intuit, Lucasfilm, Pixar and Apple have been accused of collusion to not poach one another's star employees, and hence, with keeping 'wages artificially low by preventing bidding wars for the best employees' (Wohlsen, 2012). Further, a growing body of critique now challenges some of the grander employment claims implicit in much of the established creative economy discourse. Marked as it is by uncertain career trajectories, workers engaged in the 'precarious labour' of creative industries (Neilson and Rossiter, 2005; Negri, 2006) are expected to take for granted job flexibility, casualization of the employment marketplace and all the uncertainty that goes with this. The cultural work job market is tight, with unclear entry pathways.

Is the classroom truly global? Intercultural awareness as preparation for the peripatetic life

> When citizens are to live their lives as 'self-managed projects', then the self becomes a site of labour as well as governmentality.
>
> (Ouellette and Wilson, 2011, p. 556)

Also located towards the 'tourist' end of Bauman's spectrum, but not, on the whole, quite as close to its terminal as Jason Siner, are the approximately 143,880,000 international students who not only left their parental home, city or state, but their country to pursue their personal and career dreams in 2006 (Gümüz, 2011, p. 28). Many of these students are in Australia, which for the last couple of decades has actively encouraged the enrolment of international students, especially from Asian countries, to the extent that in 2006 foreign students represented 28.5 per cent of all enrolments in Australian HE (Gümüz, 2011, p. 206). Overseas student numbers have been particularly high in courses preparing students for work in IT industries, computing and management-related professions, and they are to be found across the disciplines, including in those related to cultural work employment (notably digital content production, including animation and web design). These students are, by their very commitment to undertaking overseas training (frequently in a language which is not their first nor even second), aware of the globally competitive environment within which they seek to gain employment.

One response to the surplus of creative workers being produced in HE here in Australia, as across the global West, has been to look to the growth economies of Asia for new training, market and employment opportunities. Certainly the nations of South East Asia are emerging as major countries of origin in the global flow of international students (Gümüz, 2011, p. 36), with the more established educational markets of Singapore and Malaysia developing their own strengths as providers of HE to students from elsewhere in Asia. In so doing, both via these mobile students and domestically, Asian higher education institutions (HEIs) too are at risk of producing their own over-supply of creative graduates, as universities with an eye to the bottom line accept more students into popular courses than will be ever able to find employment in their chosen sector. Further, much university-level training for cultural work seems to assume students will be moving into ongoing, full-time creative positions in large organizations. While this might be true for many graduates in major global cities (though less so, given the GFC), for many of the industrialized world's cultural workers, their career pathways are much less clear-cut, and potentially the opportunities will be international. Many face the challenge of being owner-operators or sole-traders operating from contract to contract; others will find themselves in more marginal SMEs or micro businesses and/or embedded as cultural workers in not obviously creative industries. Given such likely career trajectories, strong personal networks and well-honed skill-sets become ever more important.

Returning to the specifics of how this precarious global labour situation plays out in the classroom, we need to pose the question: how can we realistically prepare students for the globalized world of cultural work, personally and vocationally? Despite all the talk of creative worker mobility as an inherent affordance, indeed necessity, of the global knowledge economy, a search of scholarly writing and research indicates little focus on the intercultural aspects of innovation, creativity and networking in the cultural work curricula. Partially, this is a function of the sampling approach employed, with most reports tending to focus on local employers' attitudes towards local institutions' graduates (for example, in the Australian context 60 Sox, 2010). Obviously, not all students enter our classrooms from similar backgrounds, and a key differential is that between those who have already made a major leap of faith on the road towards being a globally mobile cultural worker, and those students for whom the HE class space is their 3 pm appointment on their way back to the suburban family home three kilometres away. In a globalized world where many young people are motivated to seek 'the best education they can afford anywhere in the world so that they can compete in the global labor market, and, in the process, also make friends and meet future business partners' (Gümüz, 2011, p. 19), students in highly diverse classrooms should be at a tremendous advantage. Thus, it would follow that this would especially be the case in those countries who receive far more students than they send overseas (such as the US, Australia, New Zealand and the UK). With the 'world coming to them', local students share classrooms with highly motivated (in the Australian context), mostly Asian students from source countries flagged as those driving the global economy in the 21st century. Surely this would be seen by students as a major plus as they develop their professional skills and networks. But a number of issues coalesce here which suggest that the opportunities for cross-cultural skills development offered by multi-national classrooms are not yet being fully realized in cultural work-related degrees in English-speaking nations, either in terms of curriculum design or student approaches to it. Specifically, in the space remaining in this chapter, I wish to consider students' attitudes to group-based assessment work – the pedagogical classroom manifestation of cultural industries' demands for 'teamwork' skills, not to mention the prevalence of start-up micro-enterprises more likely to consist of teams than single individuals – and to argue for greater attention to intercultural awareness and interpersonal communication competencies in cultural work curricula.

Successive studies into the kinds of skill-sets required of cultural work graduates by employers have consistently identified such essential abilities as: communication skills; motivation; problem solving skills; adaptability; self-confidence and self-management; creativity; collaborative learning approaches; multidisciplinary working; self-employment, entrepreneurship and business skills; client-facing skills; and, notably, teamworking skills (Ball, 2004; Ball et al., 2010; Haukka et al., 2010). Given that the majority of these skills are personal or social, as much as technical, and involve networking and/or the ability to work with people, it is timely in the 21st century that a strong intercultural emphasis should be added to these lists. The need for greater intercultural awareness has an added imperative within the Anglophone world, where cultural industries are coming in for increasing censure, given the absence of women and people of colour, especially in the higher-profile, higher-paying and more secure positions within the cultural industries hierarchy (Smallbone et al., 2005; Christopherson, 2009; see also Part IV this volume). Networking, the professional sociality at the heart of much cultural work practice, requires a particular interpersonal skill-set and disposition which, as Ashton notes (drawing upon key Anglo-Australian scholarship in this area), 'is not simply a means of "making contacts" but can be explored in terms of personal tensions and anxieties, and identity performances and questions of exclusion in terms of race, class and gender' (Ashton, 2011, p. 557; see also Part IV this volume). Indeed, the writing was 'on the wall' early on for racial exclusion as something hard-wired into the networks underpinning the creative industries. As Richard Florida conceded in his early mappings:

> My own research shows a negative statistical correlation between concentrations of high-tech firms in a region and nonwhites as a percentage of the population, which is particularly disturbing in light of my other findings on the positive relationship between high-tech and other kinds of diversity – from foreign-born people to gays.
>
> (Florida, 2003, p. 80)

These exclusions go to the heart of the myth of universal creative mobility, underpinning the boosterish discourse prevalent in some sectors of the creative policy marketplace: 'Focus group participants expressed a preference for places where they can readily plug in and develop a support structure of colleagues and friends. This is particularly important to recognize as many of these young people are relocating without the support structure of friends and family' (Florida, 2005, p. 86).

Such patterns of exclusion seem to start early for some aspiring cultural workers. International student mobility brings with it the presence of the 'Other' into the domestic classroom. While some embrace (or simply take for granted) this scenario, already operating as they are as cosmopolitan citizens, many other domestic students can find this, if not daunting and too much 'hard work', then certainly not an opportunity for cross-cultural learning. All too often, non-native English speaking and writing skills, which admittedly can be less than desired in a university classroom, are seen as a barrier to easy communication and are seen to metonymically represent the broader capacities of individual international students. Whatever other skills and knowledge they possess becomes secondary to such surface appearances. That they are able to operate in at least one other language other than their own, ironically, rather than being seen as evidence of skill and capacity is frequently judged in terms of lack. Certainly my own classroom experiences concur with more systemic studies conducted across Anglophone countries which have 'revealed that despite growing numbers of international students and increasingly diverse domestic student bodies, there is strong evidence of minimal interactions between culturally diverse students' (Kimmel and Volet, 2010, p. 2; see also Volet and Ang, 2006; Summers and Volet, 2008). Such 'keeping to one's own', which is a tendency which exists among all parties to the studies, negates the capacity to build precisely the kinds of intercultural capacities which will enable students to engage in professional lives not only of physical mobility, but also in everyday local business and social worlds marked by globalization and cultural diversity. Interestingly, in the Australian context at least, Australian-born students of Asian descent also manifest a desire to seek out groups of local Australian students (Volet and Ang, 2006), highlighting the linguistic and cultural, rather than more overtly racist, reasons for the barriers to mixing. The presence too in the Australian undergraduate classroom of large cohorts of students from the same Asian country works further to inhibit intermixing as international students seek out intra-cultural connectedness and a shared sense of identity through national peer groups (Volet and Ang, 2006). And very few identified cultural mixing as an important part of their reasons for wanting to study abroad (Volet and Ang, 2006, p. 11). As Kimmel and Volet proceed to observe, despite the provision of opportunities for intercultural contact on campuses afforded by the internationalization of education, this mere co-presence 'does not automatically lead to an increase in intergroup contact', thus defeating one of the central aims of educational internationalization (Kimmel and Volet, 2010, p. 2). But the truth is that classrooms will only continue to become more diverse, with the expansion of HE both internationally and domestically as a priority of governments around the Anglophone world. Yet, despite this and the fact that many (especially digital content) cultural industries are operating in a highly mobile and globalized milieu, working in a classroom that is 'simultaneously global, national and local' means the space nonetheless remains for domestic students to engage in highly safe and culturally unchallenging ways of operating.

International student mobility, higher education and cultural work: Unfinished business

That the humanities and creative arts are seen to lag behind other university sectors in terms of the global outlook of their scholarship and research should be a source of great concern when it comes to the educating of cultural workers (Marginson et al., 2010, p. 202). As we have already seen, within the English-speaking world the creative industries are coming in for increased criticism of the subtle ways in which professional sociality and networking operate to provide access to, as well as to exclude, potential cultural workers (these issues of social capital and network inclusion and exclusion, including in terms of gender and race, are discussed in further detail in Part IV). Given the central role cultural workers – media producers and artistic directors, marketing and advertising professionals, journalists, photographers, illustrators, musicians, media presenters, communication professionals, writers, artists, architects, designers – play in generating the symbolic goods at the heart of contemporary life, it is essential that this sector represents the age, sexual and ethnic diversity of the wider community.

With portfolio careers the norm, cultural workers will be faced at various stages of their career with differing levels of immersion with 'Other' cultures. Thus, in the 21st century, a basic capacity to engage with colleagues and customers with respect for cultural differences remains a baseline *sine qua non,* for not only are workers globally mobile, digital technologies mean that in this globally interconnected world, geographic location is not always a constraint on global operation. As a negative outcome, globalization leads to white collar jobs – including cultural work – being undertaken at a distance in countries with pools of cheap labour, limited employment protections and unionization (Miller, 2011). But more positively, globalization as enabled by digital communications technologies also means that a relatively small digital media company a mere couple of kilometres away from my campus here in Adelaide can provide visual effects sequences for *Harry Potter and the Deathly Hallows (Part II)*, *Pirates of the Caribbean: On Stranger Tides*, *Terminator Salvation*, *X-Men Origins: Wolverine* and *Green Lantern* (Rising Sun Pictures, n.d.), and that some graduates can build a world-class animation company 'providing stylised character animation to the world's leading console game developers, publishers and advertising agencies' by developing their business through an initial focus on providing content for the strong Asian animation markets (The People's Republic of Animation, n.d.). With culturally diverse task groups likely to become increasingly prevalent in industry (Summers and Volet, 2008, p. 358), even if they are not planning to relocate, cultural work graduates require the capacity to act globally, across time, space, language and cultures.

Richard Florida has written at length of his concern that in the race to secure US interests – and borders – following the 9/11 attacks, the US is cutting itself off from the competitive advantage skilled migrants bring and which made it the powerhouse of the 20th century economy (Florida, 2004, 2007). In particular, he has criticized moves which limit the ability of foreign students to remain working in the US upon attainment of their degrees (Florida, 2004). He quotes research figures which demonstrate that Chinese and Indian engineers were running nearly 30 per cent of Silicon Valley's high-tech companies in the 1990s; many of them were former international students within the American system: 'What if, for example, Vinod Khosla, the cofounder of Sun Microsystems and venture capital luminary who has blocked so many blockbuster companies, had stayed in India? Or if An Wang, founder of Wang Laboratories, had gone to university in Europe?' (Florida, 2004, p. 7). In Australia too, attention is being paid to retaining international students upon graduation, especially in smaller cities such as Adelaide, which loses many local graduates to the brighter lights of Sydney, Melbourne, London, New York and Shanghai (Atkinson and Easthope, 2008, p. 313). Despite the so-called death of the 'tyranny of distance' occasioned by international mobility and digital communications technologies, place still matters when it comes to, if not the quality and vitality, then certainly the depth and breadth of local cultural economies. Competing for talent or contracts in this global marketplace can be more difficult for those located outside the large cultural capitals, especially in the global North. This is particularly the case when the number of opportunities available in large cities coincides geographically with many young university graduates' urbane lifestyle aspirations. Though this is not to say that other locales do not have their own work–life attractions, especially at further stages of peoples' creative careers (Luckman, 2012).

With the entrenching of English as *the lingua franca* of commerce and global networking, the major English-speaking destination countries for international students (US, UK, Australia, Canada and New Zealand) are particularly in demand by international students. As a result, local students too have much to gain through the presence of international students from the growing markets of South East Asia, given 'internationalization helps students develop global critical thinking skills essential to contributing as citizens of the world and competing in the international marketplace' (Gümüz, 2011, p. 237). Given that 'isolation and lack of contacts' have been identified as being a serious hindrance to getting started, post-degree, in cultural work (Ball, 2004, p. 13), it is important to focus both in content and activity structure on the intercultural in the HE curriculum of cultural workers. With networking and intercultural sociality being fundamental skill-sets graduates will require in the global economy, courses whose role is, at least in part, to prepare students for employment in cultural work are well placed to see the presence of international students in the classroom as affording opportunities for the development of international connections and understanding. Greater global understanding and solidarity also bring increased capacity, at both an individual and collective level, to off-set some of the more individuating tendencies underpinning cultural work as a precarious form of labour.

As Simon Marginson, Professor of Higher Education at the University of Melbourne valuably reminds us, worldwide HE is best understood 'as a relational environment that is simultaneously global, national and local' (Marginson et al., 2010, p. 201). Yet, when it comes time for students to engage in group work, which would ideally be a perfect space in which to develop intercultural competencies, research and anecdotal evidence shared between and among students and lecturers demonstrates a reluctance for mixing between students of differing cultural and linguistic backgrounds (Volet and Ang, 2006;

Summers and Volet, 2008; Kimmel and Volet, 2010). The irony perhaps is that this comes at a time when group work itself appears to be experiencing renewed acceptance among student cohorts also increasingly accustomed to peer feedback systems as an interesting pedagogical side effect of the exponential growth in social networking. This increased recognition of the value of team-based assessment activities is in large part due to their recognition of the need to demonstrate teamwork skills in order to gain creative industry employment, especially so in team-based production environments such as the digital content sector. But even in the more individualistic vocational training environment for journalism which tends to attract highly motivated and competitive students, many motivated by the professional autonomy provided to middle-ranking and senior members of the profession, the importance of strategic teamwork is recognized. For some, it is a necessary synergistic part of getting a larger project completed; for others, working as a group can be a buffer against some of the worst individualizing and relentlessly competitive aspects of the profession. But like other creative professionals, especially those in smaller creative milieus or starting out on their careers, even in these competitive environments there is recognition that the real race is not so much in the classroom, as out in the wider world in the battle for work placements, internships and Internet profile. Local co-operation can be an advantage in preparing oneself to compete in this bigger pond. The lens of co-opetition – simultaneous co-operation and competition – is especially useful in understanding this complexity in the network-based world of creative employment (Hearn and Pace, 2006). Frequently employing game theory models as a way of unpacking the economics of this kind of relationship (Nalebuff and Brandenburger, 1997; Levy et al., 2003), co-opetition is increasingly being identified as a business model underpinned by 'the need for the "coevolution" of organisations and networks and the "bundling" of complementary functions and companies' (Hearn and Pace, 2006, p. 61). In this way, one company's capacity development is contingent upon the evolution of another – the achievement is mutual. Such a 'lift all boats' approach to the competitive marketplace is, however, not limited to the big end of town (Hearn and Pace discuss an instance of co-opetitive collaboration between Intel, IBM and Microsoft), but we can also see such strategic network alliances and acts of collaboration evident in the cultural work classroom as students become increasingly aware of the level of competition in the larger, global creative workforce.

Note

1. The trend has been one of steady increase over the last two decades (see Gürüz, 2011, p. 263). However, at the time of writing concerns are starting to be expressed that this growth will not continue owing to a mix of factors including, but not limited to: the high Australian dollar; negative publicity following a number of high-profile violent crimes against Indian students, especially in the city of Melbourne, which received major coverage in the Indian media; and changes to student Visa requirements.

References

60 Sox (2010) *From Education to Work in Australia's Creative Digital Industries: Comparing the Opinions and Practices of Employers and Aspiring Creative* (Brisbane: Queensland Institute of Technology (QUT), Institute for Creative Industries and Innovation and Australian Research Council).

Ashton, D. (2011) Media Work and the Creative Industries: Identity Work, Professionalism and Employability, *Education + Training* 53(6): 546–560.

Atkinson, R. and Easthope, H. (2008) The Creative Class *in Utero?* The Australian City, the Creative Economy and the Role of Higher Education, *Built Environment* 34(3): 307–318.

Ball, L. (2004) Preparing Graduates in Art and Design to Meet the Challenges of Working in the Creative Industries a New Model for Work, *Art, Design and Communication in Higher Education* 1(1): 10–23.

Ball, L., Pollard, E. and Stanley, N. (2010) *Creative Graduates Creative Futures* (London: Creative Graduates Creative Futures Higher Education Partnership and the Institute for Employment Studies).

Bauman, Z. (1997) *Postmodernity and Its Discontents* (Cambridge: Polity Press).

Burke, K. (2011) Coffee is Ready, and So is a Generation's New Workplace, *The Age*, 4 June 2011, http://www.theage.com.au/action/printArticle?id=2406703, date accessed 6 June 2011.

Christopherson, S. (2009) Working in the Creative Economy: Risk, Adaptation and the Persistence of Exclusionary Networks, in McKinlay, A. and Smith, C. (eds) *Creative Labour: Working in the Creative Industries* (Basingstoke: Palgrave Macmillan): 72–90.

Cunningham, S. (2009) Trojan Horse or Rorschach Blot? Creative Industries Discourse around the World, *International Journal of Cultural Policy* 15(4): 375–386.

Department of Communication and the Arts (1994) *Creative Nation: Commonwealth Cultural Policy,* released October 1994, Canberra, http://pandora.nla.gov.au/pan/21336/20031011-0000/www.nla.gov.au/creative.nation/contents.html, date accessed 9 March 2012.

Felstead, A. and Jewson, N. (2000) *In Work, At Home: Towards an Understanding of Homeworking* (London: Routledge).

Florida, R. (2003) *The Rise of the Creative Class* (North Melbourne: Pluto Press Australia).

Florida, R. (2004) America's Looming Creativity Crisis, *Harvard Business Review,* 1–9 October.

Florida, R. (2005) *Cities and the Creative Class* (London: Routledge).

Florida, R. (2007) *The Flight of the Creative Class: The New Global Competition for Talent* (New York: Collins).

Gümüz, K. (2011) *Higher Education and International Student Mobility in the Global Knowledge Economy*, 2nd edn (Albany: State University of New York Press).

Hartley, J. and Keane, M (2006) Creative Industries and Innovation in China, *International Journal of Cultural Studies* 9(3): 259–262.

Haukka, S., Hearn, G., Brow, J. and Cunningham, S. (2010) *From Education to Work in Australia's Creative Digital industries: Comparing the Opinions and Practices of Employers and Aspiring Creatives* (Brisbane: QUT, Australian Research Council, Institute for Creative Industries and Innovation).

Hearn, G. and Pace, C. (2006) Value-Creating Ecologies: Understanding Next Generation Business Systems, *Foresight: The Journal of Future Studies, Strategic Thinking and Policy* 8(1): 55–65.

Hesmondhalgh, D. (2002) *Cultural Industries* (London: Sage).

Higgs, P., Cunningham, S. and Bakhshi, H. (2008) *Beyond the Creative Industries: Mapping the Creative Economy in the United Kingdom* (London: NESTA).

Keane, M. (2006a) Once Were Peripheral: Creating Media Capacity in East Asia, *Media, Culture and Society* 28(6): 835–855.

Keane, M. (2006b) From Made in China to Created in China, *International Journal of Cultural Studies* 9(3): 285–296.

Keane, M. (2007a) Re-Imagining Chinese Creativity: The Rise of a Super-Sign, in Lovink, G. and Rossiter, N. (eds) *MyCreativity Reader: A Critique of Creative Industries* (Amsterdam: Institute of Networked Cultures (INC)).

Keane, M. (2007b) Structure and Reform in China's Television Industries, in Kops, M. and Ollig, S. (eds) *Internationalization of the Chinese TV Sector* (Berlin: Lit Verlag): 191–204.

Keane, M. (2009a) Creative Industries in China: Four Perspectives on Social Transformation, *International Journal of Cultural Policy* 15(4): 431–434.

Keane, M. (2009b) Great Adaptations: China's Creative Clusters and the New Social Contract, *Continuum* 23(2): 221–230.

Keane, M. (2010) Re-Imagining China's Future: Soft Power, Cultural Presence and the East Asian Media Market, in Black, D., Epstein, S. and Tokita, A. (eds) *Complicated Currents: Media Flows, Soft Power and East Asia* (Clayton: Monash University ePress): http://books.publishing.monash.edu/apps/bookworm/view/Complicated+Currents/122/xhtml/chapter14.html.

Keane, M. and Hartley, J. (2006) Creative Industries and Innovation in China, *International Journal of Cultural Studies* 9(3): 259–264.

Kimmel, K. and Volet, S. (2010) University Students' Perceptions of and Attitudes Towards Culturally Diverse Group Work: Does Context Matter? *Journal of Studies in International Education* XX(X): 1–25.

Leadbeater, C. and Miller, P. (2004) *The Pro-Am Revolution: How Enthusiasts Are Changing Our Economy and Society* (London: Demos).

Leadbeater, C. and Oakley, K. (1999) *The Independents: Britain's New Cultural Entrepreneurs* (London: Demos, Institute of Contemporary Arts).

Levy, M., Loebbecke, C. and Powell, P. (2003) SMEs, Co-Opetition and Knowledge Sharing: The Role of Information Systems, *European Journal of Information Systems* 12: 3–17.

Luckman, S. (2012) *Locating Cultural Work: The Politics and Poetics of Rural, Regional and Remote Creativity* (Basingstoke and New York: Palgrave Macmillan).

Marginson, S., Murphy, P. and Peters, M. (2010) *Global Creation: Space, Mobility and Synchrony in the Age of the Knowledge Economy* (New York: Peter Lang).

Miller, T. (2011) The New International Division of Cultural Labour, in Deuze, M. (ed.) *Managing Media Work* (Los Angeles, London, New Delhi, Singapore and Washington DC: Sage): 87–99.

Nalebuff, B. and Brandenburger, J. (1997) Co-Opitition: Competitive and Cooperative Business Strategies for the Digital Economy, *Strategy & Leadership* 25(6): 228–235.

Negri, A. (2006) *Empire and Beyond* (Cambridge and Malden, MA: Polity).

Neilson, B. and Rossiter, N. (2005) From Precarity to Precariousness and Back Again: Labour, Life and Unstable Networks, *Fibreculture*, 5, http://five .fibreculturejournal.org/

O'Connor, J. (2009) Shanghai Moderne: Creative Economy in a Creative City? in Kong, L. and O'Connor, J. (eds) *Creative Economies, Creative Cities: Asian-European Perspectives* (Dordrecht, Heidelberg, London and New York: Springer): 175–193.

O'Connor, J. and Gu, X. (2006) A New Modernity? The Arrival of 'Creative Industries' in China, *International Journal of Cultural Studies* 9(3): 271–283.

Ouellette, L. and Wilson, J. (2011) Women's Work: Affective Labour and Convergence Culture, *Cultural Studies* 25(4–5): 548–565.

People's Republic of Animation (n.d.) About Us, http://www.thepra.com.au/, date accessed 23 February 2012.

Rising Sun Pictures (n.d.) Home Page, http://www.rsp.com.au/news.htm, date accessed 23 February 2012.

Smallbone, D., Bertotti, M. and Ekanem, I. (2005) Diversification in Ethnic Minority Business: The Case of Asians in London's Creative Industries, *Journal of Small Business and Enterprise Development* 12(1): 41–56.

Summers, M. and Volet, S. (2008) Students' Attitudes towards Culturally Mixed groups on International Campuses: Impact of Participation in Diverse and Non-Diverse Groups, *Studies in Higher Education* 33(4): 357–370.

Tapscott, D. (1996) *The Digital Economy: Promise and Peril in the Age of Networked Intelligence* (New York: McGraw-Hill).

Tapscott, D. and Williams, A. (2007) *Wikinomics: How Mass Collaboration Changes Everything* (London: Portfolio (Penguin)).

Volet, S. and Ang, G. (2006) Culturally Mixed Groups on International Campuses: An Opportunity for InterCultural Learning, *Higher Education Research & Development* 17(1): 5–23.

Wohlsen, M. (2012) Google, Apple Accused of Ripping Off Top Workers, *The Advertiser*, 30 January 2012, http://www.adelaidenow.com.au/news/google-apple-accused-of-ripping-off-top-workers/story-fn7bfu22-1226257053237, date accessed 31 January 2012.

4
No Longer Just Making the Tea: Media Work Placements and Work-Based Learning in Higher Education

Richard Berger, Jonathan Wardle and Marketa Zezulkova

Introduction

This chapter takes as its focus the experiences of work placement students on undergraduate creative and media programmes at the Media School, Bournemouth University. The School has almost 3,000 students, most of whom undertake some form of work placement as a formal aspect of their studies. It is perhaps an axiom now that such programmes of study in the post-1992 university sector are more industry facing – the word 'vocational' is often applied – and have been the subject of a great deal of criticism (see Berger and McDougall, 2012).[1] However, we argue here that the work placement can also be an important and useful pedagogic experience if used in the right way, where students can develop further as critical thinkers. We do, however, recognize that work placements, particularly as part of a creative and media curriculum, are not without their own challenges either; as one recent report notes (Collis, 2010, p. 7; see also Allen; Lee; and Oakley – this volume):

> Unlike disciplines with established work-integrated learning programs, creative industries faculties are unlikely to have a team of professional staff whose job it is to undertake the complex administration associated with placements, may not have academic staff with experience and skill in the area of work-integrated learning pedagogy and may not have any of the technical infrastructure commonly associated with work-integrated programs.

While this may (or may not) be true, it comes at a time when the viability and integrity of the work placement (its role, its purpose) is the subject of a myriad of policy movements and increasingly closer government scrutiny. The rhetoric now seems to be that universities must provide an education focused towards a particular industry or sector (Westwood, 2012), and a work placement programme, and its attendant relationships with employers and industry advisors, is one very visible and obvious way of achieving that.

Skillset's *Guidelines for Employers Offering Work Placement Schemes in the Creative Industries* (2010) makes some clear distinctions between the different types of offerings: volunteering; placements; internships (where students 'perform' as a worker); traineeships (usually very focused and over a longer period) and apprenticeships (formal, often involving qualifications and accreditations).

Therefore, with this as a broad backdrop, this chapter seeks to explore the relationship higher education (HE) now has with industry, through the lens of the work placement at Bournemouth. In recent years, there been a great deal of pedagogy seeming to support the perceived benefits of 'experience-based learning'. In times of economic hardship, the work placement can become a vehicle for the anxieties expressed by a fractured workforce:

> Hundreds upon hundreds of excited fresh-faced graduates are aware that the only way to get their foot in the T.V door is to offer their services for free.
>
> (Holt, 2008, p. 8)

So, the belief persists that companies and organizations are exploiting young people. Many work placements, especially in the creative and media sector, are unpaid and offer the student little more than travel expenses. As tuition fees for universities are rising (as well as the general cost of living) an unpaid work placement can place further pressures on students, not just in terms of economics, but also availability; more programmes and courses are now *insisting* on work placements and this is increasing demand.

Much of this is scaremongering, however, as work placements may soon be the subject of new government guidelines, as a recent report from the Department for Business, Innovation & Skills (BIS) states that:

> Every full-time undergraduate student should have the opportunity to experience a structured, university approved undergraduate internship during their period of study.
>
> (Wilson, 2012, p. 5)

The Bournemouth model we describe here is flexible in that students can take their work placements in small discreet periods to fit in with their studies. This matches the 'portfolio' nature of many careers in the media and creative industries. Writing about the television industry, David Lee (2011, p. 550) notes that:

> Employment has moved decisively away from the more regulated framework of public sector employment (predominately within the BBC). What public sector employment remains is increasingly casualized, while simultaneously there has been a rapid growth in the size of the freelance independent sector workforce.

So, while it is clear that placements of up to 40 weeks in duration can only be viable if supported by a reasonable salary, there is still a great deal of value in the shorter 'bite-size' experience. Many of our graduates will go on to work as freelance media professionals, and some will start up their own businesses. While we do not offer this model as a solution to a problem – or as an exemplar to be adopted by other providers of a media education – there are lessons to be learned from the experiences of this constituency of media placement students. The work placement is also a pedagogically rich experience, something often overlooked by policy-makers; indeed, Oakley (this volume) claims that:

> [I]n the last few years, the problems of cultural work and the increasingly unrepresentative nature of the labour market, have become so apparent that policymakers have been forced to pay some attention.

We argue here that the placement should not be an adjunct to a programme of study focused on a specific industry, but seen as an experience which is integrated into the wider curriculum as an important learning opportunity.

At Bournemouth, whole undergraduate frameworks have been re-written and re-structured to gain valuable industry accreditations, particularly in areas such as journalism. Ashton's research (this volume) suggests perhaps that 'teacher-practitioners are seen as a form of lesser industry professional who are either enthusiastic amateurs or failed professionals'. Industry accreditations coupled with hands-on industry experience can restore prestige to these roles by further valuing and recognizing the importance of professional practice's place in the academy.

The Chartered Institute of Personal Development's *Internships that Work* (2009) report also includes the work placement as part of a wider definition of internships (which can be credit-bearing and far more

integrated into a period of study). The rhetoric surrounding work placements seems to come in two related forms: the advice given to the
employer, and the advice given to the prospective placement student.
These two rhetorical strands are broadly reciprocal, with the former
stating that:

> Graduates with experience can offer an employer both theoretical
> and proven practical experience.
>
> (Fanthome, 2004, p. 5)

The latter, however, is keen to highlight that 'Work experience is your
chance to shine.' (Wallis, 2006, p. 66). This suggests that there needs
to be more formal advice for academic staff to support (and understand
and value) such learning opportunities, and we would hope that forthcoming government policy would address this. At Bournemouth, the
placement is viewed as very much part of the learning experience; it is
formally assessed through a placement logbook, and is an integral aspect
of the curriculum across most of our programmes. The placement usually operates across a four- to six-week period of time in the creative and
media industries. It is interesting to note that the placement period used
to be a standard six weeks at Bournemouth, but it was reduced to four
weeks because students were finding it increasingly difficult to source
placements of six weeks in length while also seeking to earn money to
support their ongoing studies.

Pedagogy of the work placement

The work placement has been a formal aspect of many media programmes in HE for decades. In this regard, it is perhaps ahead of other
more 'traditional' subject areas. Some media programmes have always
been inaccurately seen as purely vocational – having grown out of the
pre-1992 polytechnic sector. Work placements have been at the heart of
creative and media programmes at Bournemouth since the late 1970s.
Whereas perhaps the value seen in a work placement is because it gives
a student an insight into the 'world of work' and can facilitate a 'transition from learning to earning' (Fanthome, 2004, p. 4), there is also
some emerging pedagogy which supports work-based learning in the
creative and cultural industries as a valuable learning experience. Little
and Harvey (2006) argue that work placements not only have tangi-
ble benefits but are also very popular with students who view them
almost completely as a positive experience. This offers a counter to

the position that views a university education – particularly one in the post-1992 sector – as primarily a means by which to generate a workforce for a particular industry or sector. This view, that training was somehow something quite different to 'proper' education, was exemplified by Kingsley Amis (1998, p. 236) in the 1990s:

What constitutes a university, and how that might differ from what constitutes a polytechnic or other establishment for vocational training, it is not my present business to expound. Nevertheless it cannot be said too often that education is one thing and instruction, however worthy, necessary and incidentally or momentarily education, another.

While students do make invaluable contacts and gain 'real world' experiences which can lead to employment opportunities on graduation, we have found in our research that there are many other benefits to undertaking a work placement.

A work placement can be seen as an arena where, what some pedagogic theorists call 'experiential learning', can happen – see Dewey (1938). This style of learning is defined by Jordan et al. (2008, p. 214) as:

Experiential learning is part of the student-centred movement, and stresses the direct experience of the student. This offers the teacher a range of strategies for engaging students in the learning process and provides a range of techniques such as problem-based learning that demands active involvement in learning.

The early proponents of this learning style focused purely on classroom practice, where education and learning are seen as social and interactive processes. Dewey strongly believed that students could prosper in an environment where they are allowed to experience and interact with the curriculum on their own terms; all students should be given the opportunity to take part in their own learning:

It is not enough to insist upon the necessity of experience, not even of activity in experience. Everything depends on the *quality* of experience which is had.

(Dewy, 1938 [1997], p. 27)

Dewey further proposes that all experience is multi-faceted and multi-layered. This suggests that students would benefit from occupying a series of different learning contexts, not just those wedded to the lecture theatre or the seminar room – so employers not familiar with these learning styles would need guidance too. The argument then follows that experiencing something is a linking process between action and thought. For David Kolb (1984, p. 38):

> Learning is the process whereby knowledge is created through the *transformation* of experience.
>
> [our italics]

This proposes perhaps that such a transformation can occur as a student moves between these different learning contexts: so it follows that what is learned in the university can be *transformed* once it is applied in the workplace; it is one of many valuable educational experiences. We would go further and suggest it works the other way around too. In a related idea, sometimes called 'applied learning' the view holds that students learn more from actively being engaged in tasks and problem solving: Today's students often learn better by doing, rather than by listening (Lomas and Oblinger, 2006, p. 5.7).

The pedagogy surrounding experiential (or applied) learning suggests that effective learning is centred on experiences the student may have already had, or experiences artificially created in the learning environment. The media work placement, however, offers scope to examine and aggregate the learning which is centred around what experiences the students are having outside the classroom much more immediately; it offers the opportunity to widen the pedagogic reach of experiential learning far further than the classroom, while maintaining a reflective critical distance which can be brought back into the classroom later – experiences of industry practice can enliven theoretical debate in all sorts of meaningful ways.

The rhetoric of the work placement

It is important to pinpoint the places where the rhetoric surrounding the work placement began, before understanding its influence on current education policy. At the end of the 1990s the *Inquiry into Higher Education* (now known as the 'Dearing Report') was published and was clear in its advice regarding the work placement as part of university study:

> We recommend that the Government, with immediate effect, works with representative employer and professional organisations to

encourage employers to offer more work experience opportunities for students.

(1997 [accessed online])

A year later, the National Council for Work Experience was established. Their *Placement Tutor's Handbook* warned that the employability of graduates would soon come under closer scrutiny, but that placements should not be an 'added extra':

Placements which are embedded in the curriculum have many advantages. They are not an add-on burden to students, but are given time and recognition in some form.

(National Council for Work Experience, 1998, p. 4)

A decade after the Dearing inquiry, the Department for Culture, Media and Sport (DCMS) published a report into the creative and media industries. *Creative Britain: new talents for the new economy* (1998) found that there were over two million people working in what it defined as 'creative roles'. This constituted 7.3 per cent of the UK economy, but the report was keen to point out that this sector was growing at twice the rate of the rest of the economy. *Creative Britain* stated very clearly that it wanted both further and HE to work closer with industry, and set the foundations for the quickly abandoned 14–19 Diploma.[2] A series of creative apprenticeships, as a vehicle to support the new diploma, were also launched in the autumn of that year.

In 2008, the 14–19 Diploma was introduced by the Labour government, and while popular with schools, the incoming Conservative administration made it clear they would halt the scheme, which they duly did upon taking power in 2010. However, what the Diploma experience did do was to lock the rhetoric of work-based learning into discourses circling HE and employability. The Wilson Review (2012, p. 1), which examined the relationship between HE and business, was perhaps the most situated utterance of this rhetoric:

In order to enhance graduate skills levels and ensure a smooth and effective transition between university and business environments, there is a need to increase opportunities for students to acquire relevant work experience during their studies.

It is also clear from this report that the post-1992 university sector is viewed (rightly or wrongly) as more geared towards specific professions and sectors than the older universities. This is likely to be exacerbated by rising tuition fees and the statutory obligation of all UK Higher

Education Institutions (HEIs) to publish Key Information Sets (KISs) detailing graduate employment data, as well as the increasing public, statutory and regulatory body accreditations of degree courses. This is something the Wilson Review is keen to see geared towards specific sectors, particularly in the Science, Technology, Engineering and Mathematics (STEM) sectors.

In terms of policy, the organizations and groups who existed to bring education and the workplace into closer alignment, were also in general agreement regarding the benefits of work experience as part of a rounded HE. The *Internships that Work* (2009) report by the Chartered Institute of Personal Development, describes work placements as being part of what it terms the 'informal economy'. While stating that work experience is, '[an] essential part of the career ladder in many professions' the report is keen to stress the benefits to businesses and organizations:

> gaining a new and motivated member of staff...bringing new skills and perspectives to your organisation...[and] improving productivity.
>
> (Chartered Institute of Personal Development, 2009, p. 3)

Similarly, Skillset's *Guidelines for Employers* (2010) also talks about the benefits to both individuals and employers while warning that the media industry is 'notoriously hard to break into'. The advice given to students is no less positive about work placement experiences, and the benefits they claim a successful placement experience can offer, closely mirrors those given to creative businesses and organizations. *Work Placements: a survival guide for students*, states that:

> Many employers now expect graduates to have undertaken work experience in the course of their studies.
>
> (Fanthome, 2004, p. 5)

In more specific advice tailored to an aspect of the creative and media industry, the advice given is even more evangelical:

> Work experience used to be an optional extra, but nowadays it's essential. And because work experience has become a prerequisite to a T.V job, getting a placement has become a serious business.
>
> (Wallis, 2006, p. 62; see also Lee – this volume)

This is placing huge expectations on HE in the UK, as work placements are expensive to set up and administer, and need staff with the sort of career guidance skills not normally associated with an academic teaching and research contract. As for recent research into the value of a work placement for university students, other than important work by Collis (2010) there has been remarkably little published research, particularly in the creative and media area. This could be because it has been taken for granted that these types of educative experiences are already closely in tune with the needs of industry and allied with the demands of creative organizations. As Collini (2012, p. 53) puts it:

> [S]ubjects which were initially introduced for broadly practical purposes have outlived those purposes and gone on to establish themselves as scholarly disciplines in their own right.

It is curious that more work has not been done in a field with such a powerful and persuasive rhetoric surrounding it:

> [Research] on work placements and the success of work placement experiences in the creative and cultural industries has been sparse.
>
> (Özbilgin and Tatli, 2006, p. 406)

One broad study from 2003, which did look closely at work experience opportunities in a variety of sectors, did highlight some problems. *Experience-based Learning within the Curriculum: a synthesis study* found that students often led a 'double-life' of education on one hand and work on the other; the report was clear that these two 'worlds' needed to be more closely aligned – the world of work should inform education, and vice versa. While the study was positive about the experiences of both students and employers regarding placements, the management of such initiatives was a cause for concern:

> A course which includes both academic studies and work experience is a relatively complex method of education. It has more parts to synchronise than have traditional styles of education. It does not depend only on keeping students sufficiently attentive to what academics think is appropriate for them to study; it also requires that a wide variety of people in the employment sector shall find the arrangements acceptable and thus contribute to them.
>
> (Davies, 2003, p. 21)

Davies was also concerned by the fact that placements have been introduced into UK HE without much thought in terms of educational theory, such as experiential learning. Mark Banks and David

Hesmondhalgh (2009, p. 417) recognize that 'distinctive' jobs have now become 'conventional careers' and that:

> Creative work is highly prized since it appears to offer workers the chance for non-alienating employment conducive to self-expression... [I]t may be that creative work has been especially earmarked as the quintessence of a supposed new occupational autonomy.

They go on to express concerns that while those working in the creative industries 'appear free' there are problems in that much of the work is project-based, short-term and there is little in the way of job protection. Despite the government's rhetoric little has been said officially about working conditions as the growth of the culture industries is viewed in purely economic terms:

> UK creative industries policy is increasingly becoming linked to educational and employment policy, but under the sign of economics rather than social reform or cultural equity.
>
> (Banks and Hesmondhalgh, 2009, p. 428)

So, it is important that the placement maintains its autonomy and offers a site to critique the conditions for industrial practice and commerce.

The Bournemouth University media placement

Christy Collis' (2010) study of the experiences of work-placement students in Australia within a creative industries curriculum is a related study to ours and has informed our own research. Like us, Collis takes the view that a work placement should not just be about increasing the economic value of the student, but that it can be a rich pedagogic experience, which can generate social and cultural capital. Lee (this volume) considers different forms of social and cultural capital. While noting that developing students' employability for the creative industries is now an international concern, she also recognizes that:

> Many creative industries graduates will never work in traditional careers; they will work in project-based 'portfolio careers'.
>
> (Collis, 2010, p. 3)

Whether this is desirable or not, the fact remains that many who work in the creative and media industries are freelance, or are contracted to specific projects and productions – see Skillset's 2010 *Creative Media Workforce Survey*. It is precisely this type of career which the Bournemouth University media placement is designed to prepare students for. Indeed, for many media undergraduates at Bournemouth, the placement itself is very much a 'portfolio' experience, with students choosing to work in a number of creative organizations, of differing sizes, over different periods of time, while others can opt for a single, sustained experience over 12 months. While this does reflect and chart the working patterns of many media professionals, it can give some students a rather fragmented palette of experiences.

Another problem for Bournemouth is that students generally have to travel to a large metropolis to carry out their placement(s). This adds a further expense in many cases, although many students have family in these larger cities. The creative and media industries are no longer as London-centric as they used to be; the BBC has invested heavily in other regions in recent years, moving whole areas of provision to Manchester, Bristol and Cardiff. The UK is small enough to facilitate Bournemouth students getting to these areas, and some students even go abroad.

Addressing the concerns of Davies (2003), Collis (2010) and others, creative and media students at Bournemouth University's Media School are supported throughout the placement process by the School's dedicated placements office. This is important because students need careers advice from professionals who are trained to give it. An academic contract in the UK usually requires a balance of teaching and research, but there is rarely – if ever – any requirement for careers guidance skills. So, the placements office at Bournemouth is staffed by a team of careers professionals who can support students in creating CVs and in approaching potential employers; the students are all able to make individual appointments with these tutors.

In the months leading up to the work placement, lectures are given on subjects specific to gaining a placement, and what to expect from a placement employer. The School also organizes a programme of events led by notable alumni entitled 'Ready for Work?' which encourages students to think about the things they need to do to prepare for their work experience (particularly networking), and they are encouraged to think further about what they hope the placement will facilitate for them. This is fed into the more industry-facing aspects of the curriculum, such as industry case-studies and the concurrent guest lecture programme. In addition, employers with whom the School have built a relationship over time are invited to give presentations.

For the purposes of our study, we interviewed eight undergraduate students, from different creative and media programmes at

Bournemouth. We also talked to the placement tutors who administer and manage the students' work placement experiences and academic staff who have programme-level responsibilities. The semi-structured interviews all took place face-to-face and typically lasted 20–30 minutes. All of the interviews were transcribed and then open coding was applied to identify important categories.

Through this process we found that the length of a placement did differ, from programme to programme. For example, Advertising, Marketing and Communications (AMC) students generally appreciated longer placements, because new projects and challenges emerge if you are inside an organization for a longer period of time. Students welcomed the opportunity to see projects begin, develop and finish. These students also felt that they were also able to build more productive relationships with colleagues, and this could lead to further opportunities as the students became more integrated into a team:

> R1: I didn't think I'd be doing as much as I was. After about two months, I was given big projects. I worked directly with the manager. I thought I'd be doing a lot more menial stuff so it worked out better than I thought.

Some students, however, seem to prefer a longer placement:

> R2: I did a total of seven placements throughout the year... I wasn't given enough responsibility because I was never there long enough... Whereas they [classmates] would get set bigger challenges to do each time or new projects and clients they had to look after, which I never really had. Sometimes I retrospectively regret not doing that.

> R5: I'm really happy that I did a year [in addition to studies] because doing six weeks I would have missed out so much... I don't think you get enough out of six weeks so a year is appropriate... at the end the result was amazing.

> R8: On my course... placement is only for six weeks, but I did a year, because I felt like I hadn't really learnt enough and hadn't discovered what I want to do once I graduate. In six weeks you don't really get a grasp of how things are working... which is a shame.

Students from other programmes, such as Television Production (BATV) prefer shorter placements. Some of the reasons given for this are that entry-level jobs in the television industry (such as runner or production assistant) can quickly become rather repetitive, which for many is something of a wake-up call. Also, BATV students are keen to make as many contacts as possible in the industry, and then exploit these for further part-time work in their final year, and potentially full-time employment after graduation. So, our research suggests that media students can be quite strategic in the value they place on work experience, and what they want from it; a fat contacts book is sometimes seen as more useful than a pay cheque. Therefore, a balance needs to be made between working unpaid and gaining valuable experience; this tension will only increase as tuition fees rise. For Lee (2012, p. 552):

> My research [in the UK television industry] indicates that 'getting on' in the television industry as a freelancer is inextricably linked to creating and maintaining a large network of contacts, a process which involves presenting one's self as flexible, enthusiastic and mobile.

This position is also supported by our research:

> R2: After the first placement, they found out that I was then free to help out a bit more and they wanted to pay me and carry me on...I've done some work for them recently as freelancing...In my Linkedin account is silly amounts of people I met on placements...I've been also offered out of two of my placements to come back after uni...Definitely networking has been a great improvement.

Students work hard and seem keen on maintaining relationships with colleagues post-placement:

> R3: I've made friends for life through my placement. I still keep in touch with all directors and they still like to know what I've been doing. If I read an article that I think it's interesting, I send it to them. It shows the interest in the company and the people you've gained relations with.

Networking is the key outcome for many media students at Bournemouth:

> R4: Networking was brilliant! I've added a lot of people on Facebook who I was there with. I've got a game on my iPhone, which I still play with some of them...I can work there during the weekends, because

when I went back to ask if I could work on the TV show for another week and as a freelancer...Now I can say I know people in the TV industry.

R6: It was very useful for networking. I've got quite a lot of contacts there, directors, designers, producers...It's definitely given me people to talk with after the course and...that is something really important.

Some even manage to make the switch from unpaid intern, to paid employee, often during their post-placement studies:

R7: The guy who looked after me gave me feedback and said it was all good. He told me to get back in touch with them after I graduate for some freelance work...Also one of the guys, who owned the company making short films, asked if I would be the cameraman on one of their films.

This illustrates that the placement can close the gap of the 'double-life' of a student (Davies, 2003) quite effectively by bringing together social and cultural capital; the students own free time can become an opportunity for future work and projects, which can develop after a successful placement. Despite the view that this could be seen to be exploiting students, the fact remains that because of the 'portfolio' nature of many careers in the media and creative industries, establishing a network of contacts is now essential, something which Pollard's study (this volume) also supports:

Graduates felt that building relationships with peers, tutors and industry professionals whilst in HE was fundamental and provided the foundations for finding work, for the creation of work opportunities and networks of support for maintaining confidence and motivation.

The view that students now tend to work in a variety of places over an average four to six week placement is also supported by our findings – although desirable for some, longer placements are rare. Course tutors admit that this was not the original intention of the work experience scheme, but it does now at least match the 'portfolio' nature of media careers; work placements have to be flexible. If the market reverts back to more secure and long-term career trajectories – which is unlikely – then this model is able to be adapted:

A few years ago students would attempt to secure a single six week placement. But when those became increasingly difficult to source, it forced students to pull together a portfolio of different activities – from bits of freelance work, to work shadowing, to a week's standard work experience.

(Bournemouth Lecturer and Level Tutor)

The students we interviewed valued being able to talk about the many topics related to the industry and to use the correct terminology, some of which can be very technical. This 'professional vocabulary' not only helps in securing a placement in the first instance, but also enables the student to establish professional relationships with prospective employers and colleagues.

The students all valued the transferable skills they had learned on their undergraduate programme. Communication and presentation skills were seen as being of particular use, but also the self-confidence gained from seminar presentations and the other 'performance' aspects of their studies was very important as well:

R1: I worked out... that every business has their own individual way of running, so the things you learnt [at university] are often irrelevant to the placement, but organisational and writing skills helped... The amount of group work we do at university meant we can't ever get used to working with the same people... that's definitely something that has come from the course.

R2: The modules obviously helped me with analysis, creative tasks, and presentations. [Because] our course is vocational, we are more prepared than others to act in the working environment, present to clients and write reports instead of only academic essays with many reference.

R3: If you are willing to work hard, if you are a confident person, if you are able to publicly speak quite well and have a solid head on your shoulders, then you will get on.

R6: I guess on the course you work in groups and that's a learning curve, dealing with people and working as a team.

The most useful parts of their studies seem to be the 'practical' knowledge the students had gained. From the students we interviewed, this largely described the types of technical equipment the students used at university, such as the particular types of cameras or editing software, and seeing that same kit replicated almost identically in an industry context. However, Pollard (this volume) found that:

> [G]raduates often recognised the resource constraints of having up to date software and facilities to deliver appropriate learning.

The students did find it more difficult to articulate the benefits of the theoretical and contextual knowledge, which can be critical of working practices in the media industry (particularly in relation to the division of labour along gender lines), of their university studies and its direct application. Some felt, however, this would reveal itself in time – and our research certainly supports this – particularly if they reached more senior positions in the industry where they would perhaps have more autonomy, and where they would have the space to apply this knowledge. However, not all university work should or needs to have a direct application in a field of work and those of us in HE need to be better at explaining why this is.

At Bournemouth the work placement is far from the 'add-on' of which much of the literature warns. Students are expected to reflect on their experiences, and to bring that back into their final year of university study with specific assignments, which ask the students to directly draw on their work placement experiences. As Davies (2003, p. 131) agrees:

> Logbooks should be encouraged, with emphasis of assessment on the progress shown in, for example, choice of relevant material, clarity of presentation, critical evaluation and development of understanding.

Informally, the placement clearly shapes the ways in which students behave in their final year; there is more professionalism in physical spaces which mirror industry practice – such as labs and studios – and an urgency that final level work be as pragmatic and as realistic as possible. Tutors also brief and de-brief students before and after they temporarily enter the world of a creative professional, and this is all linked back to the preparation for the final year. The logbook directly asks students about the learning that they experienced on the placement:

> R4: My placement has been a good grounding and insight for what is to come. All that I have learned regarding the industry, role specific insights/knowledge, effective communication, useful contacts and

understanding the pressures involved with running a professional business are invaluable.

Students are also directed to look back at their studies prior to going on placement:

> R2. I found that my knowledge of narratives learned during *Critical Media Concepts & Contexts* allowed me to organise the clips in a linear way that told the 'story' of the festival as it happened.

These mechanisms are there to ensure that the experience of the professional media world is brought back into the university curriculum, and is aggregated into further learning experiences. It also offers a further mechanism to track students through their placement. During this post-placement reflection the students generally felt that they now had better organizational skills and time management. Many students were now able to think more critically about the nature and structure of the media industries; topics such as the gender divide in the UK film industry and issues of ownership and control became far more vivid post-placement. Students also seemed to feel that they were now far more likely to pay more attention to detail. Many articulated how they saw more relevance in their studies than they did prior to the placement; they felt they had taken their studies seriously, but are now more likely to value all subject areas, whereas before some topics were perhaps seen as having little practical use. So, the type of transition articulated by Kolb (1984) can be quite marked in terms of the more theoretical and contextual work:

> R5: I have already done some work on my [dissertation] proposal, however I intend to go over it all again and refine my idea. In the early stages of my third year I plan to research a lot more . . . and make sure I research with a lot of depth.

The students were sure that they were now more highly motivated and more engaged in their final year of study; they wanted to learn as much as possible, before 'going back'. The work placement also shaped more realistic aspirations in the students and many felt that they had now 'discovered' the job they really wanted to do:

> R1: It's made me much more motivated and focussed this year . . . It's showed me that my course choice is right. It's the field I want to go

into. I saw people in higher positions and I thought I'd like to be doing that, so it's made me want to work more.

The placement can clearly frame and focus a student's future career plans; it can be part of a pedagogic process which serves to highlight the value of careers guidance opportunities available in all colleges and universities:

> R2: The placements enlightened me... If you do a placement and absolutely hate it, at least you know that you cannot go back into that area... I definitely think everyone should go on placement, because you need to know what you're in after uni.

It can take time for students to see the value of the subjects they have been studying before they went on placement, but over time, some topics and themes come into sharp relief once they have returned:

> R3: In the position I was in it was hard to apply theory I have learnt at university, because people in professional industry don't necessarily come from academic backgrounds... I can see now more than ever in a fourth year, that the courses and the units we're doing will apply immediately to industry. I am definitely more passionate. It makes me want to learn more.

Of course, for some students the work experience means a complete re-evaluation and reflection on their chosen career. A placement can indicate to a student what areas of the labour market they no longer wish to aim for. Therefore, the experience can shape a student's aspirations and directions in other ways, and lead them to more specialist postgraduate qualifications or into other areas entirely, such as teaching. Some students find that working in the creative industries is not as glamorous as they expected, so the post-placement period can see a total rethinking of career aspirations.

Some conclusions

It is clear from our research that students believe that moving from the lecture theatre to the workplace, albeit temporarily, is crucial for their current and future career prospects:

> R7: I think the placement should be compulsory for everyone. I learnt a lot about working in industry just through the placement. The combination of the course theory and placement practice is a good

balance. Learning theoretical stuff at university is one thing, but using and applying it in a professional environment is completely different. It's good to get that link.

In this, the rhetoric of government, sector skills councils and students seem closely aligned:

> The evidence is that placements, internships and other work experience are extremely valuable to students, both in terms of their academic performance and their employability skills, is strong.
>
> (Wilson, 2012, p. 37)

From an academic perspective, however, getting the right pedagogic framework in place is crucial. Without a placement, creative and media students at Bournemouth felt that their university course would not sufficiently prepare them for the world of work; they would not see the relevance of their studies, and would not know what to focus on. The placement experience can shape how students value their university experience, once they return from industry. This is why a dedicated placement office, staffed by careers professionals is integral to the success of the scheme. Not only that, institutions need to continue to develop and maintain their links with industry, either through controversial accreditation programmes or through guest speakers and institutional enterprise activities.

Tutors also commented that students who undertake a placement are usually much more alert to 'the possibilities of the final year' and are much more motivated as learners. According to Bournemouth University's 2009–2010 DLHE survey, 85 per cent of Bournemouth media graduates secured work in the media and creative industries within six months of graduating (although this can be quite short-term work, or even further unpaid placements). Indeed, our study fully supports that of Pollard (this volume) who also found that:

> [V]irtually all creative graduates had experienced employment of some kind since graduating, whether in creative roles or industries or wider roles and sectors...The majority were in permanent work or had held a permanent job and the likelihood of permanent work increases over time in the labour market; although working on short-term contracts and part-time was common.

Critically, without a placement, students felt that they would be less confident after graduating, and would not have a network of industry contacts – something all media students seem to value highly. Returning to the experiential pedagogy, the placement students we interviewed believed that the variety their university programme offered them, combining team and practical projects with placement opportunities and relevant teaching, provided a good balance of experiences which better prepared them for the real world.

However, providing such experiences offers real challenges to those of us who teach creative and media students in HE. Universities must now be far more flexible in providing learning experiences, which relate and build on the workplace – from undergraduate degrees, right up to professional doctorates. Instead of a work placement being a discrete element of a programme of study, the professional context can act as the foundation of an entire curriculum and programmes must be carefully designed to take account of this.

Pinpointing the pedagogic reason for the placement should be a key part of the design of any degree programme. Yet because courses can treat the placement as an 'add on' or a pass/fail module, detailed unit information is often not available or it is buried within an existing unit/module descriptor. Therefore, the value to students and its place within the curriculum is often implicit as opposed to being explicit and the pedagogic approach of experiential learning is often underdeveloped. If done well, the placement becomes the lens through which much of the work done in the final year is viewed.

Experiential learning as detailed in this chapter is not a synonym for 'anything goes'; the placement unit needs to be supported in the same way standard taught units would be. Typically, this would involve a series of pre-placement workshops and lectures on what to expect. Students should also be directed in how to prepare a logbook, in a way which actively considers the learning process. This should ensure that a student gets the full benefit from transforming their experience into knowledge (Kolb, 1984, p. 38). In addition the placement must be assessed via the logbook and students must receive feedback on their logbook reflections and their performance – via comments of employers/ clients – through a summative assessment process to ensure the learning process is fully credited and rewarded.

It is certainly true that students returning from work placements can be far more motivated and the work they produce can be geared to much more realistic employment prospects if the placement is structured appropriately. However, there also needs to be a real pedagogic reason for giving students work placement opportunities and experiences; it should not just be entirely for economic or employability reasons – although this is important. The work placement can be a powerful pedagogic tool, if used in the right way, and it is this we need to aspire to. For example, students are likely to be more rigorously critical of industrial practice and working conditions:

> R7: [W]hen I got into placement, [the hours] were a bit of a shock... They obviously can't teach you how long you're going to work... but, like, going into placement, having to go in quite early and finish quite late – getting home at, like, half-nine... was a shock. I wasn't expecting that.

Indeed, issues of working conditions, hours of employment and access (particularly for women and ethnic minorities) will often form the basis for final-year dissertation work. Some even use this large piece of critical writing to examine the dynamic nature of the media industries from an economic and business perspective.

Finally, in addition to the work placement becoming an increasingly important pedagogic tool, work-related learning more broadly is on the rise and for some students their entire HE experience is framed through a professional practice lens. For example, Skillset is currently working with a number of Media Academies to establish provision where students spend 50 per cent of their time in the HEI and 50 per cent in employment. While this is unlikely to be achieved in an insecure labour market such as the media and creative industries without considerable investment, it is clear that placements are a significant agenda item in HE. In addition to this aspiration, a number of Media Academies are developing a new model of provision – entitled 'Build your own MA' – at Masters level, where courses are designed to mesh with a participant's full-time employment, and are therefore delivered via a mix of block teaching and online learning. The assessment here is entirely work related.

The challenge is clear, HEIs must be more flexible in providing learning experiences which relate and build upon the workplace. The theoretical and contextual aspects of an undergraduate degree are still relevant, but a positive placement experience can instil a new confidence in students to think more critically and to understand and relate complex ideas to their own lives and experiences. Instead of work experience being a discrete element of a programme of study, the professional context can act as the foundation of an entire curriculum, if the pedagogy is right.

Author's note

With thanks to Karen Ephram and Janice Jeffrey.

Notes

1. In 1992, the more vocational and industry focusing 'polytechnics' were awarded university status and their own degree awarding powers. Soon this will be widened to allow smaller and more specialist HE institutions – such as Arts and Drama colleges – to apply for the title of university.
2. The 14–19 Diploma was part of a Labour government initiative to completely revamp the 14–19 age-group's curriculum by replacing existing high-school qualifications with a diploma which would act as a 'vessel' for academic and vocational qualifications. The incoming Conservative administration abandoned the scheme in 2010.

References

Amis, K. (1998) *The King's English: A Guide to Modern Usage* (London: Harper Collins).
Banks, M. and Hesmondhalgh, D. (2009) Looking for Work in Creative Industries Policy, *The International Journal of Cultural Policy* 15(4): 415–430.
Berger, R. and McDougall, J. (2012) What Is Media Education For? *The Media Education Research Journal* 3(1): 5–20.
The Chartered Institute of Personal Development (2009) *Internships That Work: A Guide for Employers* (London: CIPD).
Collis, C. (2010) Developing Work-Integrated Learning Curricula for the Creative Industries: Embedding Stakeholder Perspectives, *Learning and Teaching in Higher Education* 4(1): 3–19.
Collini, S. (2012) *What Are Universities For?* (London: Penguin Books).
Davies, L. (2003) *Experience-Based Learning within the Curriculum: A Synthesis Study* (Sheffield: Association for Sandwich Education & Training).
Dearing, R. (1997) *National Committee of Inquiry into Higher Education* (London: Department for Education & Employment).
Department for Culture, Media & Sport (2008) *Creative Britain: New Talents for the New Economy* (London: DCMS).
Dewey, J. (1938 [1997]) *Experience and Education* (London: Collier-Macmillan).
Fanthome, C. (2004) *Work Placements: A Survival Guide for Students* (Basingstoke: Palgrave Macmillan).
Holt, R. (2008) Work Experience or Worst Exploitation? *Phoenix* 125: 8–10.
Jordan, A., Carlile, O. and Stack, A. (2008) *Approaches to Learning: A Guide for Teachers* (Maidenhead: Open University Press/McGraw-Hill).
Kolb, D. (1984) *Experiential Learning: Experience as the Source of Learning and Development* (New Jersey: Prentice Hall).
Lee, D. (2012) Networks, Cultural Capital and Creative Labour in the British Independent Television Industry, *Media, Culture and Society* 33(4): 549–565.
Little, B. and Harvey, L. (2006) *Learning through Work Placements & Beyond: A Report for HECSU and the Higher Education Academy's Work Placements Organisation Forum* (Sheffield: Centre for Research & Evaluation).
Lomas, C. and Oblinger, D.G. (2006) Student Practices and Their Impact on Learning Spaces, in Oblinger, D.G. (ed.) *Learning Spaces* (Educause): 5.1–5.11.

The National Council for Work Experience (1998) *The Placement Tutor's Handbook: A Guide to Higher Education Institutions on Arranging Placements and a Compendium of Current Best Practice in the UK* (London: NCWE).

Özbilgin, M. and Tatli, A. (2006) *Scoping of London Based Higher Education Institute Work Placement Practices within the Creative and Cultural Industries* (London: Arts Council England and London Centre for Arts and Creative Enterprise).

Skillset (2010) *Guidelines for Employers Offering Work Placement Schemes In the Creative Industries* (London: Skillset).

Wallis, S. (2006) *How to Get a Job in Television* (Oxford: Howtobooks).

Westwood, A. (2012) Universities and a Vocational Economy: Why We Should Rethink HE's role, (Online: *Guardian* HE Network) http://www.guardian.co.uk/higher-education-network/blog/2012/jan/16/vocational-economy, date accessed 12 February 2012.

Wilson, T. (2012) *Review of Business-University Collaboration* (London: Department for Business, Innovation and Skills).

5
Media Enterprise in Higher Education: A Laboratory for Learning

Annette Naudin

Introduction

This chapter explores enterprise pedagogies in media courses by drawing on the experience of postgraduate students in higher education (HE). The risks and challenges associated with media work are discussed with reference to two key discourses: firstly, literature from media and cultural studies, which tends to be critical of ideas of entrepreneurship (see Banks and Hesmondhalgh, 2009; McGuigan, 2010; Oakley, 2011); and secondly, investigating enterprise education literature in general and as it applies specifically to media education. Entrepreneurship in media education is explored through a case-study based upon observations in the classroom, along with interviews and feedback from postgraduate media students. The case-study builds upon earlier research conducted by Carey and Naudin (2006), and on a recognition that entrepreneurship and self-employment are increasingly important in UK media courses, as discussed in the report *Creating Entrepreneurship* (ADM-HEA and NESTA, 2007).

Entrepreneurship in this context is taken to include aspects of self-employment, freelancing, social enterprise (trading for a social purpose) and intrapreneurship (entrepreneurship within an organization). More precisely, it applies to media students at all stages of their professional careers working as freelancers, starting a small business or developing a portfolio-style career.

In contrast with general enterprise education (usually based in business schools), which has a tendency to view entrepreneurship as the answer to all ills, this study opens up critical questions for enterprise education in media courses. The case-study offers a non-formulaic, contextualized approach to enterprise curricula, which reveals significant issues for media education, particularly at postgraduate level. Firstly, the contextual element is important. Enterprise education needs to be relevant to the student's personal context including their cultural background, personal aspirations and the specific media they are interested in. Media enterprise education cannot rely on British models of working and should not make assumptions, for instance, on the best approaches to networking in the media.

Secondly, there are difficulties in encouraging a critique of aspects of entrepreneurship while teaching for enterprise. Students find it difficult to simultaneously engage with critical debates on entrepreneurship and media work, alongside adopting entrepreneurial practices to fulfil assessment criteria. Much of the popular material available to students (such as a large variety of websites, LinkedIn discussion groups and Twitter accounts) encourage enterprise but lack any critical dimension.[1]

Finally, the research reveals a confusing relationship with the language associated with business and entrepreneurship. Indeed, varied definitions of entrepreneurship and media add a level of complexity but as the experience recounted in this chapter suggests, this can also be a starting point for debate, encouraging students to be reflexive about entrepreneurship and their practice. Students develop their version of an entrepreneur, appropriate to their personal aspirations and values, and to the specific sector of the industry they work in. As a result, there is evidence of students recognizing that they are already involved in entrepreneurial activities but they would not have described it that way.

Within media education, definitions can also pose problems and, for the purposes of this study, 'media' will relate to the subjects commonly found in vocational media degrees which tend to include new and established industry sectors. They comprise sub-sectors of what the UK's Department for Culture Media and Sports (DCMS) describe as the 'Creative Industries' including journalism, television, public relations, the music industries, radio, events, photography and emerging sectors such as social media. However, DCMS definitions tend to lag behind the realities of media work, which are more fluid. One person might encompass several of the listed sub-sectors and new roles are being created sometimes with titles, sometimes not.

Enterprise and the creative industries

In his research into cultural entrepreneurs in Manchester, Banks identifies individuals who 'are pursuing careers underpinned by a diverse assemblage of motives and moral principles, and, as such, contrast markedly with the dissocialised drones distinctive to the fatalist critique' of cultural entrepreneurship (2006, p. 467). Banks argues for the need to collect further empirical data in order to explore issues of identity in the workplace and to contest the dichotomy between a celebration of flexible work and a critical perspective. An investigation of the lived experience of entrepreneurship reveals an opportunity to simultaneously extend our understanding of the contemporary creative workplace and its evocation of the rhetoric of the enterprising self, and at the same time contest the dominant popular discourse of enterprise. Banks' contribution is important because he does not reject the critics of entrepreneurial approaches to cultural and media work but his research is more optimistic and offers evidence of reflexivity and social action. This suggests that an emphasis on personal values, personal agency and encouraging reflexivity might offer an alternative to the popular perception of the entrepreneur.

The entrepreneur tends to have a fixed identity and a set of attributes defined by the narratives associated with the celebrity entrepreneur, and captured in UK television shows such as *The Apprentice* (BBC, 2005–) and *The Dragon's Den* (BBC, 2005–). According to Couldry and Littler (2011), in *The Apprentice* the 'reality' of work and enterprise is normalized through the contestants' performance on screen, emphasizing values such as passion and competitiveness. In the context of this study, it is important to note that programmes such as *The Apprentice* have international versions familiar to many students, who will be influenced by entrepreneurial characteristics being depicted in these programmes. Discussions in class reflect how students assimilate notions of entrepreneurship through popular media and celebrity entrepreneurs. Furthermore, dominant discourses of entrepreneurship in academia reflect an emphasis on the entrepreneur as having specific personality characteristics (Chell, 2008), often associated with figures such as Richard Branson. According to Jones and Spicer (2009), entrepreneurship research tends to be dominated by US academics and is either focused on the economic benefits of entrepreneurship or on the entrepreneur's character and personal attributes. In contrast, there is a more critical debate elsewhere in entrepreneurship theory, such as in the work of du Gay (2007) and a rising interest in social entrepreneurship, which aims to disrupt dominant discourses (Hjorth and Steyaert, 2006; Jones and Spicer, 2009). A challenge to the dominant discourse of entrepreneurship offers opportunities to question existing paradigms and to explore the specifics of entrepreneurship in different and more useful contexts, as is the case in this study. This resonates with the work of Hjorth and Steyaert (2006), whose book explores non-conventional examples of entrepreneurship, including the experience of women and of non-traditional business models such as the Hultsfred rock festival. This is useful in highlighting the specificity of cultural and media work, which begins to play a role in our understanding of entrepreneurship.

Critiques of cultural and media work also provide an alternative to the overly optimistic discourse of recent cultural policy (see Ellmeier, 2003; Toynbee, 2003; Banks, 2006; Oakley, 2009; Hesmondhalgh and Baker, 2010; McGuigan, 2010). Detailed accounts of creative work explored by writers such as Hesmondhalgh and Baker (2010), McRobbie (2002) and Gill and Pratt (2008), contrast with the celebratory tone of publications such as *The Independents* (Leadbeater and Oakley, 1999) and much recent cultural policy. Instead, they stress difficulties such as the blurred line between work and social life and the expectation that insecure working conditions are acceptable. In more recent research Oakley (2011) critiques New Labour's legacy and the assumptions made about the potential of entrepreneurship:

> The belief in the inherently democratic nature of small business ownership and the liberating power of entrepreneurship meant not only that the public paid little attention to the sometimes exploitative conditions of creative labour markets, but when it did so, the policy responses proposed were inadequate for the scale of the problem.
>
> (Oakley, 2011, p. 287)

While the difficulties in cultural and media work should not be ignored, this research proposes that there is the possibility of negotiating socially responsible forms of work. Structural conditions of cultural and media work can be challenged to create more progressive approaches. Empirical research exposes a more complex relationship between work, identity and personal agency (see Banks, 2006; Berglund, 2006; Naudin, 2012) revealing how cultural entrepreneurs face up to the challenges described by Oakley.

As Banks (2006) suggests, a more context-specific examination of the lived experience of entrepreneurship may reveal new perspectives. The next section focuses on the development of enterprise education and how it relates to media education. This presents the background context before introducing the findings from a study with postgraduate media students.

Enterprise education: Policy, practice and research

In the UK, enterprise education has developed predominantly through
the public body, the National Centre for Entrepreneurship in Education
(NCEE), formerly the National Centre for Graduate Entrepreneurship
set up in 2004 by Gordon Brown, Chancellor of the Exchequer at that
time. The NCEE has been driving enterprise education policy since
its inception, along with the university lobby group Enterprise Educators UK (EEUK). In collaboration, the NCEE and EEUK run a series
of events, awards and the annual International Enterprise Education
Conference, a major event for UK enterprise educators. In contrast
to traditional business school practice, which tends to focus on corporate business practices and on entrepreneurship theory, EEUK and
NCEE's focus is on developing enterprise in all students from a wide
range of disciplines. They aim to encourage confidence and practical
skills in entrepreneurship by embracing small business practice and 'creating empathy with the entrepreneurial life world' (Herrmann et al.,
2008, p. 31). In particular, the NCEE's training course challenges traditional business school curricula as experiential learning approaches
are favoured, similar to pedagogies found in art, design and vocational
media courses as discussed by Berger et al. (this volume). This includes
live industry briefs, opportunities for selling one's work, guest speakers
from industry and educators who are also industry professionals (Carey
and Matlay, 2011). In that context, recent enterprise education developments fit well with vocational media courses, yet research on the
subject is in its infancy. Apart from a few notable exceptions (see Rae,
2004; Carey and Naudin, 2006; Carey and Matlay, 2011; Boyle and Kelly,
2012) academics have not responded to policy discourse advancing
entrepreneurship in media and cultural education.

As stated earlier, scholars from media and cultural studies have tended
to engage with a critical debate focused on cultural policy rather than
entrepreneurship as a theme in cultural work. There is relatively little
evidence that enterprise discourse explicitly is commonplace in media
education except in some specific cases, such as the work of Jeff Jarvis
in the US, who teaches entrepreneurial business models for journalism
(Jarvis, 2009). This is partly because of terminology: many UK vocational courses in art, design and media have developed professional
studies programmes which include some enterprise activities but under
the label of professional studies.[2] It could be argued that a focus on
professionalism as it relates to specific subjects has made enterprise

education invisible, yet research by the Higher Education Academy Subject Centre and by the DCMS suggests that plenty of it goes on, even if in an ad hoc manner (DCMS, 2006). As Pollard's (this volume) research suggests, graduates do not always recognize entrepreneurial skills which have been embedded in the curriculum and it is only with hindsight that students see the need for practical skills in business and enterprise.

In 2007, National Endowment for Science, Technology and the Arts (NESTA) published *Creating Entrepreneurship: Entrepreneurship Education for the Creative Industries'* (ADM-HEA and NESTA, 2007) written by David Clews as part of his work for the Higher Education Academy Art Design Media Subject Centre (ADM-HEA). Written in the context of New Labour's focus on the creative economy, the publication largely supports the cultural policy objectives, such as a focus on economic growth, but applies them to a HE context. It maps current practice across art, design and media education, demonstrating the range of 'good practice', but highlights an ad hoc approach to enterprise education and a lack of research. Clews' work was preceded by a DCMS policy report (DCMS, 2006) also articulating key issues for entrepreneurship education in the creative industries, namely: a lack of a policy framework; a lack of evidence demonstrating what works; a lack of incentives for institutions to focus on that area; a lack of relevant learning opportunities; a lack of common terminology; and a tension between creative expression and commercial realities.

As a mapping exercise, both publications are helpful, but neither explores the specific nature of cultural entrepreneurship in practice or from a critical perspective. Focused on meeting economic and cultural policy demands of the time, they embrace the idea of entrepreneurship as an appropriate means of delivering vocational education: skills-based training for setting up a small business. As Ashton (2011) describes, the increasing importance of employability in HE puts pressure on universities to address professionalism, including self-employment, in the curriculum. Professional studies modules provide some career guidance for students including topics such as how to start a business, managing a portfolio career or working freelance. However, according to the authors of the DCMS report, *Developing Entrepreneurship for the Creative Industries* (2006), there is an ambiguous attitude from educators and students towards entrepreneurship. The research collected for the *Creative Entrepreneurship* report (ADM-HEA and NESTA, 2007) echoes these sentiments, stating that students do not identify with what they perceive to be the negative aspects of being an entrepreneur:

> Students often associated entrepreneurship with negative behaviour such as confrontation, poor environmental performance and focus on commercial gain at the expense of social benefit and see these as antithetical to their own creative practices.
>
> (ADM-HEA and NESTA, 2007, p. 57)

According to *Creating Entrepreneurship*, if teaching is carried out by a teacher-practitioner, this increases dramatically the delivery of entrepreneurship education 'ensuring course content and delivery is aligned with real-world practice' (ADM-HEA and NESTA, 2007, p. 42). The teacher-practitioner scenario described in *Creating Entrepreneurship* suggests the educational experience is based on professional experience in the 'real world' and not within an academic discourse of entrepreneurship. In that context, the lived experience of the teacher-practitioner presents a more nuanced version of entrepreneurship. In a similar vein, guest speakers offer further alternatives and contradictory tales of entrepreneurship, based on subjective experience.

NESTA's *Creative Pioneer* programme launched in 2003 facilitated the entrepreneurial development of creative individuals through innovative methods tailored to challenge the dichotomy between creative practice and enterprise by emphasizing how creative skills can translate into business. As a result of its success, NESTA created a *Creative Enterprise Toolkit*, a free educational resource for use in HE by art, design and media students. The Toolkit includes activities which enable students to think through the business implications of their ideas by asking simple, but practical questions in a language they can relate to. This appears to fit very well in vocational universities, where practical skills for professional employment or self-employment are seen to be desirable. However, as Thornham and O'Sullivan (2004) describe, there is criticism that a focus on practical skills for setting up a media enterprise does not offer students the opportunity to question and challenge perceptions of entrepreneurship. On the other hand, the practical experience can be a space for debate if there is an opportunity for students to reflect on their practice through, for example, a reflective essay.

Having explored some of the developments and challenges in enterprise education, in the next section I provide the findings from a study with postgraduate media students. The findings tend to further problematize the issues raised but also offer new perspectives for consideration.

Postgraduate student experience of entrepreneurial learning

Context and methodology

Informing this research is an ongoing project first started in 2010, which involves MA-level media students who attend a core enterprise module at a post-1992 UK university. The module has an emphasis on 'doing' in order to experience first-hand the entrepreneurial 'life world' (DCMS, 2006, p. 31) and engages students in initiating individual enterprising projects such as new business ventures, a one-off project, an event or a social enterprise. A range of experiential teaching methods are used including activities such as: the elevator pitch; group work to discuss enterprise problems; some conventional business tools (e.g. Strengths, Weaknesses, Opportunities and Threats (SWOT) and Political, Environmental, Social and Technological (PEST) analysis); communication through the use of social media; talks from guest speakers; case studies and critical engagement with academic texts. The emphasis is on experiencing the specifics of creative and media enterprise by investigating appropriate markets and audiences, by identifying opportunities and developing the means to plan and capitalize on their ideas. Students are asked to actively test their enterprise idea, by exploring a product or service directly with the target audience rather than working hypothetically. As they start the process of articulating ideas through various networks, students are faced with the realities of the real-life entrepreneurial environment and all its complexities. Other MA modules in this programme complement this by offering theoretical frameworks, not necessarily specific to entrepreneurship but to the media discipline linked to the student's MA award, for example, 'Popular Music as Culture', 'Social Media as Culture' or 'Creative Industries and Cultural Policy'.

The sample in this study includes 12 students (including recent UK and EU graduates, mature UK students and international students) who were interviewed for between 30 and 45 minutes each. The students are developing entrepreneurial skills for a career working in a range of disciplines including freelance journalism, photography, web design, cultural events and festivals, public relations, music industries, social media, creative and social enterprises and consultancies. Again, this demonstrates a broad range of work practices which are not always reflected in DCMS definitions of the sector but which are considered (by the university) to reflect current labour markets. In terms of their previous work experience and education, this is a highly diverse group including students from non-media backgrounds and others (a minority) with years of experience working in a professional context. In addition to the interviews, other material such as module feedback forms, social media and assignment reports have been collected from the wider student group which includes approximately 90 students from a study period of over two years.

For the interviews, the focus was on questions directed at autobiographical and narrative approaches, with the aim of revealing personal experience, self-expression and the process of individualization (Steedman, 1999). The process was deemed to be particularly appropriate for this kind of research as it encourages the notion of self-discovery and ultimately an attempt to give voice to the interviewee and reduce the level of questions and directions from the researcher. The methodology seeks to illuminate what is particular rather than universal: the version of events as constructed by individual students. The intention is that individuals speaking from the 'margins' or from unexpected perspectives, might reveal or expose unpredictable outcomes (Gray, 2003). Importantly, the purpose of the interviews is not to evaluate the module, but to hear the students' 'enterprise story' including their expectations, previous experience and response to entrepreneurship in practice. The approach is partly derived from Rae and Carswell (2000), who emphasize the subjective experience of the entrepreneur as playing a role in exploring the entrepreneurial learning process. The process of sense-making, of reshaping identity in an evolving manner, informs the learning experience. Rae and Carswell identify themes such as personal values, motivation, the development of personal theories and evidence of active and social learning.

In this research, students give the impression of playing with their potential entrepreneurial identity, testing it out to see how it feels. The findings articulate some of their responses to enterprise through three themes: firstly, the idea of students coming to terms with the subject of enterprise; secondly, the use of reflection to encourage critical debate; and thirdly, networks and networking as part of being enterprising.

Coming to terms with enterprise

Given the growing number of international students on postgraduate courses, one of the challenges is managing the range of cultural perspectives, experiences and competencies of students. Some international students demonstrate a traditional view of media work, as represented by the corporate media sector and are less familiar with the freelance and enterprise culture. One student describes how on gaining this new knowledge she was 'not comfortable', finding it 'a bit challenging at the beginning' and explains that:

> It was very new, enterprise is very new, to be honest when I was thinking of enterprise this is not what I had in mind.
>
> (Postgraduate student A, 2010)

Perhaps the student herself does not know what she had in mind but this demonstrates how some students need a few sessions before they fully understand what is being asked of them and how it relates to their media practice (e.g. online journalism or social media). In particular, international students are concerned with failing and are surprised by the fact that they can base their project on their own professional interests (see Brown, 2007).

In comparison, the notion of a portfolio career, freelance work or starting a business is familiar to many of the UK and EU students who, at postgraduate level, may already have a high level of experience and engagement within their specific sector. Commenting on the idea of being an entrepreneur, an EU student says 'I'm trying to be comfortable with it, because I know it's going to happen to me' (Postgraduate student B, 2011). However, while accepting what she thinks will be inevitable, namely, working as a freelance journalist, she also states that it horrifies her and that she is 'a bit frightened' by the prospect (Postgraduate student B, 2011). During the interview, the manner in which this student reacted to the idea of enterprise is ambiguous (she does not want to offend the enterprise educator but has many reservations about enterprise) and demonstrated a nervousness and lack of confidence. However, she expressed excitement when faced with the opportunity of kick-starting her own projects and of experimenting with new ideas, which she does very successfully. A different student describes entrepreneurship as being about 'how to bring together messy things and bring them together to make a pattern'. She illustrates this further by stating that:

> One thing was leading to the other. And without knowing it my research was being formed by my actions. So it wasn't about me thinking I need to do ABC anymore, it was about A taking me to B.
>
> (Postgraduate student D, 2010)

This suggests a willingness to engage with taking risks; exploring an idea without knowing if the outcome will lead to failure or an opportunity. As Deuze (2007) describes, contemporary media work is characterized by individuals navigating risk and having to be self-reliant. Student D reveals tentative steps which help to manage the risky nature of the entrepreneurial process. An opportunity to test, evaluate and review entrepreneurial ideas creates a less pressured environment than the media image of enterprise, particularly in programmes such as *The Apprentice*, where taking risks tends to be celebrated.

Indeed, it has emerged that, as a result of this study, the reflective nature of the interviews has contributed to the students' opportunity to connect their personal enterprise projects within the broader context of their own personal background and aspirations. The student also relates her previous experience to a business language introduced in the enterprise module, demonstrating how she is processing this new knowledge:

> I've never thought of myself as an entrepreneur, like others in the class, I've always liked the restaurant idea, always wanted to own my own job and have my own team and a restaurant, bar, cafe thing has always been in the plans, with my friends back home. We even have a name for the place, but I never realised that this was what we were actually doing, but we were brainstorming and doing SWOT and PEST but not realising that's what we were doing.
>
> (Postgraduate student D, 2010)

An educational context which values reflection and questioning can slow down the entrepreneurial process. Although reflection is encouraged as part of the learning process there is evidence of students over-analysing how they feel about their assignment to the detriment of the entrepreneurial project. Students can be seduced by the opportunity to reflect, resulting in some good critical reflections but a poor level of execution in terms of the entrepreneurial product, service or event.

Critical reflection

Critical reflection is a central ethos of the curriculum and we argue that it works in tandem with a practical enterprise education curriculum. The process of writing a report and evaluating their practice invites students to reflect and discuss their ideas, skills, abilities and entrepreneurial attributes. Students tend to start exploring critical issues when they are at the final stages of this enterprise module, usually while writing their final assignment. Indeed it is helpful to view this module as phase one of their award, and progression into further core modules tend to extend the student's knowledge and skills. Moon's (2005) work on reflection and critical thinking in education describes the process as stages, stating that some students cannot hold ambiguity and a critical discussion until they reach the second stage of their learning development. In this enterprise module, those who achieve this earlier tend to be mature students or students with the ability to contextualize their enterprise practice within a wider industry debate, often drawing on complimentary theory modules.

A relatively mature student describes how working on her enterprise project has enabled her to understand the industry context for her work in more detail and to think more strategically. For instance, by researching the market she is able to identify 'what I want to do and what I don't want to do' (Postgraduate student B, 2011), while reflecting on her professional position and the competition she might face. The realization that risks and responsibilities are a feature of media and cultural work is seen as a positive element of the module. Yet, such difficulties can be underestimated in over-celebratory accounts of entrepreneurship (Baines and Robson, 2001).

Student reports reflect a growing confidence about how they have developed skills in negotiating, bringing individuals together to collaborate, using some basic business and management tools, taking some (limited) risks and allowing their projects to grow in a realistic environment. They express how the projects have broken down popular definitions and stereotypes of entrepreneurship, enabling them to see how they could be entrepreneurial in their own way. This mature student quoted below, for example, despite his vast practical experience of entrepreneurship, identifies the purpose of undertaking entrepreneurial activities within the academic context as offering reflective and critical thinking time:

Enterprise and the whole reflection process has enabled me to, I suppose, in some ways, to think about my journey. If you remember when I started the module, I was kind of a bit uncomfortable with the whole term 'entrepreneur', as a label, and I think I'm becoming more comfortable with it as a result of the module which I think is a good thing. I think when I started, I was very much of the opinion that entrepreneurs are born and I think that's where my discomfort was from. And I think that I've completely changed my opinion on that. And looking back, I'm quite surprised that was my view because my first degree was in psychology and it's always about the nature and nurture debate.

(Postgraduate student C, 2011)

The reflective element of the student's report in this module enables a further critical discussion of both entrepreneurship generally and of their own entrepreneurial aptitudes. Students have the opportunity to explore their entrepreneurial identity by reporting on the way in which they negotiate relationships, perform tasks and manage risk. In particular, students are asked to produce a second report to review the initial stages, identify problems and weaknesses, further develop the project (in some cases, students deliver an event or some element of product testing) and reflect on their professional aspirations. For some, the opportunity to reflect is baffling and they struggle with the task of combining an enterprise report (focused on the logistics of enterprise) with reflecting on the experience of being entrepreneurial (focused on their personal development and transferable skills). The result can be pedestrian and purely descriptive such as a list of entrepreneurial tasks to be completed against a timeline. This is potentially due to the lack of attention paid to the reflective process and the mystery associated with 'critical thinking', which Moon (2005) addresses in her work. In other practice modules it is perhaps easier to see the difference between the professional practice element (for example, a piece of video or a set of photographs) and the written reflective report which supports the practice. As discussed earlier, there is an expectation that students should be entrepreneurial and also demonstrate the ability to contest popular discourses. Some students find the dual purpose of the assignment, simultaneously reporting on the enterprise itself and reflecting on their own entrepreneurial journey, as simply confusing.

In the module structure, talks from guest speakers raise issues for discussion, both online and in the classroom. These also provide students with material to reflect on in their reports. Often, guest speakers are not always reflective or good at analysing entrepreneurial processes within their own practice, revealing an inability to pin down strategies for their success. One speaker expressed the need to 'just do it' or 'stop thinking and just get on with it'. Another speaker was adamant in saying 'I'm not strategic about networking, I'm just not that kind of person, it would feel uncomfortable', after clearly demonstrating the opposite in her outstanding ability to develop and nurture good business relationships. This can become a useful point of discussion, exposing the difference between what is said and done in entrepreneurial practice. The 'push' to pragmatic solutions is in conflict with the 'pull' to construct an identity synonymous with a particular type of media professional, namely the element of 'cool' and 'alternative', un-businesslike approach described by McGuigan (2009, p. 81). Again, the cultural diversity of students adds a level of complexity in exploring why an individual might want to appear to be casual in their networking style. Conversely, making this part of the discussion can initiate an exploration of the way specific language is used to describe entrepreneurial activities. The resulting debate presents the opportunity to highlight differences and contrasting cultural perspectives. Students can start to reflect and re-evaluate their position, their emerging entrepreneurial identity, in relation to others in the group.

Some students make use of social media platforms (predominantly student blogs and Twitter) to further articulate their thoughts on the subjects discussed in class and to engage their online community in the debate. This fosters the individual student's ability to communicate with a wider network and to establish a reputation as a reflexive practitioner. Past students have expressed how initial contacts made for the Enterprise Module have developed into a live brief for another module or have remained part of their business network after the MA. The student's ability to articulate an opinion or to test an idea in a public sphere such as Twitter, demonstrates commitment to their work and a level of confidence. While a significant number of students are inclined to pursue this level of commitment, many lack the confidence and/or motivation. Yet, engaging their potential target market or media industry networks can give confidence and is perceived as critical to entrepreneurial practice. In the next section, the social space for entrepreneurial activity and education is discussed.

Networking and developing relationships

Chell and Karatas-Ozkan (2010) argue that entrepreneurial practice does not take place in a vacuum but is embedded in a social context represented by a complex web of strong and weak ties depending on the individual's position in a network (see Granovetter, 1973; Chell and Karatas-Ozkan, 2010). In this context, networking and developing relationships is crucial to enterprise and involves ongoing sharing, exchange and mutual learning by members of the network. Indeed, networks and networking skills are considered an individual's asset base for entrepreneurship. The informality of networks in the media industries is both attractive to some and intimidating to others. While it is noted that networks can exclude as well as include, collaboration and creating a support network can counteract the difficulties faced by entrepreneurial media workers (see Lee, this volume; Oakley, 2009).

Students are encouraged to share information about their enterprise projects, giving each other valuable feedback and ideas for adapting their idea. A few students have concerns about the value of sharing and defend this position with arguments about preserving their intellectual property. This line of reasoning is a legitimate concern but is problematic in a context which seeks to emulate the networks and relationships which entrepreneurs construct to launch new ventures. It may seem counter to the idea of entrepreneurship as an individualistic activity (Hesmondhalgh and Baker, 2011), indeed, in sectors of the media such as the print media, there is evidence of a fiercely competitive environment (Baines and Robson, 2001). However, as Chell and Karatas-Ozkan (2010) argue, entrepreneurial ideas are often generated and improved through interactions with others. This student expresses her concerns but also the benefits of group discussions:

> At the beginning I thought we will talk a lot and it will not come to anything. But then it started to be good, even if I'm not talking and I'm just listening to my peers – they are from different backgrounds and they have different ideas and projects and are even on different courses. So listening to them in order to get feedback was a good thing.
>
> (Postgraduate student A, 2010)

A former student interviewed after completing her MA describes one of her fellow students as still being her best critical-friend and support. She also articulates competitiveness between them as a positive characteristic of their friendship and work relationship. Friendly competition may indeed be healthy but it can also create awkwardness, as Lee (2011) describes in his research. The differences between friends and professional networks are easily blurred and are difficult to interpret in the early stages of a career. As Lee suggests in his study of the British independent television production sector, you can be in or out of the network depending on your personal social and cultural capital. Typically, students attempting to immerse themselves in local networks find that they don't have the social or cultural capital required for meaningful interactions. However, tutors, alumni and guest speakers can play a role in brokering the often invisible structures which govern social ties and the networks they form. Proactive students in this research build on opportunities to establish their networks, often starting with tutors who actively support the use of social media and invite students to industry events whenever possible. In this case study, students often benefit from studying in a school of media which engages with the local and regional cultural industry networks.

The guest speakers invariably express the importance of their networks in establishing business or career opportunities. One speaker described how much she hated networking and gave the students a series of tips for overcoming this barrier. Being immersed in networks and engaged with the market is a challenge and students soon come to realize the level of investment necessary to develop their own networks. They are asked to articulate their ideas and contribute to debates through social media platforms (e.g. Twitter, blogs, LinkedIn and Facebook) as part of establishing a professional identity. In this context reputation and social capital can be enhanced even if only tentatively at this stage. This is encouraged through the guest speaker sessions and illustrated by this tweet:

> @*** enjoyed your session, especially about sticking with one idea. Re-echoed what @***** said. #Ma***.
>
> (Tweet from postgraduate student F, 2010)

Some international students demonstrate many difficulties with building their network and developing social capital, resulting in poor achievement levels in relation to the learning outcomes. There are cultural differences at play which inhibit the networking expected of the student and a lack of social capital creates stumbling blocks in the early stages of establishing relationships within the student's sector (Lee, 2011). Others thrive on this approach, making good use of strong ties (Granovetter, 1973) through personal networks such as family and friends to support or help in developing initial ideas into opportunities. There is always a handful of students who have the impressive ability and confidence to generate a network from scratch in a matter of weeks. A journalism specialist explains that she is starting to realize the importance of networking and is developing strategies before the end of her Masters degree to enhance her career opportunities:

> I think I'm gonna work a lot online, so I'm going to get in touch with people. I've started to build up my profile on LinkedIn.
>
> (Postgraduate student B, 2011)

As postgraduate students with a focus on their professional development, students want to make a link between their studies and future employment or self-employment. Enhancing their networking capabilities is perceived as part of the broader MA awards, as well as the enterprise module described in this study. Raising awareness of the challenges and level of personal investment in networks and networking becomes an implicit aspect of the educational experience.

Conclusion

The author's motivation for this research is to challenge perceptions of enterprise education, particularly as it applies to media education. Critiques of the creative industries' policies which endorsed entrepreneurship as a means of boosting the economy (Hesmondhalgh, 2008) have rightly pointed to the inequalities and evidence of exploitation in media and cultural work. This chapter does not seek to brush these under the carpet, however, the author argues that engaging with the practice of entrepreneurship can include an exploration of the nature of being entrepreneurial, including the difficulties. Media students can engage with entrepreneurship without being slaves to a fixed notion of the entrepreneur or of entrepreneurial practice.

The chapter draws heavily on a case-study which explores the lived experience of postgraduate students, highlighting three key themes. Firstly, the need for reflection to support critical thinking and to develop an awareness of the challenges in media entrepreneurship. However, embedding reflection as part of a practical enterprise curriculum can be confusing for students. Secondly, given the opportunity, media students analyse their own approach to being enterprising. Students reflect on their experience and that of others, such as guest speakers, to explore entrepreneurship. This is fruitful in exploring a more bespoke version of enterprise. Thirdly, it is well documented that a key aspect of entrepreneurship and media work is the ability to be well networked and to develop good networking skills. This research suggests that a lack of social capital and confidence can hinder a student's progress with their enterprise. Despite that, a curriculum which insists on students immersing themselves in various networks can raise students' awareness of the challenges ahead.

This chapter explores an enterprise curriculum for media students while acknowledging that entrepreneurship is imperfect. Encouraging reflection enables students to explore entrepreneurship in context, whether it is through their cultural background, personal values or experience to date. As with many postgraduate courses, the diversity of students and the range of expectations bring a specific dynamic to the classroom. In particular, the international element in postgraduate study challenges more conventional enterprise curricula, which tends to be influenced by UK policies and UK industry needs. As discussed, DCMS and NESTA policy documents (DCMS, 2006; NESTA, 2006; Herrmann et al., 2008), which have helped to frame UK policies, are defined by Ball et al. (2010) as a 'supply' model; an instrumental approach which assumes that educational provision exists to meet creative business needs. This becomes less appropriate with postgraduate students given the increasing number of international students who will not necessarily contribute to the UK's economic development.

This research suggests that when students engage with the practice of entrepreneurship, they can start to re-shape it. As the authors of *Unmasking the Entrepreneur* propose, Schumpeter's 'creative destruction' is a good starting point for creating new models of entrepreneurship (Jones and Spicer, 2009, p. 3). In the case of media education, the more context-specific, the better the opportunity to explore the specificity of entrepreneurship as it is experienced in this sector and in new models of work. The study of entrepreneurial theory alone cannot engage students in the process of reinventing models of work in the way that practical experience can. Indeed, many careers in media, such as social media consultants or data journalists, did not exist a few years ago and are being shaped by the students and practitioners 'making it up' as they go along. When students start a course, they have a tendency to think that they will be 'trained' for a specific career, yet, even on vocational courses, this has probably never been the case. Entrepreneurial students can experiment with these new roles as they create them through their individual projects and reflect on the process for assignments. Critical debates of cultural work can inform students and initiate a less passive approach by engaging the students with different perspectives. Combined with practical experience this can lead to a more reflexive practitioner, potentially engaging with issues of inequalities and exploitation, in practice.

There is no textbook, but it is possible to create an environment which encourages critical reflection alongside experimenting with entrepreneurial ideas: a laboratory for a new generation of entrepreneurial media workers.

Notes

1. Websites such as http://www.creative-choices.co.uk/; http://www.springwise.com/; http://blog.davidparrish.com/ and http://www.entrepreneur.com/

2. Professional studies in vocational media courses include skills such as CV writing, developing a portfolio of work (on and offline), tools for personal assessment such as undertaking a SWOT analysis, live briefs and work placements, reflecting on work placements/live briefs in relation to personal aspirations and interview skills. It tends to focus on employability skills rather than self-employment although the author suggests this is changing and is reflected in The Centre for Excellence in Media Practice (CEMP) 2012 conference programme.

References

ADM-HEA and NESTA (2007) *Creating Entrepreneurship: Entrepreneurship Education for the Creative Industries* (London: ADM-HEA and NESTA).

Ashton, D. (2011) Media Work and the Creative Industries: Identity Work, Professionalism and Employability, *Education and Training* 53(6): 546–560.

Baines, S. and Robson, L. (2001) Being Self-Employed or Being Enterprising? The Case of Creative Work for the Media Industries, *Journal of Small Business and Enterprise Development* 8(4): 349–362.

Ball, L., Eikhof, D. and Stanlay, N. (2010) *Creative Graduates Creative Futures* (Brighton: Creative Graduates Creative Futures Higher Education Partnership and the Institute for Employment Studies).

Banks, M. (2006) Moral Economy and Cultural Work, *Sociology* 40(3): 455–472.

Banks, M. and Hesmondhalgh, D. (2009) Looking for Work in Creative Industries Policy, *International Journal of Cultural Policy* 15(4): 415–430.

Berglund, K. (2006) Discursive Diversity in Fashioning Entrepreneurial Identity, in Steyaert, C. and Hjorth, D. (eds.) *Entrepreneurship as Social Change* (Cheltenham: Edward Edgar Publishing Ltd.): 231–250.

Boyle, R. and Kelly, L. (2012) *The Television Entrepreneurs: Social Change and Public Understanding of Business* (Farnham: Ashgate).

Brown, L. (2007) A Consideration of the Challenges Involved in Supervising International Masters Students, *Journal of Further and Higher Education* 31(3): 239–248.

Carey, C. and Matlay, H. (2011) Emergent Issues in Enterprise Education: The Educator's Perspective, *Industry and Higher Education* 25(6): 441–450.

Carey, C. and Naudin, A. (2006) Enterprise Curriculum for Creative Industries Students: An Exploration of Current Attitudes and Issues, *Education and Training* 48(7): 518–531.

Chell, E. (2008) *The Entrepreneurial Personality: A Social Construct* (Sussex: Routledge).

Chell, E. and Karatas-Ozkan, M. (2010) *Nascent Entrepreneurship and Learning* (Cheltenham: Edward Elgar Publishing Limited).

Couldry, N. and Littler, J. (2011) Work, Power and Performance: Analysing the 'Reality' Game of the Apprentice, *Cultural Sociology* 5(2): 263–280.

DCMS (2006) *Developing Entrepreneurship for the Creative Industries: The Role of Higher Education* (London: Department of Culture, Media and Sports, Creative Industries Division).

Deuze, M. (2007) *Media Work* (Cambridge: Polity Press).

du Gay, P. (2007) *Organizing Identity* (London: Sage).

Ellmeier, A. (2003) Cultural Entrepreneurialism: On Changing the Relationship Between the Arts, Culture and Employment, *International Journal of Cultural Policy* 9(1): 3–16.

Gill, R. and Pratt, A. (2008) In the Social Factory? Immaterial Labour, Precariousness and Cultural Work, *Theory, Culture and Society* 25(7–8): 1–30.

Granovetter, M. (1973) The Strength of Weak Ties, *American Journal of Sociology* 78(6): 1360 1380.

Gray, A. (2003) *Research Practice for Cultural Studies* London: Sage.

Herrmann, K., Hannon, P., Cox, J., Ternouth, P. and Crowley, T. (2008) *Developing Entrepreneurial Graduates: Putting Entrepreneurship at the Centre of Higher Education* (London: NESTA).

Hesmondhalgh, D. (2008) Cultural and Creative Industries, in Bennett, T. and Frow, J. (eds) *The Sage Handbook of Cultural Analysis* (London and Los Angeles: Sage): 552–569.

Hesmondhalgh, D. and Baker, S. (2010) A Very Complicated Version of Freedom: Conditions and Experinces of Creative Labour in Three Cultural Industries, *Poetics* 38(1): 4–20.

Hesmondhalgh, D. and Baker, S. (2011) *Creative Labour: Media Work in Three Cultural Industries* (London: Routledge).

Hjorth, D. and Steyaert, C. (2006) *Entrepreneurship as Social Change* (Cheltenham: Edward Elgar Publishing Inc).

Jarvis, J. (2009) *What Would Google Do?* (New York: Harpers Collins).

Jones, C. and Spicer, A. (2009) *Unmasking the Entrepreneur* (Cheltenham: Edward Elgar).

Leadbeater, C. and Oakley, K. (1999) *The Independents* (London: Demos).

Lee, D. (2011) Networks, Cultural Capital and Creative Labour in the British Independent Television Industry, *Media Culture Society* 33(4): 549–566.

McGuigan, J. (2009) *Cool Capitalism* (London: Plutopress).

McGuigan, J. (2010) Creative Labour, Cultural Work and Individualisation, *International Journal of Cultural Policy* 16(3): 323–335.

McRobbie, A. (2002) From Hollyway to Hollywood: Happiness at Work in the New Cultural Economy? in du Gay, P. and Pryke, M. (eds) *Cultural Economy* (London: Sage): 97–114.

Moon, J. (2005) We Seek it Here...A New Perspective on the Elusive Activity of Critical Thinking: A Theoretical and Practical Approach. The Higher Education Academy Subject Centre for Education ESCalate.

Naudin, A. (2012) *An Exploration of Personal Agency in Cultural Entrepreneurs*, in proceedings of the 7th International Conference on Cultural Policy Research, Barcelona, July 2012. Unpublished conference paper.

NESTA (2006) *Creating Growth: How the UK Can Develop World Class Creative Businesses* (London: NESTA).

Oakley, K. (2009) *Art Works – Cultural Labour Markets: A Literature Review* (London: Creativity, Culture and Education).

Oakley, K. (2011) In its Own Image: New Labour and the Cultural Workforce, *Cultural Trends* 20(3–4): 281–289.

Rae, D. (2004) Entrepreneurial Learning: A Practical Model from the Creative Industries, *Education and Training* 46(8/9): 492–500.

Rae, D. and Carswell, M. (2000) Using a Life-Story Approach in Researching Entrepreneurial Learning: The Development of a Conceptual Model and its

Implications in the Design of Learning Experiences, *Education and Training* 42(6): 356–365.

Steedman, C. (1999) State-Sponsored Autobiography, in Conekin, B., Mort, F. and Waters, C. (eds) *Moments of Modernity Reconstructing Britain 1945–1964* (London: Rivers Oram Press): 41–54.

Thornham, S. and O'Sullivan, T. (2004) Chasing the Real: 'Employability' and the Media Studies Curriculum, *Media Culture Society* 26(5): 717–736.

Toynbee, J. (2003) Fingers to the Bone or Spaced Out on Creativity? Labor Process and Ideology in the Production of Pop, in Beck, A. (ed.) *Cultural Work: Understanding The Cultural Industries* (London and New York: Routledge): 39–55.

Part III
Identities and Transitions

6
Smashing Childlike Wonder? The Early Journey into Higher Education

Caitriona Noonan

In the past decade, much government policy has centred on helping young people discover and nurture their creative talents and leverage these as possible career opportunities (Banks, 2007; Oakley, 2009). Documents like *Creative Britain* (Department of Culture, Media and Sport (DCMS), 2008) prioritized the need for young people to develop creative talents at school and called for more structured pathways into creative careers. These ambitions were to be achieved through pilot programmes like 'Find Your Talent' and through better access to apprenticeships in the creative industries.[1]

Along with these early 'nurturing' programmes, further education and skills training was also seen as paramount to a successful career in the creative industries and now 68 per cent of the creative media workforce are graduates (Skillset, 2010). While this figure is fluctuating (increasing from 69 per cent in 2005 to 75 per cent in 2008 but with a decline in the 2010 figures), higher education (HE) still remains a popular route for many students with the decision to go to university and the choice of degree an important part of a young person's work–life biography and their own identity formation.

It is against this backdrop that this research focuses on the experiences and aspirations of first-year media undergraduates as they begin their journey through HE, extending the literature on transition and identity which is emerging within the field of cultural labour. While previous studies, including those covered in this volume and beyond (Ball et al., 2010; Ashton, 2011), have focused on the transition from graduate to professional, this chapter considers the first major step in one route to the creative industries workplace – entering and completing a degree. It considers three main questions:

1. How is creative labour understood by these young people, particularly in relation to the rewards and challenges which such work offers?
2. How do young people conceptualize their own professional identities with respect to current and future employment in the creative industries?
3. What are some of the factors influencing this conceptualization?

Even at this early stage of their degree the students demonstrate a sophisticated and critical understanding of the creative industries labour market and already reveal many of the values of the ideal creative worker. Therefore, this research extends our understanding of cultural workers 'in the making' (Ashton, 2011) and provides important insights of relevance to policy-makers, educators, the industry and those interested in competing discourses around cultural work.

Context for this study

This research considers some of the aspirations, expectations and knowledge that young people have of work in the creative industries. This research is situated within a very particular context, therefore, the conclusions generated here are not necessarily applicable to the diverse student population, the range of national and regional policy contexts and the variety of HE institutions which exist in the UK and internationally. However, the study does point to some areas of discussion around cultural labour which have been overlooked and so it should be read as intended – an attempt to broaden the debate and incorporate the student voice within that discussion.

Students on a generalist BA degree covering media, culture and journalism were the focus of this study. This course is predominantly a theoretical course but in recent years a number of core and optional practice modules have been introduced. This mirrors the change in many counterpart institutions and the prominence of the 'critical-vocational' paradigm in HE in the UK (Lindahl Elliot, 2000, cited in Thornham and O'Sullivan, 2004, p. 723).

The university itself is recognized as a 'new' university, having evolved from polytechnic to university in 1992. Today it actively markets degrees leading to careers in sectors including media production, theatre, film, journalism, animation, fashion, music and radio. Although the main campus remains in the Welsh valleys, the faculty which delivers awards relating to the creative sector is based in the Welsh capital, Cardiff, signalling the urbanization of much creative industry activity. This provision also highlights the ways in which 'new' universities with their background in vocational training and managerial structures have been able to respond to the labour demands of the new economy through the provision of industry accredited courses and capital investments programmes designed to support a growing employability agenda in HE (Thornham and O'Sullivan, 2004).

It is also worth recounting the specific context of Wales, one of the nations which make up the UK. HE is a 'devolved' area of government, which means that most decisions that are made about HE in Wales are taken by the Welsh government. HE institutions in Wales receive a portion of their income from public funds along with the income they derive from student fees, through research projects and commercial activities. Following publication of the *Review of Higher Education Funding and Student Finance* (the 'Browne Review') in 2010, the Welsh Assembly opted to provide financial support for students who study *in* Wales – whether from Wales, the rest of the UK, the European Union or the rest of the world (Higher Education Funding Council for Wales (HEFCW), 2012) – differing significantly from the position taken by Westminster for the provision of HE in England.

At the same time, creative industry policy remains a 'partially devolved' matter with broadcasting regulation subject to UK-wide governance (including Welsh-language broadcasting), while cultural funding and business development are Assembly areas of responsibility. In 2009, the Welsh government commissioned a review of the creative industries in Wales, which reaffirmed the importance of the sector for Wales but warned that significant challenges lay ahead (Hargreaves, 2010). The review examined skills development for and within the sector, concluding that Wales has strong educational assets in the areas of film, broadcasting, publishing and some areas of new media. It reported that the perception of stakeholders was that the demands for skilled labour for the creative sector and broader digital economy in Wales were being addressed but that strengths must continue to be nurtured through efficient and well-targeted knowledge transfer. HE was viewed as a key supplier.

This complex policy landscape highlights some of the challenges to any coherent discussion of the intersections between HE and creative industries. This intersection brings together a variety of interests and agendas, many of which are historically embedded yet shift subtly in terms of power, autonomy and public backing as various stakeholders evolve. Any attempts to introduce change to the experience of creative workers, students and HE staff must negotiate a battleground in which ideals become celebrated and compromised. The nearer one gets to the detail needed to explain and resolve the situation the more fragmented it appears with economic, political, social and educational goals relentlessly contested.

Note on methods

To fulfil the aims of this research the methods adopted were mixed, combining a survey, group discussion and a series of interviews. The survey was intended as a first step, capturing demographic and attitudinal data along with details of experience and future career aspirations. It shaped later interviews around key themes; for example, in the survey the Welsh capital Cardiff emerged as a key part of the responses and so the significance of broader issues of place were then probed in more depth in the interviews.

There are 30 students in the cohort which began level one in September 2011, with 25 taking part in the survey and 7 participating in the follow-up interview.[2] The students are all aged between 18 and 23, with the majority identifying themselves as British. The cohort is predominantly female (76%), reflecting a wider trend in creative sector degrees (ECU, 2011). For all students this was their first experience of HE and 40 per cent of the group are the first generation in their family to attend university. Again, this is often a characteristic of 'new' universities who are cited as promoting greater access to HE and widening participation among under-represented social groups (Harris, 2011). Despite their relatively young age, 28 per cent had work experience specifically in the creative industries. This was across an impressive array of positions which included writing for a local newspaper, contributing to local or community radio, co-ordinating some of the public relations activities for an arts organization and working in a market research firm.

The remainder of this chapter reports the findings from this research, mixing the various methodological tools in order to illuminate specific themes. The themes which proved most insightful were: how these students saw the industry and approached the issue of professionalism; the role of place, creative institutions and wider creative policies in their decision-making and expectations for the future; and how they viewed the role of education and the tensions they recognized between developing a critical understanding of creative work and needing to be 'industry-ready'. The chapter concludes by considering what this means for the curriculum and the future of HE provision, in particular, how students' views of professionalism and expert authority could have major implications for our own academic identity as educators and researchers.

Views of work and professionalism

Irrespective of whether they had experience or not, all of the respondents to this study were highly aware of the rewards and challenges of cultural work. They recognized that for many it would seem like a glamorous job, as Maria describes: 'I think because people enjoy consuming it, because it's glamorised, people think "I'd like to do that job" '. However, the survey suggests that students were doubtful about whether this was actually the case. They reasoned that as it is the media which perpetuates this view such an image is likely to be partial:

> It's what we see and we automatically think that it is going to be great [...] you think its media so all fashion shows but its not like that. We build our opinions based on what we see in the media. We are learning about working in the media through the media. And if that is what we are doing there are obviously some parts of it that you might not see. [...] It's not all perfect, it's not all great.
>
> (Leona)

While they were doubtful about how glamorous work would be, they were very clear that creative work was competitive and precarious. When asked in the survey to 'describe work in the media' typical responses included:

> Something that excites me and that I am always consuming. It is not an easy industry as there are always pressures to be better than everyone/every other brand.

> Competitive, fast paced, ambitious, modern, over-crowded, enjoyable.

As a result of this competitive nature, the respondents in both the surveys and interviews believed strongly in a specific 'rite of passage' to gain acceptance. In order to enter the industry, one had to start at the bottom, irrespective of whether they had a degree or not:

> I always think that it is such a competitive industry that you have to start at the bottom; you have to work yourself up. You gotta meet people and get your name about and then you will end up getting higher and higher in the jobs that you want. I don't think that you can go into an industry and just be like 'I want to be a TV presenter' and then be one, go straight there. You gotta completely work your way up with people you know.
>
> (Laura)

Many felt that their degree did not allow them to bypass the bottom as they believed it to be only a partial statement of their skills. They attributed this to the ambiguities of media work and the variety of creative occupations which were possible with a media degree. For many this variety was part of the attraction of media degrees, however, it also meant a certain professional rite of passage would be expected later.

Additionally, the competitive nature of the industry was cited by the students as one of the factors which prohibited any real challenge to the structural conditions of cultural work:

> [T]here is a sense you do need to be paying your dues, so you have to work hard to climb up the ladder. I'm not sure how I feel about that... that's the sort of message you get across from everyone else, you have to start at the bottom [...] I can see it is there but I don't know what to do about it. Them is the rules. There is not much you can really do about that cos that is standard practice now, enforced, and you can go against it but if you try and go against it, someone who isn't going to go against it will come along and go 'I'll do it' and now I'm out of a job.
>
> (Adam)

Creative industries policy promotes an individualistic logic and matters of employability are primarily seen as personal development (Banks, 2007; DCMS, 2008). This makes collective bargaining to improve conditions difficult to instigate or maintain (Neilson and Rossiter, 2005) and in many ways runs counter to the networked culture which characterizes the industry. This then necessitates a more 'calculating relationship' between students, HE and the labour market which is endorsed in policy-making for both the creative industries and HE

(Oakley, this volume). As we can see in the quote above, Adam is already acutely aware of these countervailing logics and adopts a calculating, albeit defeatist, response.

In order to compete and improve their future opportunities, the interviewees had all developed strategies to promote themselves to prospective employers; engaging in the meaningful arrangement of their own biography for themselves and others (Beck, 1992). They enthusiastically talked about developing their own 'brand', a concept which would offer them a convenient and distinct identity to be created and commodified within the labour market. In the interviews they had some understanding of what elements were important within that brand, in particular, work experience, social skills and digital proficiency. A mastery of social network technologies (like Twitter and Facebook) was an important element of this branding with these platforms being used instrumentally in a self-conscious project of both self-promotion and professionalization (e.g. seeking work experience, discussing news and promoting events). These new platforms undoubtedly offer appreciative students access to information, networks and opportunities not available even five years ago. However, this practice also raised specific anxieties for young people in the transition between youthful freedom and professional accountability:

> [W]e are digital natives... I think you have to actively participate, you can't just be on it [Twitter], you have to be active with what you are doing... I have been using it for years, not just to write 'lol, having a coffee'. [...] You have to build your own brand and one way of doing that is being on Twitter especially. So yeah you have to build a brand [...] I probably should have two accounts, one professional and one personal but... I wouldn't like to separate them because all the different bits come together to make them the person that they are, all the different aspects of your personality come together to make people who they are.
>
> (Alex)

The interviewees articulated a narrative of personal risk (Beck, 1992) and the sometimes negative consequences of their attempts to convey a more professional persona; particularly in online environments where they feared a threat to their authenticity and a fragmenting of the self. Since beginning university some of these students have begun to see prospective employers as part of their 'imagined audience' and this meant they now had to navigate multiple contexts adapting their mode of address and content to the expectations of this enigmatic audience in response to an uncertain and competitive labour market (Marwick and Boyd, 2011). For others the use of online media to communicate an emerging professional identity was something they resisted as they reported a wider unease with the idea of being professional.

The employability and professionalism agenda is now prevalent within HE institutions and their mission statements finding its way into the curriculum in a variety of ways (e.g. industry placements, work simulations, etc.) (Thornham and O'Sullivan, 2004). As in the research in this volume and elsewhere (Thornham and O'Sullivan, 2004; Ashton, 2011) there is a complex discourse of professionalism in the accounts given by some students, or at least a recognition that this will develop over the course of their degree:

> *Do you feel professional?* Yeah in a sense, as you are thinking 'I am doing this, I am getting in contact with people', yet you are constantly thinking about the way you have to talk to them and you have to maintain a professional manner about yourself [...] If they see you as a young person who is professional they may have a bit more respect for you rather than saying 'they are just a student, they are not very good'... they make take more notice of you.
>
> (Katie)

This research suggests that many of the transitions to becoming professional have already begun when the student begins university. Many of these ideas of being 'industry ready' are already well established and this tentatively suggests that programmes to realize the economic capacity of young people in school have been successful. However, there was unease among the students with the idea of being 'professional' as many cited that they were not ready in terms of skills or emotion:

> Labeling something as professional doesn't leave any room for mess ups. For me, as a student who has done internships, this is your playground. [...] Its better that you fail here, then fail in real life because that is going to be harder to get back up from. So I don't think I am a professional, at least not yet.
>
> (Ahmed)

> This word professional has just seemed to appear, everyone doing their job in a way they are being professional. [...] It's a very grown up word, you think of adults being very professional. I'm a child, I'm still learning.
>
> (Adam)

The levels of accountability and the ability to make mistakes were important parts in this resistance to being perceived as professional. This suggests that care is needed when putting students into a context where they are expected to be professional (i.e. work placements or professional pitches) – experiences they increasingly encounter in their curricula today. These responses to the pressure of being seen as professional highlight the importance of stressing that failure is acceptable and an essential part of the learning journey. This also needs to be communicated to external groups who collaborate with HE on these 'professional-making' experiences (i.e. industry partners) that such failures, while not accepted within a commercial context, need to be tolerated here.

This section demonstrates the complex ways in which students function as critical agents in relation to their own occupational choices and subsequently the impact this has on their identity formation. Researchers note the individualized focus of media work and how the capacity for significant disruption of this system is tempered by the structure of the labour market especially in relation to the number competing and perceived lack of alternative prospects (Gill, 2002; Banks, 2007; Oakley, 2009; Hesmondhalgh, 2010). However, what is clear in this research is that this bind not only impacts on those already working in the industry but also those aspiring to, and that clear 'institutional biographical patterns' (Beck, 1992, p. 131) have already emerged for these young people. The need to network, self-promote and develop social capital, along with demonstrating flexibility, self-governance and an absolute willingness to contribute (as the quote from Adam and his evocation of 'the rules' suggests) is integral to this value system. Many exhibited a tacit view that they are unable to restructure the rules and therefore police themselves, exchanging acceptance and access to the system for compliance and partial sovereignty. Therefore, in media work both professionals and 'would-be' professionals are elevated to be the master of their destiny and simultaneously rendered insignificant. The interviews visibly demonstrate the anxiety that this creates for many of these young people at a key stage of their personal development as they grapple with projecting an authentic and coherent identity while succumbing to the individual pressure to compete and always succeed.

Creative place, creative institution?

Within the field of creative industries policy-making the contribution of place has received significant attention; for example, the clustering of creative firms, worker and policy mobility, the contribution of the sector to urban development and regeneration, and the use of creative outputs as important symbolic and financial resources for countries engaged in various levels of trade and globalization (Banks, 2007; Allen and Hollingworth, 2013; Luckman, this volume; Oakley, 2009). In the nexus between place, the creative economy and HE institutions, policy-makers have tended to instrumentalize this relationship as simply the provision of skills and qualifications, and the commercialization of creative and technical research knowledge for economic development. They have largely ignored the role that universities play in the local cultural milieu (Oakley, this volume) and what the construction of a place as 'creative' might mean to the individual. However, as Allen and Hollingworth (2013) argue place-specific habitus shape how the creative industries feature within young people's imagined careers and it is clear from the interviews conducted here that students in HE see a clear triangulation between their institution, the creative economy and the geographical place both occupy.

Various DCMS programmes have attempted to provide a strategic plan for the UK's creative industries with the majority of policies focused on the neoliberal economic development of urban areas in an attempt to revive those cities which have been decimated by the decline of heavy manufacturing and brand them as creative places in which companies can be nurtured and sustained with the ultimate goal of contributing to the economic agenda of the region. This centralization of support to metropolitan areas is problematic as it means rural areas and those not associated with creativity are often overlooked in the allocation of resources.[3] Therefore, despite the prominence of globalization within creative industries rhetoric, in media work (and thus media education) locality still matters; however, not all places are equal.

Throughout both the surveys and interviews, 'place' appeared prominently within the narratives (for example, in discussions of Cardiff and/ or South Wales). Cardiff, in particular, played a major role in the decision of many of the students to attend the faculty – nearly three-quarters (72%) directly cited 'Cardiff' as a factor in their decision to pick the university as a place to study. In later group discussions many believed that they would have not chosen the faculty had it been located in the Welsh valleys. This has implications for universities in less urban areas and also in those places which are not actively engaging in activities which can be branded as creative; something that will be considered later.

Despite the existence of local media (including radio and newspaper) and perhaps a less aggressive job market, less urban areas were simply not recognized as creative by the interviewees. The frequent description was of curtailment, of being from a town in the 'middle of nowhere', and for people like Laura this was a professional hurdle to overcome: 'If I said I was from my little town they would be like "what experience do you have". I feel like they would think that you haven't experienced anything properly'. Inevitably, and however problematic this may be, the city became associated with opportunity, autonomy and social mobility:

> I thought if I am going to spend three years I want to be somewhere that I can get connections and stuff. [...] I come from a little tiny village in the middle of nowhere with builders and farmers, but here there are all these creative jobs and you can see it in the people all these creative people walking around.
>
> (Adam)

As indicated in this quote from Adam, place is part of the learning process, but significantly this research argues that this is not in terms of citizenship or cultural identity but solely in a further form of professionalism and occupational mobility. This view was not limited to Adam as we see through Alex's account how access to networks and work experience (as enabled through place) was yet another resource to be operationalized in similar ways to technology for instance:

> I also thought it would be easier for me to get work experience here, hopefully, because there is more stuff going on in the media. [...] I think it would be easier to get work experience living in those places [London, Manchester and Cardiff] than to be anywhere else ... I think these is a lot of opportunity here... [...] you would have contacts and knowledge of the area and that can help you on the ladder to your first job especially if you have networked a bit when you are at university, it's not that you can call in favours, but you have got more of a chance.
>
> (Alex)

The recent international success of television programmes like *Dr Who* (BBC, 2005–) and *Torchwood* (BBC, 2006–) has been the catalyst for further investment in a drama production centre in Cardiff. As well as these locally developed series, a number of established BBC dramas (including *Being Human* (2009–), *Sherlock* (2010–) and *Casualty* (1986–)) have relocated to a specially developed site in the bay area of the city, Porth Teigr. Blandford et al. (2010) report that having these programmes produced and filmed in the area provides a source of considerable pleasure to local audiences. This is also further reflected in the interviews for this research where many of the students highlighted their pleasure at being 'near to the action' and the professional opportunities it offered them:

> I saw it filming once and it was like 'wow they actually film stuff like that here'... it means things go on in Cardiff not just in London. [...] It makes Cardiff a lot more well known to know that programmes, really big programmes like *Dr Who* have been filmed here... It's making a name for itself.
>
> (Laura)

> [T]here is a lot of stuff going on in the Bay... and because they are putting the BBC Wales down there that is going to give us a lot of opportunities, especially if we want to do work experience because we are very close. [...] By being closer to it there is always a chance someone might talk to you, which is something that appeals to me.
>
> (Katie)

> When I was younger, when *Dr Who* came out in 2005, I was 13 and that was the first time Cardiff came on my radar and that I became aware of it. *Dr Who* went really well and they started making more things nationally in Wales and the attention that brought, and directed attention to South Wales especially from audiences. It might have peaked but who knows, hopefully not.
>
> (Alex)

As these quotes show, many of the students felt that this new production capacity could offer professional credibility through association with that internationally successful output and furthermore provide access to the structures and networks which it has nurtured. The emerging status of Wales as a production centre also raises their professional status, hence it would offer specific career opportunities both now (in terms of work experience) and later (in access to professional networks). However, as Alex alludes to in the final quote above, places are not static (Massey, 1994) and often these periods of creative expansion are cyclical. They are often driven by political will, access to public and private investment and, as with all creative products are subject to risk and changing audience and commissioning tastes. Furthermore, as Allen and Hollingworth (2013) argue, in order to mobilize place as a resource, converting this place-related capital into professional and economic capital, requires young people to harness other stocks of social capital (such as the ability and confidence to network); this then becomes a crucial, often invisible part of the curriculum (see Lee, this volume, for a comprehensive discussion of the television industry and the mechanisms of exclusion associated with low levels of cultural and social capital).

Also worth highlighting in relation to the quotes above are two further points; first that decisions relating to creative careers are related to consumption patterns. In all these narratives the interviewees occupied both the position of audience and future cultural producer. Without such consumption would the lure of Cardiff have been so great? Second, the BBC features prominently in their discussions of creative work and the future of the creative industry in Wales. According to the surveys, the students engaged in a variety of media activities including uploading videos, contributing to social network sites, blogging, writing music, etc. When asked what media brands they consume most often, it was interesting to note that traditional institutions like the BBC, the *Guardian* and Channel 4 featured as prominently as newer brands such as Facebook, YouTube and Twitter. Later in the survey they were asked to complete the statement 'My ideal first job would be...' and some students signalled their aspirations to work with or for the BBC:

> *My ideal first job would be...?* Working within the BBC, behind the scenes research or at a local newspaper to gain experience to progress into the BBC, as that is my main goal.

The interviewees also recognized the opportunities that the BBC represents as a major source of work experience, training and subsequent professional experience:

> [T]hey are putting BBC Wales down there [Porth Teigr, Cardiff]. That is going to give us a lot of opportunities especially if we want to do work experience because we are very close. It's a half an hour walk so we can just go down and assert ourselves down there saying 'I go this university, I am very close if you ever need anyone to help' [...] you get a sense of what is going on and from observation and a closer proximity you can see what they are doing.
>
> (Katie)

Students recognize the need to network with these organizations and to incorporate these into their social network. The BBC was often cited as a more accessible organization due to its size, public role and formal work experience programmes. Increasingly, universities are encouraged to develop more links to enable that network. However, the future potential of these links may become problematic as the BBC increasingly commissions programmes externally through systems like the Window for Creative Competition (WOCC) directly impacting in-house production units which provide the bulk of 'below the line' work experience for students.[4] Furthermore, the BBC is currently the biggest source of training and development within broadcasting, however, it is likely that successive cuts to its funding will have an impact on that role and its provision. What might that mean to students and new entrants to the industry who are often reliant on the BBC as a destination, not only locally but nationally?

It is worth highlighting that Cardiff was not the only place appearing in the student narrative, underscoring the high degree of mobility that these students already exhibit. Much of their discussions extended to other cities including Manchester; indeed one student talked about a 'golden triangle' between the developments in MediaCityUK (in Salford, Greater Manchester), Cardiff Bay and London:[5]

> I think things are quite centralised in England and Wales...it is probably easier to have everything in the one place starting out...so yeah it's like a golden triangle between places like Cardiff, London and Manchester...and when starting out it is good to be there for access to people With internet connection and more Skype maybe in a few years you won't have to be in a central location, but when we graduate we will have to be.
>
> (Alex)

It is not surprising that London features so visibly in their career aspirations. It has long been the centre of British economic, political and cultural life, and continues to dominate in terms of economic development and investment. London has 32 per cent of all the creative jobs in the UK with many of the key players in Britain's creative sector based in the city (GLA Economics, 2010, p. 4). In the last decade, a number of different policies have been introduced to decentralize creative industries outside of London and support regional production (e.g. regional quotas in television, capital investment projects like MediaCityUK). However, the impact of these is questionable as London continues to dominate the creative industries. Where secondary clusters have developed the local universities have all played a major role in supporting these through research, facilities, business incubation and advice, along with supplies of talent. However, although the lure of London remains strong for many, it is not for everyone:

> I know the main stuff happens in London but you think that some of the industry does happen in Cardiff and it is close to home if you wanted to work here and be in the industry. London is such a big and scary place and it's quite overwhelming.
>
> (Laura)

> I'll go to Cardiff or Manchester...not really London because it is big and it is scary and it is so competitive.
>
> (Alex)

These comments highlight how while London is still central to their career development, other places have a unique offering which is often linked to the quality of experience and lifestyle choice.

While some scholars argue that social relations are becoming increasingly dislocated from locality and face-to-face interaction (Giddens, 1991), this research suggests that this view overlooks the ways in which place, location and geography still matter to people (Allen and Hollingworth, 2013). In this case the young people who informed this study identified with their locality in specific ways, often within the context of their emerging professional identity. Locality, in particular the virtues of cosmopolitanism, still hold considerable value for both their personal development but also features in a range of functional ways – access to work experience, access to contacts and networks, direct exposure to creative practice. For researchers interested in cultural labour it suggests that locality and geography need to be attended to in much greater ways in order to understand how identity is constructed and exchanged. Indeed one of the most interesting points of departure for this research is how professional identity travels to other parts of the UK and beyond. As cultural work and economic productivity become increasingly consolidated within policy-making, and geographical mobility dominates creative worker experiences, what transactions occur between cities, regions and places?

The narratives reported in this study also highlight how, in linking education and creative work, place is a really important factor. This has implications for universities and policy-makers. Writing about place within culture work, Banks argues that for cultural producers, 'the feel or sense of a place might provide a focus or inspiration for alternative forms of cultural production based on aesthetic, practice-based or social/ethical endeavour' (2007, p. 145). How might the alternative forms suggested by Banks represent a substantial challenge to the exclusionary practices of the industry and the problematic routines of cultural work? Surely universities as non-profit-making organizations are well positioned to create an enduring sense of place which goes beyond the degree experience and nurture these alternative forms? Furthermore, if authentic creative experience is associated with cities, and policy-makers and government departments work hard to develop creative cities, what does that mean for more rural areas or cities with a less creative modern image and the HE institutions which occupy these places? How do they compete with the lure of the creative city rhetoric and marketing which places like Cardiff are keen to promote?

Questions of pedagogy: Smashing childlike wonder?

One of the dilemmas for those researching in the area of cultural labour, especially where their conclusions point to structural issues within the industry and a challenge to the image of the industry as 'cool, creative and egalitarian' (Gill, 2002), is how to translate this work into effective teaching. As discussed in this volume and elsewhere, while genuinely positive experiences exist within the creative workplace, various barriers, inequalities and suggestions of exploitation do condition many worker narratives (Banks, 2007; Hesmondhalgh, 2010). Therefore, how can the critical perspectives which emerge from some academic research be incorporated into the learning experience without painting an overly pessimistic picture, and what is at stake for students encountering this new knowledge?

In this study, students are clearly excited about the future. This is evidenced by the survey where across the attitudinal scales the statement 'I am excited about my future career' elicited the highest mean score (6.36 out of possible 7). This is despite the competitiveness of the industry and the challenges they recognize within the work culture. As researchers and teachers, one of the main challenges is how to balance this enthusiasm for the future with an understanding of some of the uncomfortable realities of the industry.

The interviewees felt they had a right to know what they might encounter:

> If you are going into work thinking it's going to be great and it's not, they [students] are going to feel let down; they are going to feel betrayed by the people who are teaching them. [...] Let them know

the pros and the cons cos if you say it's all perfect and it's not, they will end up thinking 'you lied to me about this' and that you did not educate me for this.

(Leona)

There is childlike wonder and then you smash it; some people are a bit fragile. Whereas I think we do need to be introduced to the real-life, the reality of what it is going to be like when we get out of here. It would be silly to hide things and be like 'everything is brilliant' and then they get out and it's not like that. People might not like that, but in the long run it is necessary.

(Adam)

When asked why some students might find critical discussion of the industry unpalatable, they put any resistance down to individual failure or immaturity and distanced themselves from such naivety. They clearly saw that it was a difficult balancing act for educators and that in many ways they could never be fully prepared:

I don't think you can actually fully prepare people for what they are about to see...On the one had it's probably not fair to let people blindly think it's going to be fun and games, an 'Alice in Wonderland' kinda career. But on the other hand try not to crush our spirits...once you work you realise that nothing anyone could have told you absolutely prepares you for what you are about to see [...] I think you have a responsibility because you guys have already worked in the industry before, you actually know what it is like. Although you can't completely relay what is going to happen and what we are going to go through, I can see that there is an effort to tell us what it is going to be like.

(Ahmed)

The students were also very clear in terms of who should deliver this knowledge. External perspectives (e.g. through guest lectures from industry professionals) were most highly valued and the students were keen to go outside the academy for expert answers (see Ashton, this volume, for a discussion of how teacher-practitioners within the academy were equally keen to share their experiences but in a way which allowed them to reflect 'from a distance'). Today, this external contribution features as a well-established part of any degree curriculum and increasingly outside perspectives are brought into the academy as a way of strengthening collaborations and opening up new networks. However, the considerable value placed in the external experiences represents uncertainty for the academe as a professional culture in itself. It raises questions about the credibility and authenticity of teaching staff without professional experience and in many ways undermines the professional value of academic training and qualifications. It also allows a discipline such as media studies, which is already subject to pedagogic debate (Thornham and O'Sullivan, 2004), to become defined elsewhere and potentially marginalizes critical engagement with the practices of media work.

Conclusion: 'this industry is good but it's not all great' (Leona)

As stated at the outset, this chapter is an exploratory study drawing attention to some of the experiences and aspirations of students as they begin their journey through HE. While small in scale it is clear when reading the other contributions to this volume that many of the issues outlined here appear in different guises elsewhere. Like the other chapters in this part of the volume, transition is an important element in the career biographies of creative workers. Here we see the transition to university and the anticipation and anxiety this causes, particularly around the cultivation of a professional identity. This chapter opened by framing this transition as the first major step towards a professional identity and for many it is. However, for a growing number this first step is already taken with many already experienced in the professional culture of the creative workplace and exhibiting many of the values and concerns of cultural workers. The need to be distinct and individual in a crowded labour market was one of the primary concerns of these 'professionals in the making'.

This research adds two further features to the intersection between cultural work and HE: the role of place and locality in that intersection and the role of external institutions like the BBC. Place features in the narratives of these students as a further resource in their career biography and conditions their view of the creative industries and the (mainly urban) spatial context they occupy. It also raises questions about the continued role of institutions like the BBC in these interactions and their role as pathways to a creative career. Cuts to funding and a shift in how public service obligations are interpreted, delivered and valued by the public will have consequences to that role.

The chapter also argues that there is room in the curriculum for an engagement with some of the challenges of cultural labour, however, this needs to be treated with care and creativity. How do we ensure that critical knowledge of the industry is an important asset in their future as citizens, consumers and cultural producers? In their respective chapters in this volume, both Anamik Saha and Kim Allen make suggestions regarding how this might look in practice. This author would add to these perspectives by saying that while such knowledge is important for students, it is *as* important that this knowledge is 'owned' by HE. This author finds problematic the arguments that the only perspective with any credibility comes from external professionals. This ignores the interests which sometimes underpin professional engagement with the academe, and also points to a worrying future where academic skills are displaced by professional ones. If this happens can critical distance and change really be effectively nurtured?

Undoubtedly these questions warrant further study. Longitudinal studies are conspicuous by their absence from the literature on cultural labour. Studies are also needed in order to compare experiences across 'new' and 'old' universities, and in the different nations of the UK which operate under different cultural and educational experiences and policy structures. These studies would also give us a better appreciation of the education system and media landscape along with the diversity of identities and experiences which they encompass. Without such understanding we are in danger of smashing childlike wonder.

Notes

1. This scheme ran from 2008 to 2010 across ten pilot areas in England. According to its site (www.findyourtalent.org) the programme 'offered children and young people regular involvement with arts and culture – both in and out of school. The programme gave young people the chance to learn musical instruments, perform on stage, attend performances and experience the great cultural heritage of the country. It also helped them develop new skills and get work experience in the fast-growing creative industries, including radio and television'. This highlights how both cultural and economic goals were combined within this programme.
2. All interviewees provided written consent and any quotes used in this work have been anonymized.
3. See Allen and Hollingworth (2013) for a discussion of the differing narratives of career aspirations in three urban areas of the UK; in particular the ways in which Stoke on Trent can be viewed as one of the 'losers' in the knowledge economy.

4. In 2006, the BBC introduced the Window of Creative Competition (WOCC) as a new system for commissioning content, leading to a greater integration of the independent sector into the process. For further details see http://www.bbc.co.uk/commissioning/tv/how-we-work/the-wocc.shtml
5. MediaCityUK is the latest large-scale development in the British government's support of the creative and cultural industries. It provides a dedicated space for media production with the BBC as its 'anchor' tenant.

References

Allen, K. and Hollingworth, S. (2013) Social Class, Place and Urban Young People's Aspirations for Work in the Knowledge Economy: 'Sticky Subjects' or 'Cosmopolitan Creatives'? *Urban Studies* 50 (3): 499–517.

Ashton, D. (2011) Media Work and the Creative Industries: Identity Work, Professionalism and Employability, *Education and Training* 53(6): 546–560.

Ball, L., Pollard, E. and Stanley, N. (2010) *Creative Graduates Creative Futures* (Brighton: Creative Graduates Creative Futures Higher Education Partnership and the Institute for Employment Studies).

Banks, M. (2007) *The Politics of Cultural Work* (Basingstoke: Palgrave Macmillan).

Beck, U. (1992) *Risk Society: Towards a New Modernity* (Newbury Park, CA: Sage).

Blandford, S., Lacey, S., McElroy, R. and Williams, R. (2010) *Screening the Nation: Wales and Landmark Television: Report for BBC Audience Council Wales*, http://culture.research.glam.ac.uk/documents/download/13/.

DCMS (Department of Culture, Media and Sport) (2008) *Creative Britain* (London: DCMS).

ECU (Equality Challenge Unit) (2011) *Equality in Higher Education: Statistical Report 2011* (London: Equality Challenge Unit).

Giddens, A. (1991) *Modernity and Self-identity: Self and Society in the Late Modern Age* (Cambridge: Polity).

Gill, R. (2002) Cool, Creative and Egalitarian? Exploring Gender in Project-Based New Media Work in Euro, *Information, Communication & Society* 5(1): 70–78.

GLA Economics (2010) London's Creative Workforce: 2009 Update. Working Paper 40, http://www.london.gov.uk/who-runs-london/mayor/publications/business-and-economy/londons-creative-workforce-2010-update, date accessed 21 June 2012.

Hargreaves, I. (2010) *The Heart of Digital Wales: A Review of the Creative Industries for the Welsh Assembly Government*, http://wales.gov.uk/docs/det/publications/100324creativeindustriesrpten.pdf.

Harris, S. (2011) *The University in Translation: Internationalizing Higher Education* (London: Continuum Publishing Ltd).

HEFCW (2012) *About Higher Education in Wales*, http://www.hefcw.ac.uk/about_he_in_wales/about_higher_education_in_wales.aspx, date accessed 6 June 2012.

Hesmondhalgh, D. (2010) User-Generated Content, Free Labour and the Cultural Industries, *Ephemera: Theory and Politics in Organization* 10(3/4): 267–284.

Marwick, A.E. and Boyd, d. (2011) I Tweet Honestly, I Tweet Passionately: Twitter Users, Context Collapse, and the Imagined Audience, *New Media & Society* 13(1): 114–133.

Massey, D. (1994) *A Global Sense of Place: From Space, Place and Gender* (Minneapolis: University of Minnesota Press).

Neilson, B. and Rossiter, N. (2005) From Precarity to Precariousness and Back Again: Labour, Life and Unstable Networks', *Fibreculture*, 5, http://five.fibreculturejournal.org/.

Oakley, K. (2009) *'Art Works'* – *Cultural Labour Markets: A Literature Review* (London: Creativity, Culture and Education).

Skillset (2010) *2010 Creative Media Workforce Survey*, http://www.skillset.org/uploads/pdf/asset_16988.pdf, date accessed 11 January 2012.

Thornham, S. and O'Sullivan, T. (2004) Chasing the Real: 'Employability' and the Media Studies Curriculum, *Media, Culture and Society* 26(5): 717–736.

7
Negotiating a Contemporary Creative Identity

Stephanie Taylor and Karen Littleton

Introduction

More than two decades of discussion of the cultural and creative industries by academics, educationalists and policy-makers has led, inevitably, to considerable interest in the experience and motivations of the people working in these industries. One interpretation is that such workers are drawn into a form of 'self-exploitation' (McRobbie, 1998) by their creative ambitions, becoming wholly subject to the requirements and interests of industries and employers. In this chapter, we draw on theory from social, narrative and discursive psychology to propose a more complex form of identification or subjectification (see Wetherell, 2008), which is linked to the multiple positionings and meanings in play around creativity and creative work. Our analyses of this complexity and multiplicity offer new explanations for the choice of a creative career and for problems confronted by creative workers. In particular, we explore conflicts around the taking up of a creative identity. These conflicts are shown to be associated with, and impact on, certain categories of workers, reinforcing previously ascribed 'deficit' identities (Reynolds and Taylor, 2005). The chapter therefore challenges previous arguments concerning the motivation and experience of creative workers. In addition, it offers a new understanding of the under-representation and exclusion in the contemporary creative workforce which was noted in Kate Oakley's opening chapter and is also discussed by other contributors to this volume.[1]

The first section below sets out how we understand 'creative' and 'creative industries' and introduces the focus of the chapter on particular categories of worker who are under-represented in these industries. Later sections outline alternative theorizations of the contemporary creative worker and describe the empirical research which the chapter refers to. We then discuss conflicts which are experienced by many creative workers and the particular difficulties encountered by certain categories of workers, with particular reference to the example of women creatives. We propose that in some cases, their response to the difficulties may further limit their participation in creative work. The conclusion of the chapter discusses possible implications of this research for educationalists, including higher education institutions (HEIs) such as art colleges.

Contemporary aspects of creative work

This chapter adopts 'creative' as a broad term embracing two relevant areas of practice. The first is the 'creative industries' as originally defined by a UK government paper in 2001 (Department of Culture, Media and Sport, 2001). These industries supposedly encompass the various activities and occupations associated with the production of meaning, signifiers and intellectual property (Howkins, 2001), already known as the cultural industries, together with the various specialist occupations of the creative arts and design. The original list of industries was 'advertising, architecture, the art and antiques market, crafts, design, designer fashion, film and video, interactive leisure software, music, the performing arts, publishing, software and computer services, television and radio' (DCMS, 2001). The term 'creative industries' has subsequently been taken up internationally, with some varying references in its use by different governments (Keane, 2009; Power, 2009) but with a general emphasis on '*individual* creativity, skill and talent' (emphasis added) as well as 'a potential for wealth and job creation through the generation and exploitation of intellectual property' (DCMS, 2001).

The second, overlapping and connected reference of the term 'creative' as we use it in the chapter is to the spectrum of specializations associated with art schools or, using the British term, art colleges. The definition of the creative industries cited above gives a new status and function to these HEIs as entry points for creative careers. Their range of courses reflects the expanded reference of supposedly creative occupations which has been noted by McRobbie (2002, p. 517) and others. In addition, the colleges can be seen to function more conventionally as points of connection to the networks and communities associated with the arts and design. These creative 'worlds' (cf. Becker, 1982) are of continuing importance for creative workers and sustain their claims to a creative identity, especially under circumstances of precarious employment in the contemporary creative industries (Taylor and Littleton, 2012).

Following from the often noted under-representation of certain categories of workers in the creative industries, one point which our research has explored is exclusion (Taylor and Littleton, 2008a). It is widely accepted that women are under-represented among creative workers (see Allen, this volume), as too are people from black and ethnic minorities (BME) (see Saha, this volume).[2] Our programme of empirical research, described in detail in a later section, consisted of a series of interview-based studies with participants recruited through London art colleges so our participants do not include people who are absolutely excluded, since all of them had at least begun a creative career by attending art college. Oakley (this volume) has noted that in HEIs like art colleges, there is often 'a general reluctance to acknowledge problems of inequality'. Furthermore, in statistical terms under-representation in the wider creative workforce is to some extent obscured among art college students. One notable point is that women form the majority of art college students on many courses (Pollard et al., 2008), even though this does not follow through into subsequent employment in the sector as a whole. Another is that art colleges, like those through which we recruited our research participants, often have a high intake of international students, from most parts of the world, and therefore include people who might be categorized in the UK context as BME. In this chapter, we explore conflicts around a creative identification and discuss reasons why they may impact unequally on different categories of people. We then outline a process by which, we suggest, some people may be diverted from a creative project towards a different focus and away from participation within the contemporary creative workforce.

Theorizations of the creative worker

Discussions of contemporary creative workers invoke different theorizations of the person or subject. Some more celebratory accounts, for example, of the opportunities available through portfolio working (see Leadbeater and Oakley, 1999; Bridgstock, 2005), adopt a minimal theorization of a rational economic actor. In this view, the worker coolly appraises all the available options and chooses the one which will result in maximum personal advantage. More critical discussions of the hardships and difficulties of contemporary creative work, such as low pay and precarious employment (Gill and Pratt, 2008) have drawn on the theorizations of a contemporary subject associated with the writing of

Giddens and Beck, among others (e.g. Giddens, 1991; Beck, 2000). The worker is understood to be engaged in an individual project of self-actualization (e.g. McRobbie, 1998) which provides a motivation for tolerating the difficulties of creative work.

A somewhat different version of this argument draws on theories of subjectification, such as the work of Nikolas Rose (following Foucault), that is, of the creative worker as subject to the larger interests of neoliberal industry (Rose, 1989, 1996). The interpretation here is that difficulties and hardship are accepted as part of a project of self-regulation and discipline by a worker in pursuit of future creative fulfilment which will never be attained. As in the previous account, the rewards of creative work are assumed to be largely illusory. Creative working is theorized as a site of subjectification in that the worker is subject to the needs and interests of the cultural and creative industries. These industries are interpreted as a phenomenon of late capitalism, a global sector in which market fluctuations and risk are passed directly to the individual self-employed worker, without the cushioning of a meso-layer of institutional employers providing long-term contracts and some degree of insurance and benefits.

Discussions of contemporary creative workers in these terms rest tacitly or explicitly on the apparent congruence between theorizations of the contemporary subject and the classic image of the artist or variants, such as auteur (see McRobbie, 1998). The theorization and the image both emphasize the personal and individual, and a commitment to a project of self-actualization. Creative making, in all its forms, can appear, therefore, to be an opposite occupation for a contemporary subject.

A somewhat different theorization of the contemporary creative worker can be derived from the work of Ian Burkitt (2008), who suggests that accounts of subjectification (such as those based on Rose's work) fail to take account of 'the relational contexts of everyday life with its various cultures and subcultures, social networks and groups, out of which emerge fully-rounded, if always unfinalized selves' (2008, p. 242). These contexts are multiple. Burkitt particularly emphasizes a split between, on the one hand, the work contexts in which the power relations of neoliberal capitalism might be seen to operate, and on the other, private life and personal relationships. Given that creative work is supposedly characterized by a merging of the two contexts, through its personalized nature, Burkitt's argument might not seem relevant to creative workers. However, his emphasis on multiple contexts accords with the complex nature of identity proposed by social and discursive psychologists (e.g. Wetherell, 1998, 2008; Edley, 2001). Following his work and theirs, we suggest that the contemporary creative worker exemplifies a situation of incomplete subjectification. A creative identity is not a simple self-categorization and nor is it adopted 'once and for all'. Rather, there is an always incomplete project of identification as a constrained and negotiated ongoing process involving conflicts and dilemmas around the multiple sites and meanings in play.

In our view, the nature of a creative identification is therefore more complex than many other writers have allowed, at least tacitly, in their accounts. Our interest is in the creative person as multiply positioned, by others *and* in her or his own accounts, claims and projects. In the remainder of this chapter we explore some of this complexity. We look at conflicts which, we suggest, are encountered by many or most aspirant creative workers and other difficulties which are associated with particular categories of worker.

Before exploring this argument in more detail and summarizing our evidence for it, in the next section we describe the empirical work through which the evidence was gathered, and we discuss in more detail the particular theorization of the person associated with our methodological approach.

Researching creative workers

The research we refer to in this chapter consisted of a series of interview-based projects conducted between 2005 and 2007 with participants recruited through London art colleges. The first two projects were with current and recent students doing postgraduate study in a range of art and design-related specializations. For the third project, we recruited participants through the student populations and alumni lists of four colleges, interviewing both current and former students. The latter included people who were several decades beyond their main period of study for a degree, although many of them had returned to take further courses subsequently, and also to teach. This research is reported in detail in Taylor and Littleton (2008a, 2011, 2012). As with other qualitative research, the sampling or choice of participants was not statistical. In addition, following the broad reference of 'creative' set out in the introduction to the chapter, participants were not selected as representing particular creative specializations.[3]

As noted in the introduction to the chapter, participants were recruited through art colleges but the research is not predicated specifically on educational contexts or issues. These HEIs were relevant to our research interests as entry points into careers in the contemporary creative industries. In addition, as we will discuss in more detail, art college was a site in which creative identities were aspired to and salient for participants. Various assumptions about and meanings attached to creative working circulated and were negotiated and interpreted within colleges and were given additional affective loading for students (and therefore former students) by their associations with particular people, both peers and senior figures.

Our empirical research employs a qualitative analytic approach based in narrative and discursive psychology (see Taylor and Littleton, 2006). As already noted, this entails a conceptualization of identity as complex, conflicted and processual, in the making but always incomplete or not fully resolved. In this view, who people are, and who they can become, is understood to be shaped by larger social contexts including through the ways these people are positioned by others, the cultural or discursive resources available, and an ongoing project of self-making which is both active and constrained. Following this approach, our research differs in several key respects from most other discussions of workers in the contemporary creative and cultural industries.

First, although we are interested in an insider view of workers' experience, rather than the more macro-scale discussion which accompanies writing with a focus, say, on policy, we do not analyse workers' accounts as straightforwardly expressive or descriptive of individual thoughts and feelings. We are interested in language and meanings as situated, and in talk as functional, constitutive and performative. What our participants say is, therefore, not treated straightforwardly as information, as in many qualitative research studies. Instead, the talk is analysed as a complex aggregate in which well-rehearsed accounts, for example, of early experience and memories, are re-versioned for the situated purposes of a particular telling. The talk is assumed to be functional within multiple contexts, including those of the interview, the art college and the participant's various relationships and life situations. The talk is a practice through which meanings are constituted and identity is constructed, negotiated and also performed.

A second difference concerns how we present our research findings in this chapter. In particular, we have avoided the widespread practice of presenting short illustrative quotations from pseudonymous participants. This is because such quotations can carry unintended implications. For example, 'A single quotation can be presented as if it represented the speaker's entire and unchanging world view, and one speaker can appear to stand for a wider category or categories of people' (Taylor, 2012, pp. 11–12). This would not be consistent with the assumptions about the talk, and the speaker, summarized above, so in this chapter we have chosen to discuss our data without presenting direct extracts.

Thirdly, we analyse the meanings in play which are resources for our participants' talk. Although we are interested in the negotiations of identity which take place in talk, we do not assume that such meanings are purely linguistic or confined to language. Rather, we explore the cultural or discursive resources which derive from the larger society. These resources are part of the shared knowledge in circulation and the society's 'common sense' (Edley and Wetherell, 1995). Such meanings tend to be banal (cf. Billig, 1995) and taken for granted. However, for individuals, these social resources can carry additional affect-laden meanings and associations from previous contexts. For example, a truism about artists never making money (part of the classic image of the artist referred to in the previous section) acquires new affective weight as advice from respected senior figures, such as tutors (Taylor and Littleton, 2008b). We suggest that this 'local' quality of resources has an additional importance in relation to continuity (Taylor, 2006). To reject or challenge a meaning becomes linked to a rejection or challenge of those from whom it is received, a potential conflict of loyalties and, in the terms of our approach, 'trouble' in the identity work or processes of negotiating a creative identification (Taylor and Littleton, 2006). An additional form of local resource is a speaker's own accounts and positionings in the contexts of previous interactions and relationships, and the talk these involved. To 'tell' oneself differently will be to risk accusations of inconsistency and even disloyalty so that, again, identity claims and positionings are troubled. Our analytic approach investigates such resources or ideas in circulation through a close analysis of participants' talk. In the following sections, we discuss recurrent images, constructions, conflicts and also absences, which we detected in an analysis of multiple interviews from across the datasets of the several projects we have referred to, and we generalize on the basis of these robust patterns.

Two images of the creative maker

One such resource has already been mentioned. This is the image of the artist or creative maker as a gifted individual engaged in a personal project of exploration and making, following inspiration in search of creative fulfilment. This image is invoked not only in writing about the contemporary creative industries, as noted in a previous section, but also in the talk of our participants. In the terms of our analytic approach, set out below, it is a discursive resource which shapes their understandings of themselves and their choices and prospects.

However, there is more than one image of the artist or creative maker in play. Our research revealed a contemporary version which is different in several key respects to the Romantic vision of the artist cited by Angela McRobbie (1998), among others (Taylor and Littleton, 2012). One aspect of this different image is the value which is placed on connection. Howard S. Becker (1982) discussed connections as integral to the 'art worlds' or networks through which creative activities (art, crafts and others) are variously enabled, evaluated and categorized, for example, as art or not art. He was arguing against the Romantic image of the individual artist as a 'myth'. We suggest that for the contemporary creative, doing your 'own' work remains an ideal but one which is recognized to depend on others for the realization of ambitious creative visions, as exemplars for a creative career and, in particular, as connections into the milieux which enable creative working. Such milieux are construed by creatives themselves as necessary not just in the functional ways which Becker outlines, but also as a stimulus to individual work and as a validation of both the worker and work as belonging to a larger, recognized field. This is the kind of connection, we suggest, that is associated with the cities such as New York and London which other writers have discussed as 'global hubs' in the creative industries (e.g. Banks, 2007). A characterization of creative workers solely in individual terms denies or understates such vital connected aspects of their lived experience.

Conflicts around a creative identification

The image of the 'connected creative' would suggest that connections with other people are important for creative making and a creative career, and our research findings did support this. However, the interviews indicated that the multiple life relationships which provide both resources and audiences for a creative identification were also a source of conflict for many participants.

One source of conflict which we found to be particularly relevant to novice and aspirant creative workers, including those still at art college or recently graduating, was relationships with parents and families of upbringing. Participants benefitted from and often depended on the support offered by relatives, whether in the form of money, board or practical help with assembling exhibitions. However, many families expect that art college courses will provide an entry point into secure employment, whereas the colleges themselves prioritize creative practice and the importance of doing your 'own' work (Taylor and Littleton, 2008a).[4]

To have someone in the family who could understand the insecurity of a creative career was said by our participants to be very helpful. However, to have a relative or partner in a related creative field was potentially problematic. Several participants had changed their specialization in order to distance themselves from the work of a creative parent. This may have been because the expectation that creative work will be your 'own' conflicts with the notion of a shared or inherited family project (in contrast, say, to the seeming logic of family members being involved in the same business). In addition, the possible competition and, most of all, potential criticism from an insider position was apparently not tolerable, perhaps again because of the difficulty of claiming success in terms recognizable to others.

One consequence of the conflict between family and college priorities, and perhaps also the different images of the individual and connected creatives, is that aspirant and novice workers, when pressed, often present composite ambitions. The aim, they say, is to work for someone else *and* do your own work; to work freelance and eventually have your own business or practice or studio; to earn money doing something else in order to support yourself in the creative work which is the priority.[5] This kind of 'double life' (Taylor and Littleton, 2008a) is not only potentially exhausting but can also have an informal, makeshift quality. A further problem which follows from the double life is therefore the need to assert the professional nature of the activity; there was great aversion to creative work being relegated to the status of a 'hobby', even when the amount of time allocated to it compared to other employment might seem to justify this categorization.

This situation also partly explains the need for validation. Art colleges had a further function in relation to this (Taylor and Littleton, 2008a). Of course educational qualifications are relevant to most careers but they acquired an additional status for creative workers given the prevalence of precarious employment and low pay within the contemporary creative industries; it is more difficult to present yourself as successful to others in the absence of conventional success markers of career advancement. Having the name of a 'good' art college on a CV conferred practical advantages and even the fact of being admitted could be presented to others as a marker of success and calibre in the chosen creative career. Many participants referred to the importance of showing their families that what they were doing was, after all, worthwhile. This was also important because for many participants, their actual practice or field was incomprehensible to both their families of upbringing and their partners.

The importance of validation became linked to another conflict around continuity. We have argued that a claim to a long-term creative interest or talent, going back to childhood, can function for novice workers to confirm to their families and others that their career choice is appropriate (Taylor and Littleton, 2006). By constructing a narrative of continuity from 'who I was' to 'who I am', novices validate their current situations, even, if necessary, in the face of low earnings and insecure employment which might mark it as unsuccessful to an external viewer. This kind of 'identity work' is particularly relevant for someone at a career entry point, trying to get established, as it legitimates a claim to a creative identification.

However, continuity might also be problematic. The positive implication of continuity from childhood derives from the assumption that this logically carries a forward momentum into a future career. Yet such a forward projection also sets up a conflict with a creative work process and, in relation, a creative career in which the ideal is to remain open to possibility, so *not* to plan, expect or in any way limit possibilities in advance. In short, carrying through a continuity from the past seems incompatible with the ideal of openness (Taylor and Littleton, 2012).[6]

We have noted elsewhere that our participants tended to characterize a steady progression through ascending stages as a feature of other, more ordinary careers (Taylor and Littleton, 2008a). However, for some of our participants, their careers had progressed to a situation of higher status and greater security and financial reward through very similar stages to those which supposedly characterized the alternative, uncreative career pathway. This led to a tension around definition and the possibility that creativity might have taken them forward into another place and identity. We found that many of our financially successful participants had to defend their claims to be creative, to be still, say, a designer and not a manager or property developer, a painter and not a manufacturer of interior design products.

This section has indicated some of the conflicts and dilemmas confronting creative workers in general, and some solutions, living 'the double life' and seeking validation through continuity, which themselves raise further issues. In the next section, we discuss difficulties faced by particular categories of creative workers and a response to these which, again, may contribute to their difficulties.

The project of repairing deficits

We have noted elsewhere the importance of confidence for creative workers (Taylor and Littleton, 2012; see also Pollard, this volume). They need to be confident enough to pursue interests which may appear 'self-ish' to others, as they themselves note (Taylor, 2011). They also need to be sufficiently confident about the quality and importance of their work to persist with it through a possibly protracted period in which they may receive little conventional reward or recognition.[7] Confidence is additionally important because of the personalized nature of creative working which implies that the work and its outputs are the unique product of the worker as maker. If 'you' are the source, the further implication is that to claim that your work is important you need to be sure that you are appropriately talented or skilled or otherwise worthy of other people's attention.

While noting that the nature and source of 'confidence' is of course a complex issue, we suggest that a lack of confidence can be equated to accepting, tacitly or explicitly, an identity as defective or incomplete or insufficiently skilled or talented, and that this is more likely in people who are *already* ascribed with deficit identities, because of particular negative experiences or, often relatedly, because of how they have been categorized socially. We note that the same categories of people who are under-represented in the creative industries are those who belong to lower valued social categories, that is, women (not men), BME (not white) people and people from working-class (not middle class) families. We suggest that existing deficit identities are *potentially* linked to a lack of confidence, which may then be reinforced as a source of disadvantage for creative workers.[8] This reinforcement occurs because the onus to be good enough to be the source of creative work opens an alternative project, to repair the self and make good deficits.

Our research indicated a number of examples of such repair projects. Some participants described how they had begun different careers then gone to art college, sometimes beginning part-time and building up to a full-time course, in order to 'go back' to previously denied interests, for example, because they had been pressured to give up studying art at school. Other examples came from the many creatives who accepted and even embraced a categorization as 'dyslexic'.[9] In itself, this need not require repair, but for some participants who had had great difficulties at school, their subsequent successes in creative careers were explicitly valued and presented as important for refuting the previous criticisms or low expectations of teachers and parents. Some other participants discussed their creative work as an informal form of therapy, referring to family issues and personal problems as motivating their work and providing its focus. Of course this is a particularly complex point given the inevitably personal reference of so much creative work and this kind of reference is also an indication of how a repair project can run in parallel with creative working. We suggest, however, that for some aspiring creatives who are not confident enough to position themselves (yet) as appropriate originators and sources of creative making, the repair project can function more negatively, dominating the creative project and even replacing it. In other words, the creative aim gives way to the project to repair the self.

The processes we have outlined have several implications for understanding the motivation of creative workers. Theoretical discussions like those summarized in a previous section tend to be primarily focussed on participation in labour markets and industry. The personalized nature of creative work is usually considered as a blurring of boundaries in which work invades the conventional territory of personal life, for example, through the long hours which are worked (Gregg, 2011). However, the processes we describe above, by which deficit identities are reinforced and made a focus for repair, suggest a blurring in a different direction, with the non-work aspects prevailing. This is consistent with our earlier argument against interpreting creative work as a site of subjectification to the needs of industry. It raises the possibility that many workers may be less interested in creative work *as* work or a career than for its personal aspects. They may seek to avoid aspects of conventional work which they expect (or have already found) to be particularly challenging, such as tasks which involve conventional reading and writing skills or, in a different example, the competitive environment of conventional offices.

Ironically, of course, more conventional occupations may offer more protection and better employment conditions. For example, other writers have noted the informality of creative workplaces (Nixon and Crewe, 2004). This can have positives (everyone is 'friends': see Taylor, 2011), but also negatives. In informal workplaces the relationships of employers and employees, or senior and junior colleagues, are probably not mediated by any regulations or bureaucratic measures to promote fairness. When laws about equal opportunity are not enforced, it will be more difficult to escape conventional and clichéd assumptions about the kind of person you are and can become, or, in other words, the limitations of an ascribed identity or, in our terms, the ways that you are already positioned.

As we have already noted, however, our participants presented themselves as avoiding the unsatisfying work, routines and dreary predictable 'age-stage' career ladders which they suggested characterize *other* careers and occupations, like a caricature of modernist factory work. This kind of talk of course functioned partly to validate their own positions and choices but it also suggested a strong prejudice against work as it has been more conventionally understood. We are not implying that our participants were lazy or trying to avoid difficulties. Rather, our argument is that for many the attraction of a creative career seemed to be that it did not 'look like' work and would enable them to remain within the territory of personal, not professional life. These motivations appeared particularly relevant to women creatives, as we discuss in the next section.

The problems of women

We suggest that women creatives are particularly likely to be ascribed with a deficit identity, for several reasons. First, there is a general argument that deficit identities are in themselves feminized, albeit available to be taken up by men as well as women. This is referred to, for example, by Ann Weatherall who discusses the association of masculinity with intactness and an absence of problems. Weatherall cites Simone de Beauvoir's claim that man 'represents both the positive and the neutral ... whereas woman represents only the negative, defined by limiting criteria' (de Beauvoir, 1952/1988, cited in Weatherall, 2002, p. 12).

More specifically, women creatives, like other women in white collar workplaces, will have to resist the subordinate female identities often (unjustly) associated with roles such as secretaries, personal assistants or catering staff, particularly since the main presence of women will probably be in such roles. In addition, Angela McRobbie (2009) has suggested that young women workers in any field must negotiate the contradictions of a 'post feminist masquerade', that is, they must be capable, but not too capable, and successful but not too successful, so that they avoid any challenge or disruption to 'existing gender hierarchies' in workplaces like offices (2009, p. 72). Allen (this volume) discusses some of the combined pressures on young women attempting to enter the cultural and creative workforce.

A further issue which women creatives will have to contend with derives from the domestic associations of many variants of creative making. McRobbie (1998) discussed 'the painting boys' and 'the fashion girls' as differently valued professional categories. However, a gendered divide which we suggest may be more relevant to contemporary creatives is the split between men as creative professionals and women as practitioners of lesser, domestic forms of the same arts or creative activities. Conventionally, for example, women have done home dress-making, but most named fashion designers, at least until very recently, have been men. Similarly, home cooking has conventionally been the task of women, even though most professional chefs are men. Women carry out a whole range of other creative practices in a domestic context (other examples would be designing interiors and arranging flowers) but professional authority reverts to men; the women's activities have the negative status of hobbies. For women creatives, this conventional division presents a further possibility of reversion to a deficit identity, that of someone who aspires to be a designer, for example, but is only a home sewer or amateur. Somewhat differently, it also suggests that creative work may carry associations of personal life contexts which make it attractive as 'not work', as discussed in the previous section.

We suggest that the confidence and status of women creatives are likely to be challenged and also that they are more likely to embrace the kind of repair project we have outlined.[10] For some, it may take over, transforming a creative project into one of long-term preparation, for example, in terms of personal therapy or further study and training. The start of the creative career is perpetually postponed. For others, more positively, the repair project may co-exist with the creative project itself, informing and sustaining it in a mutually constitutive process. This may then contribute further to the complexity of a creative identification, which we have already discussed.

Conclusion

The naming of the creative industries and subsequent discussion by academics, policy-makers and others has given a new importance to art colleges as the sites where many creative careers begin. This chapter has discussed the implications of findings from research projects which recruited participants from the students and alumni of London art colleges. Located in a city which has been recognized as a 'global hub' of the creative industries (e.g. Banks, 2007) and attracting a diverse, international study body, such colleges have an influence and level of reference beyond the UK, like the creative industries themselves. Although the research is not primarily concerned with higher education, it explores the implications of meanings around creativity and creative work which were partly derived from and reinforced in the contexts of these HEIs.

We have suggested elsewhere (Taylor and Littleton, 2011, 2012) that art colleges have a continuing importance for students and alumni, in any field of practice or specialization. First, they are sites where students learn the conventions of their chosen fields and develop their own practice. Second, they provide contexts in which the student can take up a new identification as creative. Third, they provide connections to the tutor and peer figures who contribute to students' understandings of creative work and careers and will also become part of their professional networks or creative 'worlds', including formally and informally as mentors. The art college itself is a continuing point of access to these worlds, given additional value through the image of the 'connected creative', which we have also discussed in this chapter.

The chapter has indicated other points relevant to art colleges and educationalists. We have suggested that for some creative workers the creative project may become implicated with a project of self-repair, or even taken over by it. A central issue here is the confidence, or lack of it, which is vital to the creative practitioner or maker's sense of being central to the creative process, with or without the support of others. Art colleges can perhaps help sustain this confidence through pastoral support, with an additional focus on categories of students who are susceptible to a deficit identification. This has already occurred for students identified as having dyslexia or similar educational difficulties and we would suggest that the support might extend to other students with unhappy educational histories and also to the more 'social' categories which have been noted as under-represented in the wider creative workforce. Their presence within art colleges is not enough to ensure that they can successfully extend their careers beyond them, as the example of women indicates.

These points will be particularly relevant given the recognition of the importance of widening participation. In addition, although creative projects will always entail an awareness of the self as producer, it may be desirable for colleges to encourage students' awareness of making, in all its manifestations, as a process which is also outward facing, taking place within larger contexts involving others with similar interests and difficulties. This is perhaps a departure from the Romantic image of the artist or creative maker which remains so closely implicated with the creative arts and design, yet it is central to that other, connected image we have discussed, and also to creative practice as it has always been understood and undertaken, as a form of work.

Notes

1. See chapters in this volume by Anamik Saha and David Lee, and also Susan Luckman.
2. As examples of statistics on this, Leadbeater (2004) says 'About 4.6% of the creative industry workforce is from an ethnic minority, compared with 7% of the economy as a whole. In London the gap is even starker: ethnic minorities make up 26% of London's population but only 11% of the workforce in the creative industries.' Freeman (2007) says that 'the employment of BAME workers in the creative industries has failed to improve over the last eight years in comparison with London's workforce as a whole, and ... the employment of women in the creative industries has deteriorated absolutely' (p. 44), that is, in the creative industries between 1995/6 and 2003/4 the proportion of BAME workers rose from 11 per cent to 15 per cent, compared to 15–23 per cent in the whole London workforce, and the proportion of women fell from 42 per cent to 37 per cent, compared to 44–43 per cent in the whole London workforce.
3. The research was conducted in accordance with the ethical guidelines of the British Psychological Society. Its purpose and the potential uses of the data were explained, both before and after the interviews, and participants were invited to ask questions. They signed a consent form but were told that they could choose not to answer questions and to withdraw from the research if they wished. Their interview material was anonymized and the full transcripts were seen only by those working on the project (researchers, research assistants and transcribers).
4. These priorities can themselves provide a moral or ethical imperative within creative working, and therefore a variant on the kinds of projects discussed by Banks (2007).
5. Similar ambitions are noted by Emma Pollard, in this volume, who comments that for many creative graduates 'career progression is often characterized by gravitation towards self employment from (or alongside) salaried careers'.
6. We have suggested that one way participants oriented to the valuing of openness was to emphasize the role of chance or 'serendipity' in important decision-making and changes related to their careers (Taylor and Littleton, 2008a).
7. We link this to the trajectory of a 'big break', which we suggest shapes creative workers' own expectations around their careers (see Taylor and Littleton, 2011, 2012).
8. Of course the connection is not inevitable. As just one example, Henri Tajfel's work on Social Identity Theory discusses how a socially ascribed identity category which has a low status is not inevitably taken up as a low status personal identity (see Brown, 2007).
9. As we have observed elsewhere (Taylor and Littleton, 2008a), our research can neither confirm or deny the condition this category refers to, but we noted the wide range of difficulties which it supposedly encompasses among different people.
10. In a contemporary context, Rosalind Gill (2007) suggests that there is an onus for repair placed on contemporary women more generally: 'In a culture

saturated by individualistic self-help discourses, the self has become a project to be evaluated, advised, disciplined and improved or "brought into recovery"... (and) it is women and not men who are addressed and required to work on and transform the self' (p. 262).

References

Banks, M. (2007) *The Politics of Cultural Work* (Basingstoke and New York: Palgrave Macmillan).

Beck, U. (2000) Living Your Own Life in a Runaway World: Individualisation, Globalisation and Politics, in Hutton, W. and Giddens, A. (eds) *On the Edge: Living with Global Capitalism* (London: Jonathan Cape): 164–174.

Becker, H. (1982) *Art Worlds* (Berkeley, Los Angeles, London: University of California Press).

Billig, M. (1995) *Banal Nationalism* (London: Sage).

Bridgstock, R. (2005) Australian Artists, Starving and Well-Nourished: What Can We Learn from the Prototypical Protean Career? *Australian Journal of Career Development* 14(3): 40–48.

Brown, S.D. (2007) Intergroup Processes: Social Identity Theory, in Langdridge, D. and Taylor, S. (eds.) *Critical Readings in Social Psychology* (Maidenhead: Open University Press): 133–162.

Burkitt, I. (2008) Subjectivity, Self and Everyday Life in Contemporary Capitalism, *Subjectivity* 23: 236–245.

Department for Culture, Media and Sport (2001) *Creative Industries Mapping Document* (London: HMSO).

Edley, N. (2001) Analysing Masculinity: Interpretative Repertoires, Subject Positions and Ideological Dilemmas, in Wetherell, M., Taylor, S. and Yates, S. (eds) *Discourse as Data* (London: Sage): 189–228.

Edley, N. and Wetherell, M. (1995) *Men in Perspective: Practice, Power and Identity* (Hemel Hempstead: Prentice Hall/ Harvester Wheatsheaf).

Freeman, A. (2007) *London's Creative Sector* (London: GLA).

Giddens, A. (1991) *Modernity and Self-Identity: Self and Society in the Late Modern Age* (Cambridge: Polity).

Gill, R. (2007) *Gender and the Media* (Cambridge: Polity).

Gill, R. and Pratt, A. (2008) In the Social Factory? Immaterial Labour, Precariousness and Cultural Work, *Theory Culture & Society* 25(7–8): 1–30.

Gregg, M. (2011) *Work's Intimacy* (Cambridge: Polity).

Howkins, J. (2001) *The Creative Economy: How People Make Money from Ideas* (London: Penguin).

Leadbeater, C. (2004) Britain's Creativity Challenge, *Creative and Cultural Skills*, http://www.ccskills.org.uk, date accessed 24 October 2007.

Leadbeater, C. and Oakley, K. (1999) *The Independents: Britain's New Cultural Entrepreneurs* (London: Demos).

Keane, M. (2009) Creative Industries in China: Four Perspectives on Social Transformation, *International Journal of Cultural Policy* 15(4): 431–443.

McRobbie, A. (1998) *British Fashion Design: Rag Trade or Image Industry?* (London: Routledge).

McRobbie, A. (2002) Clubs to Companies: Notes on the Decline of Political Culture in Speeded up Worlds, *Cultural Studies* 16(4): 516–531.

McRobbie, A. (2009) *The Aftermath of Feminism: Gender, Culture and Social Change.* London: Sage.

Nixon, S. and Crewe, B. (2004) Pleasure at Work? Gender, Consumption and Work-Based Identities in the Creative Industries, *Consumption, Markets and Culture* 7(2): 129–147.

Pollard, E., Connor, H. and Hunt, W. (2008) *Mapping Provision and Participation in Postgraduate Creative Arts and Design* (London: National Arts Learning Network).

Power, D. (2009) Culture, Creativity and Experience in Nordic and Scandinavian Cultural Policy, *International Journal of Cultural Policy* 15(4): 445–460.

Reynolds, J. and Taylor, S. (2005) Narrating Singleness: Life Stories and Deficit Identities, *Narrative Inquiry* 15(2): 197–215.

Rose, N. (1989) *Governing the Soul: The Shaping of the Private Self* (London and New York: Routledge).

Rose, N. (1996) *Inventing Our Selves: Psychology, Power and Personhood* (Cambridge: Cambridge University Press).

Taylor, S. (2006) Narrative as Construction and Discursive Resource, *Narrative Inquiry* 16(1): 94–102.

Taylor, S. (2011) Negotiating Oppositions and Uncertainties: Gendered Conflicts in Creative Identity Work, *Feminism & Psychology* 21(3): 354–371.

Taylor, S. (2012) 'One Participant Said…': The Implications of Quotations from Biographical Talk, *Qualitative Research* 12(4): 388–401.

Taylor, S. and Littleton, K. (2006) Biographies in Talk: A Narrative-Discursive Research Approach, *Qualitative Sociology Review* II(1): 22–38.

Taylor, S. and Littleton, K. (2008a) *Creative Careers and Non-Traditional Trajectories* (London: National Arts Learning Network).

Taylor, S. and Littleton, K. (2008b) Art Work or Money: Conflicts in the Construction of a Creative Identity, *The Sociological Review* 56(2): 275–292.

Taylor, S. and Littleton, K. (2011) New Creative Careers: The Problems of Progression and Uncertainty, in Shaw, J., Wise, J. and Rout, A. (eds) *Research in the Lifelong Learning Networks* (York: Lifelong Learning Networks National Forum): 52–58.

Taylor, S. and Littleton, K. (2012) *Contemporary Identities of Creativity and Creative Work* (Farnham: Ashgate).

Weatherall, A. (2002) *Gender, Language and Discourse* (London: Routledge).

Wetherell, M. (1998) Positioning and Interpretative Repertoires: Conversation Analysis and Post-Structuralism in Dialogue, *Discourse and Society* 9(3): 387–412.

Wetherell, M. (2008) Subjectivity or Psycho-Discursive Practice? *Subjectivity* 22(1): 73–81.

8
Industry Practitioners in Higher Education: Values, Identities and Cultural Work

Daniel Ashton

Introduction

This chapter examines cultural industries practitioners working within higher education (HE) and the contribution of those with 'industry knowledge and expertise' to students' learning experiences. Empirical research with 'teacher-practitioners' from a range of industry sectors and disciplinary fields is drawn on to explore practitioner pathways into HE. A key factor that emerged from practitioners' career stories was around working conditions, security and quality of life. Highlighting practitioners' experiences of challenging cultural workforce conditions (Oakley, 2009; Hesmondhalgh and Baker, 2011), the discussion turns to consider how industry practitioners help to shape the HE contexts through which students engage with 'industry'. Specifically, the professional knowledge and learning communities generated through dialogue between practitioners and students are examined. The discussion closes by considering how the personal and situated accounts of working in industry provided by teacher-practitioners can help students make sense of their emerging identities as 'cultural workers' and critically reflect on their future cultural work environments.

The practitioner in higher education

Within creative and cultural industries discourse (see Hesmondhalgh, 2008) the role of HE has increasingly and prominently been positioned as having a crucial supporting role. The *Creative Britain* report by the Department of Culture, Media and Sport emphasizes the importance of developing creative talent/human capital, and states the commitment to 'conduct research to ensure that academia is equipping students with the skills they need to make the most effective contribution they can to the creative economy' (DCMS, 2008, p. 25). The Confederation of British Industry (CBI) *Creating Growth: A Blueprint for the Creative Industries* report provides recent illustration of the creative talent/human capital approach. In making a case for the economic importance of and government support for the creative industries, this report suggests that 'government policy should reflect the range of skills required by creative businesses and ensure these are delivered through secondary and higher education' (CBI, 2010, p. 4). Within this 'economic discourse' (Berger and McDougall, 2012), the principal concern of studying 'media' within HE should be preparing students with skills to gain employment upon graduation.

The *Looking Out* report published by the Art Design Media Subject Centre of the Higher Education Academy (ADM-HEA) identifies student work placements, industry involvement in student projects, and teacher-practitioners as key forms of HE and industry engagement (Clews and Mallinder, 2010; see also Clews, 2010a). Teacher-practitioners are defined by Antonia Clews (2009, p. 25) as, 'those that work concurrently in professional creative practice and teach at higher education (HE) and/or further education (FE) level'. This chapter uses the phrase 'teacher-practitioners' to refer to cultural industries practitioners working in HE, but also recognizes the complexities of how different roles and responsibilities, such as research and administration, are viewed. Examining this form of involvement goes beyond recognizing that 'many media workers do bits of teaching at a local college' (Tunstall, 2001, p. 5), to take account of the diverse positions and activities described by the 239 teacher-participants that were surveyed as part of the *Looking Out* project. The *Looking Out* report surveyed 108 art, design and media departments and found that over 85 per cent employed teacher-practitioners as a way of 'sustaining current industry knowledge in the curriculum'. In his foreword to the ADM-HEA's *Stepping Out* report, Sadler (cited in Clews, 2010b, p. 2) suggests that 'teacher-practitioners have a profound impact on the student learning experience' that might be characterized in three ways: 'influence over pedagogy and curriculum development; opportunity for greater student participation, and; opportunities for skills that have employer relevance'. While these impacts may be identified across the board for HE teachers, teacher-practitioners are positioned as presenting a distinctive combination of these and the reference to skills relevant for employers resonates with the concerns stressed in the DCMS and CBI reports.

In turn, for Clews and Clews (2009, p. 267), 'although the number of teacher-practitioners undoubtedly increases the potential pool of professional knowledge [...] the processes by which professional knowledge transfer take place' are not understood. Tracing the relationship between industry practitioners and HE demands going further than noting that students are 'exposed' to ideas, practices and skills (Sadler cited in Clews, 2010b, p. 2). Rather, as Thornham and O'Sullivan discuss (2004, p. 723), professionals are not socially or discursively neutral and teacher-practitioners bring with them notions of 'professional identity, relation and order'. For example, Antonia Clews' (2009) research on teacher-practitioners highlights that an individual's identity is often wrapped up in their roles and professional behaviours. A number of commentators have highlighted questions around roles and professional behaviours, for example, in relation to freelance work (Storey et al., 2005) and networking (Blair, 2009; Lee, this volume). In terms of teacher-practitioners, distinctive roles and behaviours can be identified at the interface of industry and education. Parmar (2010) draws on research with five professional industry leaders working as teacher-practitioners to highlight that practitioners had a particular currency and were capable of offering distinctive insights. It is this distinctive position and professional identity that this research has approached through concepts of creative biographies and career trajectories.

Creative biographies: Researching practitioners

Existing research into the roles and activities of art, design and media practitioners teaching in HE have employed a range of methods including narrative interviews (Shreeve, 2009); practice-based workshops (Clews, 2009); and surveys and focus groups (Clews and Mallinder, 2010). Using existing larger scale research on teacher-practitioners in the arts (Clews and Clews, 2009) as a platform, this study sought to gain overall impressions from the sector and explore a small number of creative biographies (Taylor and Littleton, 2006). In exploring the pathways that practitioners take into teaching in HE and the connections between their practice and teaching, the following draws on survey data and semi-structured interviews with a number of teacher-practitioners. The survey data was used to provide an illustration of backgrounds, roles, and motivations, and these points were connected with interviews focusing on in-depth stories, experiences and reflections.

The survey was conducted online between October and December 2011 and was distributed within the UK via the Media, Cultural and Communication Studies subject association (MeCCSA) and Higher Education Academy mailing lists. It included a mix of closed and open-ended questions. The project was framed in terms of 'media practitioners teaching in higher education' and there was space for participants to present their own definitions and understandings of being 'teacher-practitioners'. A self-selecting sample was employed and while the response rate of 17 was low in comparison to the *Looking Out* report, there were a number of provocative comments. The self-selecting approach was combined with a range of requests for participants, and quotes presented in the following are not intended to represent the diversity of teacher-practitioners experiences. Similarly, any quotes should not be seen to present complete understandings or an 'unchanging world view' (see Taylor and Littleton, this volume), and rather they are used as a form of 'intensive' research investigating 'how processes work in a small number of cases, seeking explanation of the production of certain objects, events and experiences' (Hesmondhalgh and Baker, 2011, p. 15). In conversation with the survey responses (SR), this chapter draws on interviews with 12 practitioners in three industry sectors at five HE institutions: A (two in Television and two in Film); B (two in Journalism; one in Film); C (three in Games Design); D (one in Games Design); and E (one in Games Design).[1] When discussing 'industry' practitioners, it is helpful to echo Caldwell's (2008, p. 7) comments that care should be taken in referring to 'the industry' in a 'totalizing or unified sense'. This sample does not intend to produce broad generalizations on one single so-called 'media industry', but rather to focus on experiences across sectors.

In taking this seemingly disparate range of sectors together, Deuze's (2008, p. 6) 'media logic' approach is used to address the 'specific forms and processes that organize the work within a particular medium'. Deuze (2008, p. 6) notes the problem with the notion 'that what a journalist does is guided by distinctly different ideas and factors of influence than what informs the work of a game developer, television producer, or advertising creative – or vice versa'. For Deuze (2008, p. 6), common to all these fields is that they are examples of the production of culture and therefore this research is part of a move to focus on 'what people actually do when they work in the media, and how they give meaning to their actions and beliefs' (Banks and Deuze, 2009, p. 426). By focusing on the production of culture, analysis extends beyond an investigation of a specific industry or role to consider industry practitioners engagement with HE.

One of the challenges in this research was identifying 'teacher-practitioners'. While the wider cultural and educational policy context for addressing industry and education engagement has been set out, practical questions and uncertainties around the role remain: 'practitioners are employed because of the knowledge and experience they bring from industry. This practice-knowledge is different to the subject-based and teaching-knowledge that teachers have and yet the role of the teacher-practitioner within HE is poorly defined' (Clews and Clews, 2009, p. 266). It can be difficult to detect exact positions, roles and identities. Similarly, it is not always clear whether and how students define teaching staff as teacher-practitioners and respond to them compared with, for example, industry speakers delivering one-off sessions or well-known industry figures. On this, Ashton (2009a) examines how games design students relate to industry practitioners who teach on their degree compared to 'celebrity designers', and highlighted how it was career stories and successes from teacher-practitioners known personally that could engage students and inform their efforts to 'break into industry'.

A related concern around 'breaking into industry' can be seen with debates around professional and amateur media production. As Hesmondhalgh and Baker (2011, p. 14) argue, 'the vast majority of the cultural productions we share in modern societies are still produced by people who are trying to make a living out of that industry'. This was clear in research by Ashton (2011a) examining the understandings that digital games design students have of making games and the investment they have in the games industry as a distinct domain with career opportunities and goals. Moreover, reports such as *Creative Britain* (DCMS, 2008) illustrate the continued investment in individuals realizing their talent and following pathways into working in the creative industries (Ashton, 2011b). While recognizing tensions around user-generated content and co-creative forms of cultural production (Banks and Deuze, 2009), it is clear that for students entering HE there is often an explicit focus on developing their career as industry professionals alongside their interests in making media content. In this respect, while appreciating the changing nature of cultural industries, it is the industry insights and career stories from industry practitioners that seem to most readily resonate with students (see also Noonan, this volume for a discussion of the 'value' students place in this professional experience).

Practitioner biographies

During the survey and interviews, participants were encouraged to explore and refine Antonia Clews' (2009) definition, and one of the main revisions made in the survey was to highlight that there may be a complete move into teaching rather than supplementing income and concurrent work. One respondent flags up those, 'who were industry practitioners for a number of years, and then came into HE, as a second career' (SR6). This was echoed by another survey respondent: 'it can be that practitioners are becoming redundant in newsrooms then they try to change careers' (SR11). The concurrency point was also evident in terms of continued activity: 'I worked for over twenty years as a producer in British television. I am currently an executive producer on an ex colleague's documentary but, since joining academia in 2007 I have not produced or directed a documentary or other TV programme' (SR15). This comment indicates how it can be a challenge to maintain industry work in the same way as before entering HE (see Clews, 2009) and therefore also the distinctive multifunctional role that Sadler identifies. Noting the different circumstances and degrees of involvement in HE described by the respondents, the following section outlines some of the motivations given for entering HE.

Parmar (2010, p. 2) draws on her research to suggest that the aim for teacher-practitioners, 'was to share their own expertise and knowledge both with academic staff and with students who were eager to explore the latest media industry practices' and notes how for one practitioner, 'relaying 25 years of industry experience to interested students became fulfilling' (p. 3) (see Pollard, this volume, for student perspectives on input from industry professionals). The following survey responses resonate with this by explicitly flagging up the rewards of working with students and passing on knowledge:

> I like working with students. It's inspiring. It forces me to constantly remind myself of first principles. I like creating work within an academic context, as it allows me to think critically about the work I do, and to experiment with different forms. [It's] interesting to think critically about work, and perhaps there is an implication about not working in this manner outside of 'an academic context' (SR3)

> To share some of the professional practice and skill I have developed and help bring a greater industry understanding to the teaching of media skills (SR8)

> Interest in working with young people, passing on skills – and employment! (SR12)

This investment in sharing expertise as an activity and end in itself can be used to counter claims around teaching in HE as a diminished form of professional capacity. In describing his work teaching digital games design within a university, games designer Warren Spector suggested, 'the games education movement is kind of in its infancy', and went on to add: 'most of the people in it are either people who can't get jobs, and if they could, they would – or they're people who love games, but don't really have any professional experience' (Spector cited in Gillen, 2008, online). Here teacher-practitioners are seen as a form of lesser industry professional who are either enthusiastic amateurs or failed professionals. Interview exchanges with teacher-practitioners involved in games design degrees in HE (see Ashton, 2009a), reveals a different understanding in which the demands and aims of each domain distinguish the dual nature of the teacher-practitioner role from others in industry and education, and point to the complexity of engaging in both arenas rather than a reduced status in either one.

In terms of the differing demands of working in industry and working in HE, it became clear from the survey and interview data that there were certain push and pull factors associated with quality of life and working conditions. As Oakley (2009, p. 41) highlights, 'much of the more boosterish "new economy" literature has been criticized in particular for neglecting the aspects of insecurity, casualization and often very low pay that also characterize the cultural industries'. Issues of working conditions are clearly stated in terms of uncertainty and security, and the following responses to a question on motivations for entering teaching in HE also touch on the nature of working in HE:

Wanted to 'put something back'. Wanted to pass on what I knew. A change and a new challenge. A steady income after 20 years of freelancing. Uncertainty about finding work as a freelancer approaching 50 (SR2)

Initially, to be honest, the hours and vacations. I was finding the challenge to be a good mother with all the early and late shifts at the BBC impossible. I wanted hours that were more amenable to family life. I then discovered to my astonishment I enjoyed the work! So despite my son now being an adult, my initial intention to return to fulltime broadcasting has now changed (SR4)

Stable job/income; rewarding to work with students; to develop my knowledge and skills in the area of creative practice; to have a (occasionally) flexible work pattern (SR5)

Closely linked to this, there were a number of responses that implicitly commented on industry working practices and conditions with a direct focus on what HE could offer through a career change:

I took redundancy from the BBC and needed to think about other directions in which I could take my career. I had always enjoyed mentoring and helping to develop younger or less experienced colleagues, and thought that this was an area that I could develop more in myself. I also welcomed the opportunity to become research active and to spend some time learning myself, as well as teaching others (SR6)

A change of career – as I did not want to be shouting in a newsroom at 65. (As well as an awareness of the rarity of finding a 65 year old news editor in a newsroom...) (SR7)

It's nice to share and it's also an opportunity to reflect and develop practice – staying current is good for the quality of the learning experience and my practice (SR9)

After 25 years in the field I was not ready yet to retire so I went for a PhD in a very specialized area within media and it worked (SR11)

Initially pragmatic. Moved out of London, too far to commute five days a week, and it was one of the most readily available and reliable employments using decades of expertise. Really enjoyed the role of lecturing and also engaged more with the academic and theoretical side. (SR14)

Evident within these responses are that differences in work cultures and practices could inform practitioners' identity work: 'as practitioners who teach (practitioner tutors) move between their practice and their teaching, the two different cultural contexts require them to work in different ways, with a resulting impact on identity work that ensues' (Shreeve, 2009, p. 152). This comment is key to exploring how teacher-practitioners might not operate in a straightforward way as conduits of 'industry knowledge'. In contrast to seeing teacher-practitioners as vehicles for transporting industry knowledge, it was clear that industry and industry practices are re-encountered and reflected upon from a distance.

In addressing changing industry dynamics and requirements placed on workers, Deuze (2007) examines the challenges and opportunities of 'contingent employment' and stresses that the global economy, consumer desires, shifts in workplace technologies, and management vogues for innovation, are all part of the contingencies and uncertainty facing media industries workers. When asked about motivations, a number of survey respondents provided direct responses that focused squarely on industry working conditions and clearly connect with Deuze's wider analysis of uncertainty:

Having a family – better working hours, conditions, security (SR1)

Financial security (SR10)

Reduction of documentary commissioning in – and consequent reduced income from – UK television (SR15)

A significant number of respondents flagged up working issues as at least part of their response, and the above comments can be further elaborated on through interview data. For one documentary film-maker working in HE, the 'holiday and sick pay' provided within HE provided the security to enable them to work freelance and to have a greater capacity to pursue and reject specific projects (A2; Film-maker). This is echoed in the following comments, also from a film-maker: 'partly job security, but I kind of realized that I wasn't going to be making the kinds of films that I wanted to make professionally anyway' (B2; Film-maker). HE seems to provide both financial security and a degree of autonomy in the productions pursued with this participant noting the institutional support available to apply for research council funding on a wider range of content (see Saha, this volume). While it is clear from the first of these participants that working across HE and industry illustrates practices of 'portfolio' working (see Gill, 2002), the following section addresses the differing working patterns and conditions described when comparing the two.

Workforce issues: Reflections and responses

Recognizing how industry work practices and conditions inform the career trajectories of teacher-practitioners and act as a motivating factor in the move into HE, the following engages with recent debates on cultural work to consider the space and opportunities for teacher-practitioners to reflect on and address students' questions of 'cultural labour, political economy and social justice' (Gill and Pratt, 2008, p. 19).

Banks and Hesmondhalgh (2009, p. 417) suggest that 'in its utopian presentation creative work is imagined *only* as a self-actualizing pleasure, rather than a potentially arduous or painful obligation undertaken through material necessity'. Research with cultural industries practitioners reveals both inherent pleasure and passion, and arduous conditions. Banks and Hesmondhalgh (2009, p. 418) suggest that creative work is presented as 'unproblematic in much policy and academic discourse since it seems to be a freely chosen *vocation*' and 'the appeal of creative work has been further enhanced by its pervasive presentation as intrinsically leisure-like, pleasurable and *fun*'. While the perspective on creative work as a vocational calling could be seen, it was also clear that perspectives on the nature of cultural work as challenging and un-leisure-like were being articulated by teacher-practitioners. In turn, it was difficult to pin down the extent to which existing working practices could be challenged especially in terms of the limited resources available to do this. This is captured in the following comments from a practitioner dividing their time between working in HE and work as a film and television director:

> I don't know how you can get people to really [experience hardship]; how you can immerse them into that sense of how hard it is to work as a media professional outside of actually doing it. It's very difficult. It's never been easy to get work in the field of the arts. There is no certainty in the industry, so I don't know how you can actually get people to really appreciate that without hitting that experience themselves. I mean I would be interested to know if someone can or does offer that. I don't know how you could do that really. Until you are actually trying to earn your living doing something it's very difficult for it to be real.
>
> (A3; Film and Television Director)

For Antonia Clews (2009, p. 32), with 'freedom of time and an open brief' teacher-practitioners can 'relate their practice to their teaching within the educational contexts so that students learn about their tactics (conditions of risk, getting lost and the happy accident)'. The final sections will make a number of suggestions on the range of tactics that can be explored with students in relation to cultural workforce issues such as conditions, pay and security.

Professional knowledge and learning communities

For teacher-practitioners the move from industry into education and/or the co-occurrence of employment in the cultural industries and HE was a process of reflection and analysis and a prompt for reconstituting their own relationships with industry. The move from industry to HE is comparable with the transition between jobs that Paterson (2000, p. 498) identifies as significant for identity: 'Transition between jobs is important in working lives and each transition leads to some element of social identity being reconstructed'. The reconstruction of social identities and an examination of working contexts could prove key for how students make sense of their own emerging identities and address the potential cultural work environments they may go on to work in.

Parmar (2010, p. 7) summarizes her case study, stating how the experience of teacher-practitioners provide 'the opportunity to meet academics who have encouraged them [students] to reflect on their own working practices'. Engaging students with specific insights into the world of work could be coupled with the study of how HE can prompt reflection. Such reflections are of potentially huge significance given Gill and Pratt's (2008, p. 19) comments on 'putting questions of cultural labour, political economy and social justice on the agenda'. As they state:

> The lack of trade unionization and labour organization in many areas of cultural work is striking, and is both cause and outcome of industries that are individualized, deregulated and reliant upon cheap or even free labour, with working hours and conditions (particularly among freelancers and intermittents) that are largely beyond scrutiny.
>
> (Gill and Pratt, 2008, p. 19)

Gill and Pratt (2008, p. 20) suggest that 'this situation has been scandalously ignored by the academic fields of media and cultural studies'. While this may be the case, the *Creative Graduates Creative Futures* report (Ball et al., 2010, p. 87) highlights that in its research with graduates, contextual/critical studies received a, 'relatively low usefulness rating, perhaps due to the perceptions of the direct relevance of academic study for career development'. In turn, Ashton (2011c, p. 87) 'has attempted to survey the range of critical perspectives on media and cultural work and explore how these could be interweaved with questions of employability [and] students' industry aspirations'. The aim here is to see how the investment in employability, highlighted earlier with reference to *Creative Britain* and *Creating Growth*, may be used to frame and stress critical perspectives on problematic aspects of cultural work.

As addressed earlier, a number of teacher-practitioners made the move into HE in response to challenging working conditions. For Banks and Hesmondhalgh (2009, p. 416) reports such as *Staying Ahead* (Work Foundation, 2007), *Creative Britain* (DCMS, 2008), and *Beyond the Creative Industries* (National Endowment for Science, Technology, and the Arts (NESTA), 2008), 'have generally had very little to say about the process of creative labour – and less still about the substantive problems associated with such work'. These comments help frame a key concern of this volume on how HE might operate as a forum in which processes and problems of cultural work can be explored by drawing on first hand accounts.

Shreeve (2009, p. 157) explores the different 'teacher' and 'practitioner' positions that may be taken, and what it can mean to be a practitioner by 'helping students to understand, not only the skills of making, but to understand the emotional and affective aspects of *being* a practitioner'. Here Shreeve (2009, p. 157) signals a 'change of emphasis from what you do to how it feels to be a practitioner' and suggests that 'tutors could be said to be helping others to construct an identity as a practitioner'. This comment signals the mediating role of industry practitioners working in HE. Personal experiences and insights are central to the offering that teacher-practitioners can make, and being able to evidence this can cement the credibility of their suggestions on the career trajectories that 'cultural workers in-the-making' might take. Antonia Clews (2009, p. 29) identifies that 'it is common for teacher-practitioners to describe bringing their experience of professional practice to the students'. For one practitioner, this was less a question of 'teaching by anecdote' and seen more as reporting back from the workplace (B3; Journalism). A colleague (B2; Film-maker) was able to elaborate, highlighting how they had been, 'able to use short films as kinds of case studies in teaching'. It was also evident that workforce issues were being addressed. For example, how over-supply of graduates (see Comunian et al., 2011) and limited job opportunities are explored with students: 'in terms of job security, the students are very well aware of it [...] they're constantly investigating the state of the media industry through essays and dissertations. You do sometimes get a sense of gloom back from students when they hear about the latest lot of redundancies' (B3; Journalism). The examination of industry contexts and practitioners identities by teacher-practitioners and students can be situated as part of a learning community, and this concept helpfully highlights the forms of reflection and co-learning that are in action.

In their analysis of skills formation in the film and TV sectors, Grugulis and Stoyanova (2009, p. 136) suggest that 'newcomers learn on the job through observation and discussion with peers and their entry into a professional network'. Grugulis and Stoyanova (2009, p. 139) describe the 'community' model of skill formation as it relates to film and TV: 'people are expected to learn through employment by taking part in various projects, watching others perform tasks, appreciating what production involves and working their way through simple jobs to highly skilled work'. They go on to suggest that 'in this model new-comers are not just taught how to do a job, they are socialized in a way of life with its own particular values, priorities, and forms of behaviours' (Grugulis and Stoyanova, 2009, p. 140). This dual process of technical learning and socialization is captured in the following comments from a part-time lecturer with a background in television production:

> The studio multi camera side of things is I think a good complement to single camera productions which most of the students do. It gives them an insight into not only larger scale productions, but also larger scale in the sense of what you might use a studio for. [You] capture some of the buzz of studio working where lots of people have lots of roles to get on with.
>
> (A1; Television Producer)

Here, there is a clear rationale for providing students with hands-on experience of multi-camera shooting in addition to single camera pro-ductions and experience of working within in a particular environment. The 'buzz of studio working' is something familiar to the tutor and they strive to ensure that students can encounter this. This aim extends beyond a technical proficiency to an engagement with and under-standing of what it means to work within a production team within a particular brief and production scenario. While appreciating the impor-tance and value of the 'buzz', this example signals how there is also scope for stressing the challenges and pressures that future cultural workers *might* face. Exploring the intersection of industry and education in relation to the teacher-practitioner/student learning communities is an invaluable opportunity to pursue questions of social justice sig-nalled earlier. The following section now turns to consider the position of teacher-practitioners, and the nature and practicalities of critical reflection.

Higher education and critical reflections on industry

In relation to cultural work, Hesmondhalgh (2010, p. 282) highlights that cultural-industry jobs are often seen as desirable and goes on to explore opportunities for 'good work' and the 'positive and emanci-patory aspects of labour – including creative labour in the cultural industries – might be made more prevalent, and how negative aspects of work might be contained, controlled or eliminated'. To further explore how negative aspects may be addressed with students, this final section considers the position of teacher-practitioners. This chapter suggests that teacher-practitioners can have a role to play in exploring with students the social practices of cultural work in ways that are experientially grounded and hold particular forms of credibility and currency. As Shreeve (2009, p. 152) suggests:

> Even In the face of strong 'enculturation' individuals have choice about the positions they adopt in relation to the workplace, what they learn and how they identify with it [...] the individual can also exercise intentionality; they have some choice in whether they appropriate, transform or ignore the social practices they encounter at work.

A crucial aspect of this comes from the position(s) that teacher-practitioners occupy. In assessing transformations in workplace practices, teacher-practitioners have a career biography that may show direct experience and resonate for students more than, to recall the earlier comments, overtly academic contextual/critical studies.

Critical perspectives as articulated within media and cultural studies may be problematic in addressing working in industry. As Gough-Yates (2003, p. 23) describes: 'media professionals are understandably concerned about how they will be depicted in research, and, in my own case, the practitioners I approached seemed especially worried that I would criticize them for the ways their magazines depicted contemporary femininities'. In this scenario the critical perspective comes from an 'academic researcher' and the media professional may be positioned as an object of research. Moreover, when industry practitioners themselves engage with critical issues, such as representations of contemporary femininities, there might still remain uncertainty or ambivalence on how it connects with industry practice and working in the cultural industries. For example, Judge (2009, p. 2) in his book *Runner*, offering guidance on 'how to break into the film, TV and commercials industry as a runner and survive long enough to get your dream job', brings together experiences from his Media Studies degree with his later work and career goals: 'I could write a great essay on the representation of race and gender in television, but when it came to applying for a job, I was, quite frankly, screwed'. Judge's comments on the relevance of his Media Studies degree signals an avenue for further research on the perspectives that media practitioners have on HE provision of creative courses. While data is emerging on the career trajectories and destinations of HE graduates (Ball et al., 2010), there remains a need to examine the educational and career backgrounds of media practitioners and the extent to which the courses under discussion in this volume figure within those backgrounds. Rather than seeing issues of representation and applying for a job as a case of 'either-or', a productive step may be to see where and how the essay on representations of race and gender fits with how graduates understand their work. This is a connection that is taken up by Marcellus (2009, p. 140) with reference to the advertising professional:

> Advertising creates an imaginary world that teaches us to see the real world – and how to see ourselves. Because ads have so much social power, those who create them have a responsibility to do so in a way that does not reinforce unequal power structures. The ability to do that is one indication, in the twenty-first century, of a truly creative, truly responsible advertising professional.

With teacher-practitioners, the possibility is for critical debates around, for example representation, to take on an applied aspect in relation to industry production contexts. In this scenario, critical 'studies' research may be connected with industry knowledge and experience of working in industry in ways that allow students to employ a critical distance and dialogue and to position this in relevant, identifiable and immediate ways.

The engagement with students and the focus on links with teaching may work to highlight the value and purchase of a critical focus on cultural workforce issues. This was highlighted by Paterson and Zoellner (2010, p. 100) in their discussion of the 'efficacy of professional experience in the ethnographic investigation of production' when they suggest that researchers 'make explicit the connections between research and teaching' and 'make a stronger case that there is a clear social good resulting from an organization's participation in a research project'. Further consideration of the connection between 'theory' and application in industry contexts has been succinctly unpacked by Chitty (2011) and his call for researcher practitioners: 'instead of practitioners entering academia to pass on their production skills we need to create opportunities for them to inquire, analyse and reflect on the changing nature of the contemporary media and work with those who have the analytical frameworks'. From his 'manifesto' entry, it seems there are areas of expertise and knowledge that can be distinctively addressed by those with industry experience on the nature of contemporary media, such as creative clusters, international trade of TV formats, and decision-making in creative businesses. It is also possible that inquiry, analysis and reflection can focus on the nature of contemporary media with reference to the working conditions and practices that may have shaped a practitioner's decision to enter into teaching in HE.

In assessing this possibility, further discussion must explore if teacher-practitioners *would* explore critical perspectives with students and *what* the critical focus might be. Critical perspectives are not the exclusive preserve of those with industry experience, and there is rich body of research into media and cultural industries. Indeed, many of the concerns around cultural workforce issues raised above were drawn from scholarly research. Further to this, Noonan's (this volume) concerns around the interests that may underpin professional engagement should not be overlooked. Taking the cue again from work looking at 'research-practitioners', there is a need to consider what might be missed as teacher-practitioners investigate cultural work practices. As Paterson and Zoellner (2010, p. 104) suggest, because of 'pre-knowledge of the observed processes and routines the researcher might fail to notice specific aspects or features in the field because her professional identity accepts the conditions as self-evident and not worthy of attention'. This hugely important point of detail finds common ground with existing studies of teacher-practitioners: 'It should not be presumed that practitioners are experts at articulating their knowledge, process and experience' (Clews and Clews, 2009, p. 270). This is further acknowledged by Antonia Clews (2009, p. 36), who notes studies showing that 'teacher-practitioners find it difficult to describe how their experience and working processes inform student learning, although they are clear that they do'.

In turn, it was clear from the *Looking Out* research that working within HE could have a transformative influence for practitioners. As Parmar (2010) notes, 'practitioners have been able to engage with academic staff and find the time to reflect on their work and research related ideas'. This approach is also highlighted in the 'Confessions of an "Early Years" Teacher-practitioner' in which Kathleen Griffin, a presenter, producer and reporter with experience at the BBC, states:

> I believe teaching practitioners bring the world of work into the classroom so students can identify and engage with that world. In turn, I've learned from their energy and fresh approach and to question why I do things a certain way, why particular rules apply, and whether there are different ways of working.
>
> (cited in Clews and Mallinder, 2010, p. 95)

The following participant in Parmar's research was more explicit in suggesting that HE can be a prompt for critical reflection on media industries:

> [I] would like other industry leaders to get more involved at the university as it toughens up critical thinking facilities and makes you realize that there is a historical and cultural context for work.
>
> (Tim Wright – Commercial Producer, cited in Parmar, 2010, p. 6)

These comments illustrate how industry practitioners engage in critical conversations around cultural work. This can be elaborated on with reference to how teacher-practitioners engage with the skills approach evident in the DCMS and CBI reports referred to above. One of the concerns of an employer-led employability agenda introduced at the outset is the extent to which local and immediate recommendations on the role of HE might stand in for wider and more long-term perspectives. As Brown et al. (2003, p. 116) identify, employers can present employability as a 'technical problem of ensuring that labour market entrants have the skill sets that match the requirements of employers'. From one interview exchange between a journalist and film-maker (HEI B), it was clear that speaking from HE as well as from industry informed how the instrumental skills approach was critically tackled:

> Despite the kind of push to make courses more vocational from above, the students aren't actually ready to make decisions [...] you can give them all the skills that might fit them into, shoe horn them into jobs [but] its actually disabling them in lots of ways because they're tailoring jobs that might not be there in any case when they do want to decide. You know the notion of liberal education is going out of the window in the process.
>
> (B2; Film)

This was further addressed in relation to course accreditation: 'it's a bunch of bureaucrats meddling with education, because they're not really engaged with what the tenants of liberal education should be in a university. They're thinking we should be churning out graduates that are employable in this industry only' (B2; Film). Clearly, competing perspectives would be available from 'bureaucrats' and employers on the role of HE (see Ashton, 2009b, for a discussion of 'critical thinking'). Crucially, these comments signal a broader range of concerns beyond 'skills for industry' being articulated by industry practitioners.

This represents a form of critical distance based on industry experience and reflection through working with HE. This practitioner demonstrates a firm understanding of cultural work and 'industry' practices, but they are not beholden to a particular agenda. Similar concerns about accreditation and industry needs have been discussed elsewhere in relation to games design, drawing on interviews with teacher-practitioners from institutions C, D, and E (see Ashton, 2009a). As one contributor summarized (B3; Journalism), 'we are delivering courses that for a long time the industry was very negative about'. This teacher-practitioner is able to consider HE from the industry perspective of 'questionable courses and deficient skills' and through their time in HE respond to this by stressing critical distance.

These comments indicate that teacher-practitioners engaging with critical debates around cultural workforce issues may extend their criticisms to addressing what constitutes the 'employability agenda'. In this respect, a focus on 'skills' may be accompanied by a reflection upon the nature of the skills and the contingent cultural contexts in which they may be used. In short, set against the backdrop of reports such as *Creative Britain* and *Creative Growth* with their focus on employer needs and their silence on cultural workforce issues, industry practitioners working in HE may be distinctively positioned to extend the debate and engage with students across a host of aspirations and concerns.

Summary

This chapter addresses the role of teacher-practitioners in investigating cultural work. It is offered alongside existing commentaries on how scholarly research can prompt critical perspectives on the nature of employment in the cultural industries (see Ashton, 2009a) and how cultural industries research can be drawn on in teaching and learning (see Ashton, 2011d). As discussed elsewhere (Ashton, 2011d), a concern for students' employability does not necessarily reinforce a vocational orientation that narrowly sees HE as a pathway into working in the cultural industries. The employability framing can be used to position critical understandings of potential employment and career contexts as personally meaningful for aspiring cultural workers.

Teacher-practitioners, with the aim of passing on knowledge and first-hand experiences of cultural workforce issues may be ideally placed to frame and stress a range of perspectives on cultural work and contribute to an associated social justice agenda. Central to this is how HE provides a catalyst and context for reflection. While exploring the distinctive position of teacher practitioners, it is HE as a potential space for critical distance and interventions that must not be overlooked. As Antonia Clews (2009, p. 35) states, 'the process of articulating practice to another prompts critical reflection and greater understanding of one's own practice or at least, exposes contradictions between what one says through teaching and what one does in practice'. The aim of this chapter has been to signal the diversity of perspectives articulated by teacher-practitioners, and foreground that where critical reflection on cultural work emerges there are opportunities for both workers and workers 'in-the-making' to develop critical distance.

Author's Note

I would like to thank all those who kindly gave their time to participate in this research, and dedicate this chapter to the memory of David Clews.

Note

1. Background on institutions (see Marr and Forsyth, 2011)

   A: Post 1992 university in South West England
   B: Post 1992 former Polytechnic in Wales
   C: Post 1992 university in North West England
   D: Post 1992 former Polytechnic in North East England
   E: 1960s university in North West England

References

Ashton, D. (2009a) Making it Professionally: Student Identity and Industry Professionals in Higher Education, *Journal of Education and Work* 22(5): 283–300.

Ashton, D. (2009b) Critical Thinking across Contexts, *Politics and Culture* 10(4), http://www.politicsandculture.org/issue/2009-issue-4/, date accessed 21 February 2012.

Ashton, D. (2011a) Playstations and Workstations: Identifying and Negotiating Digital Games Work, *Information Technology and People* 24(1): 10–25.

Ashton, D. (2011b) Pathways to Creativity: Self-Learning and Customising in/for the Creative Economy, *Journal of Cultural Economy* 4(2): 189–203.

Ashton, D. (2011c) Media Education and Media Industries: Identity, Anxiety, and Aspirations, *Media Education Research Journal* 1(2): 85–93.

Ashton, D. (2011d) Media Industries, Education and Employability, *A Manifesto for Media Education*, http://www.manifestoformediaeducation.co.uk/2011/06/daniel-ashton/, date accessed 20 February 2013.

Ball, L., Pollard, E. and Stanley, N. (2010) *Creative Graduates Creative Futures* (Brighton: Creative Graduates Creative Futures Higher Education Partnership and the Institute for Employment Studies).

Banks, J. and Deuze, M. (2009) Co-Creative Labour, *International Journal of Cultural Studies* 12(5): 419–431.

Banks, M. and Hesmondhalgh, D. (2009) Looking for Work in Creative Industries Policy, *International Journal of Cultural Policy* 15(4): 415–430

Berger, R. and McDougall, J. (2012) Editorial: What Is Media Education For? *Media Education Research Journal* 3(1): 5–20.

Blair, H. (2009) Active Networking: Action, Social Structure and the Process of Networking, in McKinlay, A. and Smith, C. (eds) *Creative Labour* (Basingstoke: Palgrave Macmillan): 116–134.

Brown, P., Hesketh, A. and Williams, S. (2003) Employability in a Knowledge-driven Economy, *Journal of Education and Work* 16(2): 107–126.

Caldwell, J.T. (2008) *Production Culture* (London: Duke University Press).

Chitty, A. (2011) Practitioner Researchers Needed! – Filling a Hole in the Knowledge Base, *A Manifesto for Media Education*, http://www.manifestoformediaeducation.co.uk/2011/06/andrew-chitty/, date accessed 17 September 2011.

Clews, A. (2009) 10BY10, A Research Report on the Teaching Practitioner, in Clews, D. (ed.) *Stepping Out: Studies on Creative and Cultural Sector Engagement with Arts HE* (University of Brighton: ADM-HEA): 25–38.

Clews, A. and Clews, D. (2009) And I also teach: The professional development of Teaching Creatives, *Journal of Arts and Communities* 1(3): 265–278.

Clews, D. (2010a) *Looking Out: Effective Engagement with Creative and Cultural Enterprise (Discussions)* (University of Brighton: ADM-HEA).

Clews, D. (2010b) *Stepping Out: Studies on Creative and Cultural Sector Engagement with Arts HE* (University of Brighton: ADM-HEA).

Clews, D. and Mallinder, S. (2010) *Looking Out: Effective Engagement with Creative and Cultural Enterprise (Key Report)* (University of Brighton: ADM-HEA).

Comunian, R., Faggian, A. and Jewell, S. (2011) Winning and Losing in the Creative industries: An Analysis of Creative Graduate's Career Opportunities Across Creative Disciplines, *Cultural Trends* 20(3–4): 291–308.

Confederation of British Industry (CBI) (2010) *Creating Growth: A Blueprint for the Creative Industries* (London: Confederation of British Industry).

Department of Culture, Media and Sport (DCMS) (2008) *Creative Britain* (London: Department of Culture, Media and Sport).

Deuze, M. (2007) *Media Work* (Cambridge: Polity).

Deuze, M. (2008) Understanding Journalism as Newswork: How it Changes, and How it Remains the Same, *Westminster Papers in Communication and Culture* 5(2): 4–23.

Gill, R. (2002) Cool, Creative and Egalitarian? Exploring Gender in Project-Based New Media Work in Europe, *Information, Communication and Society* 5(1): 70–89.

Gill, R. and Pratt, A. (2008) In the Social Factory? Immaterial Labour, Precariousness and Cultural Work, *Theory, Culture & Society* 25(1): 1–30.

Gillen, K. (2008) Warren Spector Interview, *Rock, Paper, Shotgun*, http://www.rockpapershotgun.com/?p=1115, date accessed 22 February 2008.

Gough-Yates, A. (2003) *Understanding Women's Magazines* (London: Routledge).

Grugulis, I. and Stoyanova, D. (2009) 'I Don't Know Where You Learn Them': Skills in TV and Film, in McKinlay, A. and Smith, C. (eds) *Creative Labour* (Basingstoke: Palgrave Macmillan): 135–155.

Hesmondhalgh, D. (2008) Cultural and Creative Industries, in Bennett, T. and Frow, J. (eds) *The SAGE Handbook of Cultural Analysis* (London: SAGE): 552–569.

Hesmondhalgh, D. (2010) User-Generated Content, Free Labour and the Cultural Industries, *Ephemera* 10(3/4): 267–284.

Hesmondhalgh, D. and Baker, S. (2011) *Creative Labour: Media Work in Three Cultural Industries* (London: Routledge).

Judge, W. (2009) *Runner: How to Break into the Film, TV and Commercials Industry as a Runner and Survive Long Enough to Get Your Dream Job* (Will Judge).

Marcellus, J. (2009) What's the Harm in Advertising Stereotypes? in Pardun, C.J. (ed.) *Advertising and Society* (Oxford: Wiley-Blackwell): 136–141.

Marr, L. and Fortsyth, R. (2011) *Identity Crisis: Working in Higher Education in the 21st Century* (Stoke on Trent: Trentham Books).

NESTA (2008) *Beyond the Creative Industries: Mapping the Creative Economy in the United Kingdom* (London: NESTA).

Oakley, K. (2009) *Art Works – Cultural Labour Markets: A Literature Review* (London: Creativity, Culture and Education).

Parmar, N.A. (2010) Media Practitioners Engaging with Higher Education, *Looking Out: Case Study*, www.adm.heacademy.ac.uk/library/files/adm . . . / lobmsparmer270710.pdf, date accessed 1 September 2011.

Paterson, R. (2000) Work Histories in Television, *Media, Culture & Society* 23(4): 495–520.

Paterson, C. and Zoellner, A. (2010) The Efficacy of Professional Experience in the Ethnographic Investigation of Production, *Journal of Media Practice* 11(2): 97–109.

Shreeve, A. (2009) 'I'd Rather be Seen as a Practitioner, Come in to Teach My Subject': Identity Work in Part-Time Art and Design Tutors, *Journal of Art and Design* 28(2): 151–159.

Storey, J., Salaman, G., and Platman, K. (2005) Living with Enterprise in an Enterprise Economy: Freelance and Contract Workers in the Media, *Human Relations* 58(8): 1033–1054.

Taylor, S. and Littleton, K. (2006) Biographies in Talk: A Narrative-Discursive Approach, *Qualitative Sociology Review*, 2(1): 22–38.

Thornham, S. and O'Sullivan, T. (2004) Chasing the Real: 'Employability' and the Media Studies Curriculum, *Media, Culture & Society* 26(5): 717–736.

Tunstall, J. (2001) Introduction, in Tunstall, J. (ed.) *Media Occupations and Professions* (Oxford: Oxford University Press): 1–22.

Work Foundation (2007) *Staying Ahead* (London: Work Foundation).

Part IV
The Politics of Access

9
Creative Networks and Social Capital

David Lee

Introduction

This chapter explores the role of networks and associations for cultural workers within the creative economy, and then considers the implications of research findings in this area for the practices and curriculum of higher education institutions (HEIs), and their relationship to creative sectors. Networks and networking can be seen as crucial practices for finding work, sustaining a career and progressing within the often freelance and insecure labour markets of the cultural industries. Yet, who is best placed to undertake networking successfully? Research in this area raises important concerns about the network culture that has developed within cultural labour markets (Oakley, 2006; Ashton, 2011; Lee, 2011; Allen et al., 2012). On the surface the reliance upon networks as a means of recruitment and finding work appears to offer a relatively friction-less and non-hierarchical method of facilitating labour market processes in this area. Unburdened by the administrative demands of formal job recruitment, managers are able to rely on word-of-mouth and informal associations to recruit in highly freelance, contract-based labour markets. However, on closer inspection, they actually act as mechanisms of exclusion, favouring individuals with high levels of cultural and social capital. On the other hand, networks also offer the possibility for a renewal of work politics within the increasingly deunionized workplaces of the cultural industries, as the case of the highly successful TVWRAP campaign in 2005 against workplace exploitation demonstrates.[1]

A network culture has also become highly embedded within HEIs. Increasingly, the focus is on learning outcomes which develop social skills; networking activities are central aspects of degrees in fields such as creative arts, media and communications studies. In this context, students are encouraged not only to attend events with 'industry' speakers, but also to actively promote themselves and to make 'contacts'. Furthermore, personal development planning systems are now commonplace within universities as a key part of the student experience, where 'soft' skills, such as networking and gaining 'experience' outside of the classroom are included as major elements of the university student experience beyond the formal curriculum. Universities are now central to the ongoing institutionalization of a 'technology of the self' first associated with creative labour by writers such as Ursell (2000) and McRobbie (2002), whereby individuals embrace neoliberal values such as networking and entrepreneurialism at the level of self-identity (Boltanski and Chiapello, 2005). Arguably, in higher education (HE) we are seeing a mainstreaming of the highly-publicized practices encouraged by Michael Craig-Martin at Goldsmiths in the early 1990s, where fine-art students were encouraged to create their own 'brand', and to actively network and promote themselves to dealers in the protean London art scene of the period.[2]

Based on extensive field research into the British independent television industry, but also reviewing research findings within other creative sectors, this chapter examines the implications of the discursive and material shift towards a network culture at work for cultural workers, where the 'network extender' is presented as the ideal within contemporary management discourse (Boltanski and Chiapello, 2005). It then considers how such networking practices are embedded within the culture and curriculum of HEIs. In conclusion, it considers the role of HEIs in either challenging or being complicit with the classed, gendered and raced entry mechanisms to creative labour fields, which are often based on cultural and social capital. In this context, should the university be instrumental in formulating an 'ethic of cultural labour' in response to the challenges unearthed within the empirical research?

Access and the question of fairness in creative labour

The issue of fair access to creative professions has become an increasingly prominent debate within academic and policy spheres in recent years (HM Government, 2009, 2011). It has long been understood that labour markets in the contemporary cultural industries are flexible, organized around clusters and dependent on networks as sources of industry gossip, employment and talent (Pratt, 2002; Scott, 2005). Cultural industries are geographically clustered, and are predominantly comprised of dense networks of formal and informal economic and social relationships (Pratt, 2004; Scott, 2005; van Heur, 2010). These networks have an economic function, providing cultural producers with vital routes to market, and are key sources of collaboration and competition (Pratt, 2002). Networks in the cultural industries also serve a social function, supporting the exchange of ideas that drives the development of creative work (Lange, 2005). Therefore, networking is a central mode of interaction. It functions as a means of sharing tacit knowledge, fostering relationships within flexible working environments and building competitive advantage (Grabher, 2004).

As such, networks function to overcome information asymmetries (Stigler, 1961) within the project-based economies of cultural production, where an absence of familiarity leads to a reliance on personal recommendations. However, it is only relatively recently that the issue of access into those networks has come to be critically examined by scholars motivated by concerns around social justice, equality, class and social mobility (Antcliff et al., 2007; Lee, 2011).

Television networks

My own recent study of television production explores the significance of networking practices as a means of finding work and developing a career in the British independent television production sector (ITPS) (Lee, 2011). This research, involving longitudinal research on 20 participants working in the independent sector, showed the importance of networking not only as a mode of finding work, but also a mechanism of exclusion, favouring individuals with high levels of cultural capital. Drawing on network theory (Granovetter, 1973; Burt, 1995), the research considers patterns of hierarchy and discrimination within the ITPS, in a context where formal recruitment procedures are often bypassed in favour of network relationships.

Networking was absolutely critical for my respondents. They enter insecure labour markets through networks; use networks as a means of communication (for finding work and promoting themselves through employment websites); and find that 'after-hours' networking is central to success. In this precarious context, networking becomes a method for negotiating risk, enabling individuals to navigate through 'a bewildering sea of loose affiliations, temporary arrangements, and informal networks' (Deuze, 2007, p. 542). Yet the opportunities are unequal, determined by cultural, economic and social capital.

The UK television industry displays a network structure and culture. Structurally, the independent television industry is comprised of a large number of small- to medium-sized firms arranged in dense geographical clusters, providing content for a small number of broadcasters. This follows the classic *publishing logic* model of cultural production described by Miège (1989) and which is highly common in cultural industries.[3] There are high levels of movement by individuals between these companies, as work is mainly contract based (Antcliff et al., 2005). Informal and formal networking between individuals provides actors with a route to find work, and companies with a method of bringing in flexible, freelance talent and 'know-how' on a project basis. Therefore, making and maintaining contacts with people in the industry is a crucial determinant of career advancement, as evidenced in other research (BFI, 1999; Dex et al., 2000).

Networks and social capital

All of this suggests that there is a close relationship between networking and cultural and social capital within the cultural industries. Within flexible firms, high levels of social capital have been seen as modes of competitive advantage (Marti, 2004). Networking operates as a means of reducing competition within informal and flexible labour markets (Fevre, 1989). 'Getting on' in the television industry as a freelancer is linked to creating and maintaining a large network of contacts, a process which involves presenting one's self as flexible, enthusiastic and mobile (see also Allen, 2010). While networked labour markets allow for economic and managerial flexibility in the ITPS, this research shows that there is a social cost to pay as this process counteracts equal opportunity and diversity because of the high levels of cultural capital necessary to enter and succeed (Bourdieu, 1984, 1986). It is worth noting, of course, that this social critique of networks within industry mirrors contemporary concerns around limited access and participation in HE, in particular in the aftermath of the Browne Review (2010), and the shift in HE towards 'a lightly regulated market in which consumer demand, in the form of student choice, is sovereign in determining what is offered by service providers' (Collini, 2010, p. 23).

Networking is a mandatory practice to succeed within the ITPS (and increasingly within HEIs), but one which individuals may have an ambivalent attitude towards. My research suggests that while many workers embrace networking as a practice, others only reluctantly accept it. For some it is all part of the 'fun' and glamour of creative work, involving a heady mix of work and play; others see it as a normative practice which must be approached instrumentally as a source of potential economic or professional reward. Those that reject it then feel they are somehow 'missing out'.

This raises important questions about how network culture is both structural, determining the field of relations within the industry, and discursive, producing ambivalent subjective responses. For networking is a dominant discourse which functions to legitimate and regulate particular practices and modes of thinking about labour market processes. The research participants for this study have internalized a set of discursive values connected to the networking culture, suggesting that 'networking' is a potent aspect of the 'doctrine of creativity' (Schlesinger, 2007). Through the power of discourse, networking is a 'justificatory regime' utilized within contemporary capitalism to ensure its attractiveness to individual workers (Boltanski and Chiapello, 2005).

In the following section, I explore the role that social networks play in the working lives of the interviewees, and the implications of a network culture upon this sphere of employment, exploring how the reliance on networks of contacts 'frees up' the labour market, allowing a greater mobility and flexibility for the lucky few, but also creates forms of exclusion, hierarchy and discrimination.

Network sociality in the ITPS

Network sociality drives the television labour market (Wittel, 2001). 'Networking' is understood as central to economic, social and cultural relations, in contrast to the declining traditional sociality of community. This sociality is informational and intermittent in character, and 'consists of fleeting and transient, yet iterative social relations; of ephemeral but intense encounters' (Wittel, 2001, p. 51). Such relations are less based on common history and mutual experience, and more on knowledge exchange and 'catching up' (Grabher, 2004). One's success at it is dependent on class, geographical and educational variables. Indeed, Skillset research suggests, two thirds of the television workforce hold degrees, which is higher than in the creative industries generally, and much higher than in the rest of the UK workforce, where 37 per cent are currently graduates (Skillset, 2012).

My interviewees rely on this mode of interaction to find work. When asked about the importance of networking for their professional practice, they all agreed that it was vital. Jack, a producer/director, described contacts as 'absolutely crucial' when it comes to finding work in the industry. He explained that when you finish a job as a television freelancer, the 'first thing' you do 'is just start ringing around, emailing people'. Equally, Sarah, a series producer, explained why networking and confidence were critical to her entry to the industry:

> I was like dynamic, very employable, so a lot of it was through force of personality I think... I was quite good at capitalising on contacts that I'd made because by then I was generating my own contacts, but... *I was a good little networker!*

Jenny, an assistant producer (AP), described the significance of contacts and persistence. Each meeting becomes an opportunity to network, and work can come from unexpected places: 'it's just a case of trial and error, of like trying to speak to people and saying you know "can I have 5 minutes of your time?" '. In such an environment, great emphasis is placed on having the 'right' kind of personality, being persistent and constantly contacting people for work: 'some of them were like yeah, yeah, yeah whatever. And other ones were like, sort of interested... But at the same time I was making new contacts'. Rachel, a junior researcher, described how she found work: 'Well it has been through word of mouth, it's been through different directors I've worked with, they've all actually said... I know so and so needs a researcher, and they put you in touch... None of the jobs I've got have ever been advertised'.

Durable networks and weak ties

This suggests that if cultural employment is precarious, then the networks are durable. Granovetter's (1973) seminal work on the strength of 'weak ties' helps us to understand this paradox. Close relationships such as those between family members and close friends ('strong ties') do not provide the same diversity of social capital as the relationships between acquaintances and business 'contacts' (seen as 'weak ties'). Therefore, a person or an organization is more likely to maintain and build on their position in the field by actively creating contacts with 'weak ties'. There is a mathematical logic to this, in that 'whatever is to be diffused can reach a larger number of people, and traverse greater social distance (i.e. path length), when passed through weak ties rather than strong' (Granovetter, 1973, p. 1366). Strong ties involve 'bonding' social capital, as opposed to 'bridging' social capital (Putnam, 2000), are based on trust and forged around community and family (Leonard and Onyx, 2003). Conversely, weak ties are based on the thin, impersonal trust of acquaintances. These are loose networks, which means a shift from the 'getting by' dynamic of 'bonding' social capital to the 'getting ahead' culture that comes out of 'bridging' social capital.

Granovetter (1973) discovered that individuals were much more likely to find out about a job through someone with whom they share a weak tie, because they move in different social circles and have access to a greater range of information (Granovetter, 1973, p. 1371). Weak ties provide individuals with informational advantages within job markets, because they connect distant 'nodes' in the network, and are thus highly efficient as a means of overcoming information asymmetries that occur within networks (Burt, 1995).

Broadcasting is a transient industry, making it difficult for people to build up lasting, strong ties. As executive producer Anita puts it, although it 'seems like a social industry, [it is]...actually quite isolated and isolating'. Her perception of the industry is that 'people are separated off into their cliques. People move in and out of jobs so regularly there is very little sense of sort of team or kind of continuity'. Therefore, in the ITPS, weak ties function as a way for workers to keep each other informed, and act as a way for individuals to negotiate a casualized labour market. For example, Louise, a series producer who has worked for a number of 'super-indies', described how 'networking is hugely important', recounting how having worked as a freelancer in the last two years have given her more contacts through which she finds work. Equally, Anita stressed the significance of contacts in terms of finding work: 'I think it helps if you've got friends who are in good positions, and...if you know a certain number of people...there are a lot of deals that are done that are to do with socializing'.

Simon explains how 'word of mouth is very important and who you know is very important'. As such he told me, 'that's really how I've always found my work, through who I've known and when my name's been passed on to other people'. This means that access to these networks and informal routes of recruitment is vital in order to get on. The networking culture, while seemingly open and accessible, actually negates diversity, by privileging those with good contacts and social status. Moreover, the fact that entry to the industry is often unpaid means that individuals from less privileged socio-economic backgrounds find it very difficult to survive.

The industry was seen as highly middle-class by producer Emma: 'it's people who can afford to get into telly, who can afford to support themselves while they are doing work experience to get the experience you need to get a paid job'. Social position (and race) was also linked to success in television by Simon: 'Yes if I think about it everyone does talk the Queen's English. You don't get many "geezers"; you don't get many black people'. This echoes research done by Skillset (2005) which shows that 38 per cent of audio-visual workers had done unpaid work during their careers; and 70 per cent got their first job by informal routes such as via contacts.

Social mobility and the creative economy internship culture

The analysis above is indicative of low social mobility within the cultural industries, an issue that HE needs to critically engage with.[4] The cultural industries are a key area where the long-term effects of a decline of social mobility is prevalent; where access has been predicated on internships and free labour for many years; and where cultures of inequality have been developed, circulated and promoted.

The relevance of the debate about social mobility for research into the cultural industries is clear. As argued above, creative labour markets favour individuals with high levels of social and cultural capital: in short, individuals from relatively prosperous backgrounds, who are able to afford to work for nothing in order to gain an internship (the established route into the labour markets in the creative sectors), and who have the confidence and ability to network that comes from middle-class socialization and education. They use their 'cultural capital' in order to accrue social capital which allows them to access closed networks and job opportunities. Indeed, despite the political and institutional focus on widening participation which has accompanied the introduction on increased tuition fees in England, it seems inevitable that the social stratification of creative labour across the media industries will be further entrenched by the introduction of higher university tuition fees, introduced in 2012.

Internship and socially exclusive labour

The internship culture is central to getting into television. As in other high-status, highly attractive sectors, internships are ubiquitous within the creative sector, raising issues of class and access. Skillset estimates that 44 per cent of those working in the media industries had to undertake a period of unpaid work before getting their current job (Skillset, 2008). In my sample, of those who were under 30 at the time the research was undertaken (2005–2007), all had found their way into the television industry through work experience. Many had taken advantage of family and close ties.

For example, Sarah comes from a middle-class professional family. Her father was a senior civil servant, and both parents went to university. She now works as a series producer across Factual Entertainment documentary strands. Her route into television follows a classic model, based on familial contacts and networking. She got into television by going to a party with her mother after finishing university, where she was introduced to a family friend: a television series producer who eventually provided her with her first job in the industry. She describes the vital role that familial contacts can offer to those in the sector, describing how being at a family party helped launch her career:

> I was at this party, again it was one of those things where my mum said "I'm going to this party that a colleague's having and his boyfriend works at Planet 24 and you better come"...Sure enough I go to this party begrudgingly with my mum and dad and there was this guy there who you know we didn't talk about TV particularly but somehow that was enough to mean that when my mum bumped into someone at work a couple of days later he said 'Oh that guy's looking for researchers'...My experience, even though I didn't have parents who were in the media, was that just having that sort of middle-class network works as a huge advantage because if you're a kid in Wolverhampton from a council estate you just don't have access to those sort of connections, so there's no doubt that that is very significant.

Jenny also defined herself as middle class, and made use of contacts to enter the sector. Working as an Assistant Producer, she told me she had entered the industry through a prolonged period of unpaid work experience as a runner: 'I worked unpaid for a full bloody year – I wondered if I was ever actually going to get paid to do this job'. Finally, this led to a position in the company as a junior researcher. Similarly, Rachel, a researcher at the time of interview, told me 'I just don't think you've got a hope in hell of getting a job in television without doing free work'. Paul (a producer) speculated on the implications for diversity, noting that it's only possible 'if your parents can bankroll you', and that 'the industry loses out on a lot of talent because people just can't afford to work for free'.

Negotiating exclusion

But television is certainly not an exclusively middle-class industry and of my interviewees there was interesting evidence of how working-class entrants might negotiate exclusion. For example, Dave (Managing

Director of an indie) came from a working-class background in West Yorkshire, and continues to do a lot of work in the region, managing to balance public sector contracts with commercial television work. He did not go to university, and none of his family had gone into HE. His route into television was through a paid apprenticeship as a camera-operator, from which he made the move into directing. Interestingly, Dave took a much more instrumental approach to networking than some other interviewees for whom it appeared to be an extension of their social life. It was an activity which 'doesn't come naturally' to him. In fact he expressed dislike of it, but realized the importance of developing social capital in order to find work:

> I think that if you don't know what you are selling, if you don't know what your position is in that market place, if you don't know what your USP [Unique Selling Point] is, why are you networking? Unless you just want to meet people and have a nice time, but then you can go to speed-dating for that. Networking is all very good, but it has to be focused.

Jonathan (BBC Sports AP) described his route into the industry, which was also unconventional (in that it did not involve going to university). Here, humour and experience were critical in order to overcome and negotiate exclusion. He told me the story of an interview where he was asked which university he had gone to:

> So she doesn't know anything about me, and she's just got my CV in front of her and she's like 'Oh OK', it's all going fine. And then she goes 'Oh you're really young aren't you?' She went 'So how have you done all that since university?' I said 'Well I haven't gone to university'. And the look on her face because I hadn't gone to university. And she went 'Well how do you find that's affected you?' So I said 'I don't, I don't find it's affected me', and she said 'But not having a degree, do you not think that will go against you and stop you going to places you want to go?' I went 'No'... it ended really horribly. And I didn't hear anything.

For Jonathan, class remains a big issue in the industry:

> I know when I see fellow people from Essex and they find out I'm from Essex they're like 'Wahey!' Is class an issue? In the BBC, yes. Outside even yes it is I think. You see very few people with like common

accents. I've got quite a common accent, but even when I go home now to Southend I hear people I'm like ooh god I've turned into one of them.

To negotiate these class barriers, both Dave and Jonathan had to rely on reputation and 'being better' than other people: in this sense to be slightly outside of the norm can work in your favour, but it's not easy and they are exceptions to the rule. In the largely middle-class, higher-educated work of television production, having a degree is expected; it is normalized. To be outside of that requires taking on an 'outsider' identity, which is what both Dave and Jonathan articulate above (for a fruitful discussion on the relationship between class and university education, see Archer et al. (2007)). Even having 'made it' in the industry, both had a keen awareness of this status – although of course for them, the display of having made it without a degree acts as a means of self-promotion, implicitly suggesting a narrative of having made it against the odds, through pure talent and willpower.

The role of higher education

> Colleges and universities have become cheerleaders and enablers of the unpaid internship boom, failing to inform young people of their rights or protect them from the miserly calculus of employers.
>
> (Perlin, 2011b)

I shall now consider how the networking practices outlined above are embedded within the culture and curriculum of HEIs and the role of HE in either challenging or being complicit with the classed, gendered and raced entry mechanisms to creative labour fields. What role do HEIs play within the context of creative labour practices within cultural industries, where individuals are forced to work for nothing to get experience, where high levels of social, cultural and economic capital facilitate entry to the sectors and where exploitation at the junior levels of industries is rife?

An analysis of current debates about the rise of the 'internship' culture for graduates is crucial in order to explore this question. The evidence indicates that cultural industries (and many other 'desirable' sectors) now systemically rely on unpaid internship labour as a means of entry to paid work (Heath and Potter, 2011; Oakley, this volume), although more detailed empirical research into cultural industries internships remains to be done. What internships mean in practice is the prospect of endless work without pay, which favours individuals with social and economic capital. Not only does this create a structural class-based inequity in our labour market but often has a crushing effect on the self-esteem of the young people undertaking these internships.

In a systematic enquiry into the internship culture, Ross Perlin (2011a) describes the situation in the US, where internships have become standard rite of passage for movement from HEIs to paid employment. His study demonstrates the impact on the self that this has, fostering low self-esteem, depression and a continued reliance on family help. In the UK much research has been undertaken by a mixture of pressure groups, journalists and commentators. It is patchy, yet a picture is clearly emerging showing the negative impacts of internships in terms of equality of opportunity and their often murky legal status (de Grunwald, 2010). In July 2011, a report by the Institute for Public Policy Research (IPPR) and the social enterprise *Internocracy* decried the majority of internships as 'illegal', arguing that companies should pay the national minimum wage to interns (Heath and Potter, 2011). Indeed, the question of internships has reached the political radar, with a series of statements by Deputy Prime Minister Nick Clegg – statements which have been received with some scepticism, given that many of the British Coalition government cabinet themselves either undertook unpaid internships to get into politics, or have made use of interns during their careers (HM Government, 2011). Indeed, according to recent research, less than 1 per cent of the interns who worked for MPs received the UK minimum wage, and nearly half were not paid expenses (Unite, 2009).[5]

British HEIs are deeply complicit with this culture of free labour, although in this context the free labour is provided through accredited work placements, rather than 'internships'. Furthermore, students are increasingly demanding such opportunities at pre- and post-application open days.[6] For degree programmes in the creative arts, media and cultural industries, universities regularly provide 'opportunities' for students to work for nothing to gain 'experience'.

Of course, providing skills for employability has become a key part of the contemporary university mission statement, and this is set to intensify with the fees ceiling in the UK rising to £9,000 per annum for the 2012–2013 academic year. However, we need to think critically about the nature of the 'experience' being offered, and the nature of the relationship between HEIs and companies benefitting from an endlessly renewable source of free, educated labour.

This represents one more aspect of the commodification of education and the direction of travel appears clear. In the US, colleges and universities have actively opposed calls for greater regulation of internships. For example, in a letter sent to the US government Labor Department last year 13 university presidents wrote: 'While we share your concerns about the potential for exploitation, our institutions take great pains to ensure students are placed in secure and productive environments that further their education' (Perlin, 2011a). Indeed, US colleges have commodified the provision of academic credits through internship labour, charging students tuition to work in unpaid positions and then selling those credits to mediators who then sell on the internships to companies.[7] While there is no evidence of money being given to the UK HEIs in return for student labour, it can be argued that less resource-intensive work placement modules provide a relatively cheap way for some universities to provide academic credits to students, while at the same time meeting students' increasing expectations for degree programmes to provide them with networking opportunities and professional skills.

In the UK the situation is not as extreme as this. However, similar dynamics are in operation, whereby the relationship between industry and HEIs is becoming closer, with universities being expected to do much more for 'UK Plc', often under the banner of 'knowledge transfer' (Ozga and Jones, 2006). As Collini argues in relation to the highly influential Browne report on the future of HE, published in 2010: '[it] displays no real interest in universities as places of education; they are conceived of simply as engines of economic prosperity and as agencies for equipping future employees to earn higher salaries' (2010, p. 25). This instrumental, reductive view of HE connects ideologically with the function HEIs have embraced, as 'hubs' for 'knowledge exchange networks' whose role is to drive 'economic growth'.

In such a network culture, issues of access are often displaced by the rhetoric of diversity within HEIs, where inequality of access may be neglected, in favour of diversity measures (Ahmed, 2006). The discursive rhetoric of diversity (recording diversity in terms of work placements, for example) can be seen to mask more structural issues of inequality, as Allen et al. (2012) have argued in their research into work placements in the HE sector. Their work shows how staff involved in HEI creative placements faced a dilemma in regulating employers to abide by fair practice in relation to pay, and in terms of being unable to control why students are and are not taken on. As they argue, 'In an audit culture, diversity work becomes a box-ticking exercise, leaving inequitable practices unattended' (2012).

By drawing attention back to class and social inequality, it is crucial to consider the role of social and cultural capital which facilitates entry to these competitive labour markets. Of course, this focus on diversity is not coincidental. As McGuigan has argued, neoliberal discourse creates particular favoured terms, of which diversity is one. And of course it creates terms that cannot 'be spoken in polite company' – inequality being the most significant (2005, p. 233). With over one million young people now out of work in the UK, and with talk of a 'lost generation', now more than ever, universities must become sites of critical resistance to practices which perpetuate inequality, rather than being complicit with such practices. Of course, the key question is how, especially as universities face their own structural pressures such as the casualization of staff, decreasing budgets and pressures from student consumers?

Concluding comments

The creative industries are highly afflicted by the broader decline in social mobility that has occurred in the UK under the conditions of neoliberalism (Wilkinson and Pickett, 2009). Within its many sectors, cultures of inequality have become entrenched. An aggressive, neoliberal discourse of 'meritocracy' flows through the sector, perpetuating an ideal-type model of creative worker which is classed, raced and gendered (Allen et al., 2012). This discourse acts as a 'justificatory regime' (Boltanski and Thévenot, 2006) for an individualized notion of social mobility through creativity (the 'anyone can make it' argument).

So, what can we learn from the debate on internship culture and exploited labour in the cultural industries, at a broader political level? The conclusion to Alan Milburn's 2009 report into social mobility stated that 'Internships are accessible only to some, whereas they should be open to all who have the aptitude. Current employers are missing out on talented people – and talented people are missing opportunities to progress' (HM Government, 2009). Clearly structural barriers to entry need to be addressed at a political level. This will involve a reconsideration of the role of internship labour and regulation of internships through a close enforcement of National Minimum Wage Law.

But is this enough? The challenges faced are so embedded and structural that policy on internships alone will not address the issue. The emerging role of HE in either entrenching this inequality, or challenging it, is becoming increasingly critical. With tuition fees now soaring (two out of three universities are set to charge new students £9,000 tuition fees from 2012), what role does HE need to play to stimulate social mobility? As Allen's (2010) research in this area shows, HE perpetuates a particular ideal type of creative worker (a neoliberal, middle-class, 'rational' subject). Yet the resources (economic, social and cultural capitals) necessary to become the ideal creative worker are not equally distributed, which means that the production of this ideal subject is deeply entangled with social inequalities. Can HE stimulate an 'ethic of cultural work', challenging the neoliberal, middle-class stereotype of the ideal-type creative worker (one who is prepared to be utterly flexible, work for nothing, and be exploited to get on)? Can it remain a space for critique within the hegemonic project of neoliberalism (McGuigan, 2005)? Or has it become the locus for the acceleration of social inequality and stratification?

For many commentators, the signs are not good: facing extreme marketization, they feel that the long-mooted arrival of the 'neoliberal university' is now here (Nelson, 2010; Freedman and Bailey, 2011; Collini, 2012). For these critics, considering the implications of government policies towards HE, we are going back to the future, to a model of university education for the few, while other 'providers' (such as Further Education colleges and commercial organizations) look to fill the gap in the market for cheaper, quicker alternatives with compressed two-year undergraduate degree programmes to create 'market-ready' students. However, the levels of mobilization around this and other issues of social fairness in the last 18 months suggests a sea-change in public attitudes towards an accelerated neoliberalization of universities (among other areas) favoured by the right-wing majority in the Conservative-LibDem coalition – a reaction against neoliberalism that is of course global in scale (Leitner et al., 2007). Research is needed over the coming years, but clearly the 'justificatory regime' of neoliberalism in regard to HEIs is failing to achieve a consensus. In tumultuous times, the university represents a space for deliberative debate and mobilization, for proximal rather than virtual solidarity, and for imagining future alternatives to the 'commodification of everything' (Leys and Harriss-White, 2012).

Notes

1. The Television Workers Rights Advocacy Petition (TVWRAP) in the UK in 2005, which utilized the Internet to campaign against exploitation of television workers, proved highly successful as a networked mode of organized resistance which brought about industry changes to the exploitative culture

of endless unpaid work experience for individuals without any promise of paid work at the end of it (for more detail, see Saundry et al., 2007).

2. The relationship between art schools and 'innovation' within the cultural economy has been debated recently within the field of cultural policy studies and cultural sociology. While Oakley et al. (2008) have argued that artists have always played a key role in the creative economy, and the executive summary points out that 'artists have attitudes and skills that are conducive to innovation' (2008, p. 5), McRobbie and Forkert (2009) have rejected the normative basis of their report, arguing against the 'discursive imposition' of 'innovation' and claiming that the social potential of art school education should be prioritized.

3. See Hesmondhalgh (2007, p. 244) for a detailed account of this model.

4. Social mobility refers to the opportunities available for citizens to enjoy a better quality of life than their parents. It is also often called 'intergenerational mobility'. It refers to both horizontal mobility (movement from one position to another within a particular social level, such as changing jobs without altering occupational status) and vertical mobility (the ability of an individual to change status in terms of position in the social hierarchy). In this paper, I am referring to vertical mobility. Academic research in this area has shown how social mobility (in particular vertical mobility) is aided or abetted by numerous forms of capital: most significantly economic capital, but also social capital (access to networks), cultural capital (education and taste), physical capital and symbolic capital (Goldthorpe et al., 1987; Crompton, 2008). A nation's abundance (or otherwise) of social mobility denotes to what extent it offers opportunity to individuals based on ability, rather than social position.

5. See Oakley's chapter in this volume for a discussion about the political implications of internships.

6. This is based on discussions with colleagues at a number of other universities, and also through my own experiences as admissions tutor of organizing undergraduate open days at the University of Leeds.

7. For example, Menlo College in northern California sold credits to a company called Dream Careers. In 2008, Menlo made a gross profit of $50,000 (approx. £32,300) by selling Menlo-accredited internships for up to $9,500 (approx. £6,100). This provides universities with a cheap way of providing academic credit – rather than paying for teaching staff, classrooms and equipment.

References

Ahmed, S. (2006) Doing Diversity Work in Higher Education in Australia, *Educational Philosophy and Theory* 38(6): 745–768.

Allen, K. (2010) *Constituting the Self as Future Creative Worker: Young Women, Self-Formation and Cultural Capital*, Paper Given at 'Capital Ideas? Fresh Perspectives on Class, Capital and Education' Symposium. BSA Annual Conference, Glasgow Caledonian University. Glasgow. April 2010.

Allen, K., Quinn, J., Hollingworth, S. and Rose, A. (2012) Doing Diversity and Evading Equality: The Case of Student Work Placements in the Creative Sector, in Taylor, Y. (ed.) *Educational Diversity: The Subject of Difference and Different Subjects* (London: Palgrave Macmillan): 180–200.

Antcliff, V., Saundry, R. and Stuart, M. (2005) *Freelance Worker Networks in Audio Visual Industries. Working Paper No.4* (University of Central Lancashire, Business School).

Antcliff, V., Saundry, R. and Stuart, M. (2007) Networks and Social Capital in the UK Television Industry: The Weakness of Weak Ties, *Human Relations* 60: 371–393.

Archer, L., Hollingworth, S. and Halsall, A. (2007) 'University's Not for Me – I'm a Nike Person': Urban, Working-Class Young People's Negotiations of 'Style', Identity and Educational Engagement, *Sociology* 41: 219–237.

Ashton, D. (2011) Media Work and the Creative Industries: Identity Work, Professionalism and Employability, *Education + Training 53*(6): 546–560.

Boltanski, L. and Chiapello, E. (2005) *The New Spirit of Capitalism* (London: Verso).

Boltanski, L. and Thévenot, L. (2006) *On Justification: Economies of Worth*, Porter, C. (trans.) (Princeton: Princeton University Press).

Bourdieu, P. (1984) *Distinction: A Social Critique of the Judgement of Taste* (London: Routledge).

Bourdieu, P. (1986) The Forms of Capital, in Richardson, J.G. (ed.) *Handbook for Theory and Research for the Sociology of Education* (New York: Greenwood Press): 241–258.

British Film Institute (BFI) (1999) *Television Industry Tracking Study, Third Report* (London: BFI).

Browne, J. (2010) *Independent Review of Higher Education Funding and Student Finance* (London: Department for Business, Innovation and Skills).

Burt, R.S. (1995) *Structural Holes: The Social Structure of Competition* (Cambridge, MA: Harvard University Press).

Collini, S. (2010) Browne's Gamble, *London Review of Books* 31(21): 23–25.

Collini, S. (2012) *What are Universities For?* (London: Penguin).

Crompton, R. (2008) *Class and Stratification* (3rd edition) (Cambridge: Polity).

Deuze, M. (2007) *Media Work* (Cambridge: Polity).

Dex, S., Willis, J., Paterson, R. and Sheppard, E. (2000) Freelance Workers and Contract Uncertainty: The Effects of Contractual Changes in the Television Industry, *Work, Employment and Society* 14(2): 283–305.

Fevre, R. (1989) Informal Practices, Flexible Firms and Private Labour Markets, *Sociology* 23(1): 91–109.

Freedman, D. and Bailey, M. (eds) (2011) *The Assault on Universities: A Manifesto for Resistance* (London: Pluto Press).

Goldthorpe, J.H., Llewellyn, C. and Payne, C. (1987) *Social Mobility and Class Structure in Modern Britain* (2nd edition) (Oxford: Clarendon Press).

Grabher, G. (2004) Learning in Projects, Remembering in Networks? Communality, Sociality, and Connectivity in Project Ecologies, *European Urban and Regional Studies* 11(2): 99–119.

Granovetter, M. (1973) The Strength of Weak Ties, *American Journal of Sociology* 78(6): 1360–1380.

de Grunwald, T. (2010) Internships: Institutional Exploitation? http://www. guardian.co.uk/commentisfree/2010/aug/17/internships-institutional-exploita tion-young?intcmp=239, date accessed 9 February 2012.

Heath, B. and Potter, D. (2011) *Going for Broke: The State of Internships in the UK* (London: Internocracy).

Hesmondhalgh, D. (2007) *The Cultural Industries* (2nd edition) (London: Sage).

HM Government (2009) *New Opportunities White Paper* (London: Cabinet Office).

HM Government (2011) *Opening Doors, Breaking Barriers: A Strategy for Social Mobility* (London: Cabinet Office).

Lange, B. (2005). Socio-Spatial Strategies of Culturepreneurs: The Example of Berlin and its New Professional Scenes, *Zeitschrift fur Wirtschaftsgeographie* 49: 79–96.

Lee, D. (2011) Networks, Cultural Capital and Creative Labour in the British Independent Television Industry, *Media, Culture & Society* 33(4): 549–565.

Leitner, H., Peck, J. and Sheppard, E. (2007) *Contesting Neoliberalism: Urban Frontiers* (London: Guilford Press).

Leonard, R. and Onyx, J. (2003) Networking through Loose and Strong Ties: An Australian Qualitative Study, *Voluntas: International Journal of Voluntary and Nonprofit Organizations* 14(2): 189–203.

Leys, C. and Harriss-White, B. (2012) Commodification: The Essence of Our Time, http://www.opendemocracy.net/ourkingdom/colin-leys-barbara-harriss-white/commodification-essence-of-our-time, date accessed 6 May 2012.

Marti, J. (2004) Social Capital Benchmarking System: Profiting from Social Capital when Building Network Organizations, *Journal of Intellectual Capital* 5(3): 426–442.

McGuigan, J. (2005) Neo-Liberalism, Culture and Policy, *International Journal of Cultural Policy* 11(3): 229–241.

McRobbie, A. (2002) From Holloway to Hollywood: Happiness at Work in the New Cultural Economy? in du Gay, P. and Pryke, M. (eds) *Cultural Economy* (London: Sage): 97–114.

McRobbie, A. and Forkert, K. (2009) Artists and Art Schools: For or Against Innovation? A Reply to NESTA, *Variant* (Spring), http://www.variant.randomstate.org/pdfs/issue34/nesta34.pdf, date accessed 5 May 2012.

Miège, B. (1989) *The Capitalization of Cultural Production* (New York: International General).

Nelson, C. (2010) *No University Is an Island: Saving Academic Freedom* (New York: NYU Press).

Oakley, K. (2006) Include us Out – Economic Development and Social Policy in the Creative Industries, *Cultural Trends* 15(4): 255–273.

Oakley, K., Sperry, B. and Pratt, A.C. (2008) *The Art of Innovation: How Fine Arts Graduates Contribute to Innovation* (London: NESTA).

Ozga, J. and Jones, R. (2006) Travelling and Embedded Policy: The Case of Knowledge Transfer, *Journal of Education Policy* 21(1): 1–17.

Perlin, R. (2011a) *Intern Nation: How to Earn Nothing and Learn Little in the Brave New Economy* (London: Verso).

Perlin, R. (2011b) Unpaid Interns, Complicit Colleges, *New York Times* http://www.nytimes.com/2011/04/03/opinion/03perlin.html?pagewanted= all, date accessed 10 January 2012.

Pratt, A.C. (2002) Hot Jobs in Cool Places: The material Cultures of New Media Product Spaces: The Case of the South of Market, San Francisco, *Information, Communication and Society* 5(1): 27–50.

Pratt, A.C. (2004) Creative Clusters: Towards the Governance of the Creative Industries Production System? *Media International Australia* 112: 50–66.

Putnam R. D. (2000) *Bowling Alone: The Collapse and Revival of American Community* (London: Simon & Schuster).

Saundry, R., Stuart, M. and Antcliff, V. (2007) Broadcasting Discontent – Freelancers, Trade Unions and the Internet, *New Technology, Work and Employment* 22(2): 178–191.

Schlesinger, P. (2007) Creativity: From Discourse to Doctrine? *Screen* 48(3): 377–387.

Scott, A.J. (2005) *On Hollywood: The Place, the Industry* (Princeton: Princeton University Press).

Skillset (2005) *Survey of the Audio Visual Industries' Workforce 2005* (London: Skillset).

Skillset (2008) *Creative Media Workforce Survey Report* (London: Skillset).

Skillset (2012) Who does the Television Industry Need? http://www.creativeskillset.org/tv/industry/article_6776_1.asp, date accessed 4 May 2012.

Stigler, G.J. (1961) The Economics of Information, *Journal of Political Economy* 69(3): 213–225.

Unite (2009) 'Unfair' Working Conditions of Parliamentary Interns to be Discussed at Speaker's Summit, http://www.unitetheunion.org/news__events/2009_archived_press_releases/_unfair__working_conditions_of.aspx, date accessed 9 February 2012.

Ursell, G. (2000) Television Production: Issues of Exploitation, Commodification and Subjectivity in UK Television Labour Markets, *Media, Culture and Society* 22(6): 805–827.

van Heur, B. (2010) *Creative Networks and the City: Towards a Cultural Political Economy of Aesthetic Production* (Berlin: Transcript Verlag).

Wilkinson, R. and Pickett, K. (2009) *The Spirit Level* (London: Allen Lane).

Wittel, A. (2001) Towards a Network Sociality, *Theory, Culture and Society* 18(6): 51–77.

10
The Cultural Industries in a Critical Multicultural Pedagogy

Anamik Saha

In higher education (HE), media studies, perhaps more than any other discipline, exemplifies the pedagogic challenges, but also the possibilities, of teaching 'race' and difference. The impact of Stuart Hall and his work on new ethnicities (Hall, 1996) in particular has given the study of 'the politics of representation' a central role within the cultural and media studies curriculum, providing a space for teachers to confront and contest students' particular attitudes about difference, as well as potentially transform their own entrenched racialized subjectivities (Sharma, 2006). Indeed, one of the most productive elements of teaching media studies is in inspiring and encouraging students from minority backgrounds to enter the cultural industries and make their own productions – whether in television, radio, film, publishing, theatre and so on – that feature narratives and characters that challenge reductive representations of racial difference, and in the process contribute to a more progressive form of multiculture.

Yet the problem is that teaching 'race' and difference in media studies remains fixed on the text and identity, and very rarely engages with the actual experiences of minority practitioners in the cultural industries. This is a major shortcoming, since, as the industry itself has recognized, minority groups are greatly disadvantaged within, if not marginalized completely from, the media. Following Greg Dyke's infamous comment that the BBC is 'hideously white' (Hill, 2001), there have been numerous initiatives launched across both corporate and subsidized cultural sectors that have made efforts to increase and encourage participation from 'Black Minority Ethnic (BME)' groups. Moreover, HE is seen as a critical site for this, where there have been particular attempts to encourage students from minority backgrounds to enter media professions, with numerous bursaries offered for vocation-based media programmes such as broadcast journalism.

No doubt, some important inroads have been made in terms of improving access to the cultural industries, but this has not necessarily led to the improved *portrayal* of minorities in the media. As several authors have noted (Campion, 2005; Malik, 2008), while the participation of blacks and Asians in the media through these initiatives has actually increased in recent times, problematic representations of 'race' persist, defined by a post-9/11 racialized agenda centred around, as Sarita Malik (2008, p. 352) describes, issues of ' "asylum seekers", "black gun crime", "freedom of speech", the "clash of civilizations" and most of all "the war on terror" '. In fact, the disturbing reality is that rather than a case where increased participation in the cultural industries leads to better representation, we find instances where minority producers appear to be themselves behind stereotypical and reified versions of difference (Saha, 2011, 2012). It is this chapter's contention that HE is therefore the critical space in which future media practitioners from minority backgrounds can learn about these issues. I argue that a *critical multicultural pedagogy* has to be founded upon highlighting the cultural-industrial context of the politics of representation, in order to enlighten future cultural practitioners about the ways in which the commercializing tendencies of contemporary cultural production undermine and subvert the counter-narratives of difference, and in turn how these processes can be resisted. While the focus is on producers from minority ethnic and racial backgrounds, it is felt that the issues raised in this chapter will resonate with the experiences of other marginalized groups, whether based upon gender, sexuality, disability or class (see Lee and Allen, this volume).

To illustrate my argument the chapter draws from an ethnographic study of British (South) Asian cultural producers working in three cultural industries – theatre, publishing and broadcasting. The research consisted of interviews with over 50, mostly Asian, cultural producers and creative managers, and participant observation conducted over a year to see how respondents 'perceive and imagine the world in which they are working' (Negus, 1999, p. 11). The aim was to examine the actions of British Asian symbol creators and cultural intermediaries at the 'editorial' stage of production (Garnham, 1990), and their exegeses on the experience of cultural production, as a way of gaining a greater understanding of how exactly the cultural industries work to reproduce racial and ethnic stereotypes. The key finding was that increasingly commercialized cultures of media production constrain the work of minority practitioners, transforming their attempts at producing progressive representations of 'race' into the very opposite, in an insidious form such that they often do not even notice this process is occurring. As such the chapter begins by questioning the extent to which recent policy and industry efforts to improve minority representation improves the experience of non-white media workers. Yet rather than dwell solely on this issue, the chapter goes on to present two case studies which I use to demonstrate how British Asian cultural producers have managed to prise open a productive space within the cultural industries that has facilitated the production of radical cultural political interventions in the form of narratives of difference that disrupt common sense and reductive understandings of 'race'. The chapter's purpose then is to unpack the conditions of this space and to think through how the knowledge produced can inform a critical multicultural pedagogy that can empower students and help them imagine and develop their own forms of progressive (anti-racist) media practice.

Towards a critical multicultural pedagogy

To begin, we need to unpack this notion of a critical multicultural pedagogy. The term is taken from the work of Sanjay Sharma (2006, 2008), who highlights the problems and dangers of teaching multiculturalism. Here he is referring specifically to the practice of using popular media texts and representations of minority cultures as study aids, where the emphasis is placed on teaching students to celebrate diversity and appreciate minority culture – what he describes as 'multicultural education'. It is this form of educational practice that typifies the study of otherness in HE. The problem with multicultural education is that there is too much emphasis on identity. For Sharma, merely including the other in teaching does not engender a truly multicultural curriculum. As he states (2006, p. xiv):

> The use of these types of popular texts is a fraught undertaking, however. While there appears to be a contemporary political recognition of multiculture, this has also been accompanied by an increasing commodification and fetishization of ethnic difference in neo-liberal democracies. The reification of otherness makes a pedagogy for alterity a risky activity. To use 'ethnically marked' texts in teaching runs the danger that it inadvertently leads to further objectifications of otherness.

In light of this, what might a radical multicultural pedagogy look like? For Sharma, the aim is to develop 'pedagogic agency'; to shift the emphasis from identity to agency for 'innovating a pedagogy of cultural difference' (Sharma, 2006, p. xi). As he continues:

> The challenge is to develop an educational practice that eludes reifying cultural identity by engaging the racialized 'other' outside a pedagogic encounter of idealization or domination. It necessitates questioning the *logic of identity and representation* as the only grounds for a critical multicultural pedagogy.
>
> (Sharma, 2006, p. xi) [original emphasis]

As such Sharma's own approach is to tackle the politics of representation head-on, and develop methods which engage with the other without reproducing reified categories of 'race'; that is, an engagement that destabilizes the very category of otherness rather than reaffirms it (Sharma, 2006, p. xiv). To illustrate this Sharma (2008, 2006) uses a reading of the film *Bend it Like Beckham* (Chadha, 2002) to suggest the ways teachers can disrupt racist stereotypes through a more nuanced textual reading of this text, in contrast to multicultural education practices that tend to adopt an approach that presents the 'facts' or cultural truths about minorities.

As Sharma himself acknowledges, such an approach is a risky undertaking, not least since the line between destabilizing and reaffirming a stereotype is open to different interpretations and is certainly not as clear-cut as we would imagine. As Sharma himself admits, it is easy to mistake presenting positive images of difference as progressive teaching practice, since these positive images are often in terms of tropes that continue to racialize and objectify the subject. A more productive route in my view is in addressing Sharma's point regarding the commodification of ethnic difference. As he suggests, commodification complicates our reading of representations of multiculture, where difference is transformed into a commodity from which to extract surplus value, and in the process reified into stereotypes that present 'race' as something that is either feared or fetishized (Hutnyk, 2000; hooks, 1992). As a consequence, this chapter argues that a critical multicultural pedagogy needs to ground issues of 'race' and difference more explicitly within the cultural industries, to see precisely how such representations are formed, how commodities become *racialized*, and more crucially, how this very process can be disrupted. This means paying closer attention to the experience of cultural work and the labour that goes behind the production of cultural texts. The implications are two-fold. Firstly, it underlines the constructed nature of stereotypical and deeply damaging representations of difference, and the way in which the media shapes our understandings of 'race'. Secondly, it highlights how future practitioners can negotiate the racializing/reifying processes of commodification (or more precisely, particular forms of standardized cultural production) and as a consequence, contribute towards a cultural politics that produces more progressive representations of difference. It is in this way that an emphasis on the cultural industries needs to inform a critical multicultural pedagogy, through engaging directly with the commodification of otherness, and also the very ethical agency of the student, as Sharma suggests. Thus, the university plays an absolutely crucial role; providing the resources, as well as a safe environment, in which to carry out this kind of self-reflective work.

The purpose of the remainder of the chapter is to demonstrate what grounding the experience of minority practitioners within the cultural industries context brings to the discussion of minority representation. Firstly, it highlights the limitations of current policy initiatives that attempt to increase participation of those from 'BME groups'. Secondly, it presents two case studies, in order to show how minority practitioners can disrupt the racializing effects of commodification through industry practice. Then, in the final section I outline the specific ways in which this knowledge needs to inform a critical multicultural pedagogy in HE.

The numbers game

It is not controversial to suggest that students from minority backgrounds encounter greater difficulties in entering and moving within the cultural industries than their white counterparts – mirroring their experience of HE itself (Archer et al., 2003; David, 2009). As stated, in recent years we have seen an increasing recognition of how minorities are marginalized in the media, particularly following policy research on 'race' in the labour markets of the cultural industries (Campion, 2005; O'Loughlin, 2006; Mailk, 2008). The reports produced have exposed how little diversity there is in the media workforce particularly at the senior level where positions are monopolized by individuals from a particular privileged social class (and ethnicity). Such a discourse appears in all three of the industries in my study of British Asian cultural production.

For instance, the 2004 report *In Full Colour: Cultural Diversity in Book Publishing Today* (Kean, 2004) showed that, while 13 per cent of the publishing industry belong to an ethnic minority, since the industry is predominantly based in London, these figures are not actually representative of the London population, 30 per cent of whom are 'black or minority ethnic' (ibid.). Moreover, it found that diversity tends to occur at the periphery of the workforce, with 'virtually zero diversity in editorial', a consequence of the prevailing culture of nepotism that ensures that this layer of the industry remains dominated by individuals from the same networks and social class. In television, similar statistical studies and their findings have led to the launch of numerous schemes aimed at boosting diversity in the workforce. The most significant of these is the creation of the Cultural Diversity Network (CDN), a joint initiative involving all the major UK broadcasting companies, who together produced an action plan outlining its objectives for achieving 'a fairer representation of Britain's multicultural society' (Deans, 2002). A similar discourse appears in the theatre, exemplified by Estelle Morris, the former Culture Secretary, who, speaking at the launch of a theatre training scheme for individuals from minority communities, stated, 'At the moment, we are not recruiting enough people from black and ethnic minority backgrounds. The statistics are abysmal and that means, quite simply, that the arts is missing out on a whole lot of talent' (Bramley, 2004). Indeed, the Arts Council has made supporting culturally diverse theatre one of its major aims and has made a concerted effort to encourage companies to target cultural diversity – in terms of audiences, and within the organization itself (Khan, 2002). Thus in all these policy literatures the focus tends to be on the structural aspect of racism in the labour market, where diversity is discussed in terms of 'glass ceilings', quotas and diversity targets, which are geared towards improving the employment opportunities of professionals from 'BME' communities.

The lack of black and brown folk in the higher echelons of the cultural industries is an obvious hindrance to British Asian cultural production, the products of which struggle to reach wider, 'mainstream' audiences (Malik, 2008). However, even though representation in the labour market is an issue that must be addressed (particularly if black and Asian professionals are unable to further their careers because of their non-white status), I argue that such a discourse's sole focus on the quantitative, not only ignores the *quality* of output and the politics of representation, but more crucially, fails to understand the relation between cultures of production and the agency of the cultural worker through which symbols of 'race' and ethnicity are created. Exemplifying this point is a quote from an interview I conducted with an Asian television executive producer at the BBC, who describes the reality for minorities who manage to break through the 'glass ceiling' in the cultural industries:

> [A]nd I mean really breaking it. I don't mean breaking and peering over the side and taking on the values of the organisation around you, but doing it, maintaining your own values and sense of self, and having a sense of individual autonomy within the bigger beast of the corporation [...] once that happens things can open up more. We're a long way off that because I think to breakthrough to that level you have to, in a way, I feel... my fear is you almost have to take on values which may not be in keeping with your own individual values and your own kind of who you are, and I think that is the problem with society, not just broadcasting. You almost have to suppress your [cultural heritage] in order to get to where you want to go. And I think that is the biggest shame in our industry; we should never have to suppress who we are. I was always proud of my culture, my tradition, my heritage and I have managed to keep onto that, but I also want to be very successful in broadcasting. And whether you can have both... I don't know if you can have that in this current climate.

In this quote, the respondent identifies the problem as not just the supposed glass ceiling, but the difficulty in maintaining one's identity, and not conforming to the values of a particular organization, which run counter to the values of the Asian or black media professional. Indeed, the last line suggests that the respondent has resigned himself to the fact that achieving this is nearly impossible, though I hope this chapter can provide a more optimistic narrative. From this comment, I suggest that an effective cultural strategy needs to have less emphasis on the numbers of non-white bodies in the cultural industries, and a greater focus on the cultures of production through which diversity is governed. The reference at the end of the respondent's comment, to the 'climate' of broadcasting (or indeed, the public sphere itself) suggests that change needs to occur within the heart of industrial production, where quota schemes and race-relations legislation have little impact. That is not to say that these particular approaches are misguided or pointless, rather that real change within the cultural industries will only occur once the very cultures of production have been transformed. And such a notion,

I argue, has critical implications for the way HE addresses the needs and aspirations of students from minority backgrounds.

The cultural politics of minority cultural production

It is this chapter's contention that students who aspire to work in the cultural industries in order to produce texts that challenge problematic representations of difference, need to understand how the success of their productions in this way depends on how they negotiate particular commercial rationales during the manufacture of the cultural commodity. For Nicholas Garnham (1990, pp. 161–162) – one of the leading proponents of the cultural industries tradition (Hesmondhalgh, 2008) – rather than the production of the good itself, it is cultural distribution that is the 'key locus of power and profit [...] and the key to cultural plurality'. It is for this reason that Garnham argues that the focus of cultural policy has to be on this 'editorial' (Garnham, 1990, p. 162) function of production, 'a vital function totally ignored by many cultural analysts, a function as creative as writing a novel or directing a film'. Indeed, it is the editorial stage that was precisely the object of my research into British Asian cultural production. A further key principle of cultural industries research that informs this chapter is that cultural production is a contested space, capable of producing both 'good' and 'bad' art. Garnham (2000) explains this in terms of the dialectic of the market as an entity that both dominates and liberates. David Hesmondhalgh (2007) builds on this and discusses commodification as an *ambivalent* process that is enabling as well as constraining. Certainly, while my own research mostly found instances where the cultural politics of British Asian practitioners were undermined by the standardized and rationalized processes of commercial cultural production (see Saha, 2012), I did also encounter cases that at various points 'contradicted' the system. I want to reflect on two of these cases now, which will help us think through the ways in which successful 'cultural transruptions' (Hesse, 2000) – moments when the multicultural interrogates the ontological status of national and 'racial' identities – can be staged. It is such an engagement that I argue needs to be built into a critical multicultural pedagogy; drawing from examples of progressive cultural strategies should be used as a way of inspiring students from minority backgrounds to enter the cultural industries.

The first case I want to draw upon is the Channel 4 drama *Bradford Riots*, directed by British-born Bengali Neil Biswas. Based on the real-life events that took place in Bradford in July 2001, it tells the fictional story of a student called Karim who gets caught up in the riot between hundreds of Asian youths and the police. On one level the programme provides another case in which the stories of the other are reduced to standard racialized tropes – in this instance, the 'Asian Gang' as new folk devil (see Alexander, 2000). But this actually belied the content of the drama, which was both well crafted, and also a significant political intervention that exposed with damning effect the latest social injustice to have occurred in the troubled history of British race relations.[1] Gauging the actual social and political impact of *Bradford Riots* needs further dissection than can be afforded here, but its relative critical *and* commercial success highlights at the very least the mark it made on the British cultural landscape at that moment in time.[2]

Considering its provocative subject matter (which is where its primary disruptive qualities lay), I asked the director and writer Neil Biswas about how *Bradford Riots* came to be commissioned:

> Neil Biswas: I think they [Channel 4] did *Bradford Riots* because they felt politically it had to be addressed. They genuinely thought that this was something that needed to be seen, that it was actually something that was extraordinary enough ... no one else would do it, and they genuinely felt that in terms of perspective was important ... you remember part of their remit is to do ethnic programming [...] programming that is there for a minority interest, so it couldn't have been more up their street in terms of their remit. But I think in terms of their political positions they all felt this was a really important story to be told that hadn't been told.

In this quote, Neil alluded to how the programme fitted in with Channel 4's remit to produce 'ethnic programming'. Channel 4 is a commercial channel, totally reliant on advertising revenue, but it also has a public service remit to appeal 'to the tastes and interests of a culturally diverse society' (Communications Act, 2003). While Neil admits that *Bradford Riots* was 'right up their street' in this respect – and also, I would add, the channel's brand and target audience, with its focus on youth and urban themes – in our interview Neil was nonetheless keen to stress the ethical motivations of various individuals involved in the production (from co-producers to the channel executives), who felt that, from a political point of view, the story 'needed to be seen'.

While it would be naive to suggest that Channel 4 commissioned *Bradford Riots* for political reasons alone, I was nevertheless surprised to hear Neil describe their approach to the production as – in his words – 'gung-ho' and 'radical'. In one instance, Neil was specifically referring to the Head of Channel 4 Drama's offer of an additional £1 million to build a street set, following the temporary shutdown of the production as it struggled to get permission from various local authorities to stage the riot scene. Neil additionally referred to how, despite the channel's anxiety over his status as a first-time director, Channel 4 nonetheless gave him 'incredible support'. Thus, in contrast to the majority of cases I researched where symbol creators would describe feeling alienated or pressured by senior executives, Neil expressed his amazement at how Channel 4 and its co-producers flouted all the standard commercial conventions, and took *risks* over a production that would probably have generated press interest based on subject-matter alone, but was not guaranteed to be a commercial or critical hit. It transpired that *Bradford Riots* was a relative success, much of which was due to Neil's skill as a writer and director.[3] But as Neil would probably admit, the film would not have appeared as it did without the freedom and support he was given by the producers and the channel – including a significant marketing push consisting of trailers, a billboard campaign, and a two-page advert in all the daily newspapers. Thus the political agency of key individuals, and the willingness to take risks (in terms of the original commission, resource and budget allocation, and the priority it was given by Channel 4 in its overall schedule and marketing plan), no doubt aided by Channel 4's public service remit, were all factors that set the foundations from which the political potential of the drama – in terms of highlighting the injustices of the convictions of the Asian youth involved in the riots – could be realized.

A second case study that provides an example of a successful cultural political intervention is Daljit Nagra's collection of poetry *Look We Have Coming to Dover!* published by independent UK publishing house Faber & Faber. What makes the collection particularly striking is not just its beautifully crafted expression of a very particular British Asian experience (in his poems Daljit – born and raised in west London – writes in a language he describes as 'Punglish', a playful mix of Punjabi and English), but for the way in which the book was packaged and marketed, which absolutely refused to reduce the book to the author's ethnic identity when this would have been the most 'obvious' thing for a marketer to do. Indeed, the book's redesign for its incorporation into Faber & Faber's fiction department following the success of the first edition, neatly illustrates how Asianness can be represented in a way that avoids the reifying, racializing processes of commodification.

The original cover of *Look We Have...* was part of a series designed by award-winning design firm Pentagram, marking the relaunch of Faber's poetry list. This particular design recalled the typographic style of classic Faber poetry covers, connecting the backlist and the new titles within a single embracing cover. The covers are very simple, consisting of the title and author's name in a basic font, against a plain background; the only differences between covers being the size of the font and the colour scheme. While Daljit appreciated the serious, austere style of the design, he also felt that it was not in keeping with the playful and subversive tone of his poetry – not least because he would have preferred a more visible Asian presence on the cover – and he subsequently requested that his jacket featured the 'gaudiest' colours possible (settling for a clashing orange and light blue font against a mauve background). However, when the cover was redesigned for the new edition, which was an attempt to introduce the collection to the mass market, rather than amplify Asianness, the collection's ethnic themes were subtly represented through the font in which Daljit's name is written. Though the font is recognizably 'Indian', it is very muted and not as clichéd as one would imagine. In fact it reflects the convivial tone of the new cover, which depicts a pound shop (several of the poems are about shops), featuring mops and buckets and stacks of plastic chairs, a deliberate contrast to the high-brow quality of the original cover. While the pound shop can be read as connoting difference and the immigrant experience, there is an ordinariness about the depiction at odds with the otherwise exoticization of Asian cultures in particular. Daljit reflected on the redesign as follows:

Daljit Nagra: [I]t's very bright and colourful, it's yellow. And they got some Asian artist to write my name so it's slightly off-centre script.
AS: Have they accentuated the ethnic aspect?
DN: Just slightly yeah.
AS: But not in a way you feel uncomfortable with?
DN: I wanted it anyway. I like this cover. I want my books to not look as English as possible, I want to move away from that. Same with the writing there [pointing to title on the original cover] if they could have made the writing less English I would have been happy. I didn't challenge it at the time.
AS: But would you have been worried if they really exaggerated the collection's Asianness?
DN: Yeah, absolutely. I didn't have really any input in the [original] cover. I just said I wanted it as gaudy as possible whatever

happens. I don't want another serious blue or black cover. That's not the spirit of the poems. And they picked this [new] design anyway and showed it to me and I just say yeah it's fine. So there was no kind of conflict there I guess and they've instinctively gone for this kind of design. And I think it's quite tasteful isn't it? I think it works well.

A similar narrative was presented when Daljit explained the process behind choosing a title for his collection. The editors, rather than pick an obvious, or perhaps more commercial, quirky (hybrid) 'Punglish' title, adopted a riskier strategy and chose to name the collection after what Daljit considered his most difficult poem. No doubt the particular cultures of production of Faber & Faber aided what I consider the progressive design of *Look We Have* ... through its status as a well-respected, literary, non-corporate entity with a reputation that values quality over commerce (something that Daljit was keen to stress throughout our interview). Certainly, poetry does not face the same kind of commercial pressures as the trade publishing industry, as historically it has not produced large sales, which makes even more impressive how *Look We Have* ... at the time of the interview, had sold over 14,000 copies, which I was told was a remarkable feat for a poetry collection, let alone one produced by a brand new author. Yet, what I consider a greater achievement is how, like *Bradford Riots*, *Look We Have* ... was a relative critical and commercial 'splash' that crucially, managed to transgress the ethnic niche where British Asian cultural producers are usually found, fixed to the margins of the cultural industries, the market and the public realm itself (Saha, 2011). Instead, both of these cultural works, through their production and their craft, stand alone as simply good pieces of art, rather than merely 'Asian works'.

The point I wish to make, however, is that, looking closely at the production of these two texts we see that these transruptive effects were not mere random dysfunctions of the system, or spontaneous, unexplainable transgressions. Firstly, what that these two cases have in common is the way that at various points, the creative managers involved in their production took *risks*. Neither production had immediate commercial appeal in terms of repeating a known formula, yet at the commissioning level, someone felt that they were 'worth a punt'. Similarly, despite the lack of obvious commercial appeal, schedulers and sales executives both took risks when they allocated *Bradford Riots* a primetime 9 pm slot and decided to push a collection of 'Punglish' poetry into the broader fiction market. While a more predictable approach was taken at the marketing and design stage of production for *Bradford Riots* (though it did receive a national billboard campaign), the marketing team behind *Look We Have...* risked losing a potentially larger 'mainstream' audience (even going against the author's own vision for the cover in the process) by choosing a subtle, ethnically ambiguous book jacket, rather than one based upon a hammed-up (Orientalist) *East-meets-West* aesthetic that, for instance, made Andrew Lloyd Webber's musical *Bombay Dreams* such a massive hit.

My key argument is that the way in which such risks could be taken, is explained by the particular 'hybrid' cultures of production through which each production occurred. Channel 4, which broadcast *Bradford Riots*, is a commercial channel, funded by advertising revenue, but it has a public service remit that obliges it to produce minority-interest television, and more challenging work. In a less regulated setting, Faber & Faber, which published *Look We Have...* as I have shown, is an independent company operating in a highly competitive market, but has a reputation for producing literary works of value, and an independent spirit that contrasts with the corporate environs of the larger publishing houses (a reputation repeated numerous times by respondents working in the publishing industry). I argue that it is these particular cultures of production that allow symbol creators more autonomy, increasing the potential for cultural transruptions to be staged. This is not unique to these particular companies or even industries, and is not to say that the organizations to which I refer consistently produce works of artistic, cultural and political merit – sometimes, quite the contrary. However, both of these organizations were able to provide environments in which cultural workers were at important moments, buffered from the market (or state) pressures that can have potentially detrimental effects upon the cultural work. This points us towards ways in which British Asian cultural producers can avoid and disrupt the constraining effects of commodification, and in turn the role HE can play in facilitating this process.

Higher education and the cultural industries

The purpose of using these case studies on poet Daljit Nagra and film-maker Neil Biswas has been to draw attention to the processes of cultural production as a critical site for the politics of representation. According to the cultural industries tradition, cultural production is a complex, ambivalent and contested process. And as the case studies demonstrate, at certain moments – contingent on the dynamic between a specific time and place – social actors *can* harness the enabling dimension of commodification and produce oppositional texts. It is precisely this knowledge that I argue needs to inform a critical multicultural pedagogy, helping to facilitate a shift from an excessive focus on identity (which, as Sharma argues is the main preoccupation in media and cultural studies of 'race' and difference) to agency, in providing support for students from minority backgrounds in developing and staging their own cultural political interventions. By situating the study of the politics of representation within the experience of cultural production, students begin to learn how the radical potential of narratives of difference rests on the ability to negotiate commercial pressures at key moments in production. Thus the impetus now turns to educators, who I argue need to focus on two areas in particular.

Firstly, a media studies curriculum on 'race' and ethnicity needs to include a component on the actual *experience* of cultural production and what Hesmondhalgh (2007, pp. 20–21) calls the 'commerce-creativity dialectic'. As Hesmondhalgh (ibid.) and Ryan (1992) both highlight, the cultural industries can be characterized by 'loose/tight control', referring to how symbol creators are granted considerable autonomy at the design/conception stage of production, but less so at the distribution/circulation side where media companies employ increasingly rationalized processes and strategies in order to negate the unpredictability of the market. It is this latter stage – what Garnham refers to as the editorial stage – that is 'the key locus of power', and what a critical multicultural pedagogy needs to underscore as the key site of struggle for minority producers in order that their texts enter the market as they intend it. For instance, educators could draw from the growing field of empirical research conducted on marketing difference (Havens, 2000; Crockett, 2008; Saha, 2011) to demonstrate how standardized marketing strategies can have reductive effects upon the productions of minority cultural producers. A session run by a practitioner would be particularly helpful in capturing the interest of students by being able to share their experiences first-hand. At the very least, helping students engage with these issues will prepare them for those inevitable moments when certain commercial expectations attempt to steer their work into what they might find compromising directions.

Secondly, a media studies curriculum focused on aiding the aspirations of students from minority backgrounds needs to stress the importance of working with the right organization. As my case studies were intended to show, successful interventions can be held in different kinds of production settings, dependent on the autonomy experienced by the symbol creator and access to appropriate networks of distribution and marketing. For instance, working with an established independent organization that prioritizes artistic or political endeavour over profit (as the poet Daljit Nagra described his experience at Faber & Faber), I believe, is a particularly productive space in which to produce challenging and experimental work. However, such independent media companies tend to exist on the periphery of the mass media, in which case there is a danger that that the minority practitioner is further ghettoized. Consequently, cultural producers from minority backgrounds might prefer to work with larger organizations that have access to bigger distribution networks and greater marketing resources, though the risk is that it is in these types of environments that practitioners feel most constrained by commercial goals that prioritize profit over aesthetic or political goals. Public service broadcasting provides a particularly unique and potentially productive setting for black and Asian cultural production – as Nicholas Garnham (1990, p. 166) believes, it is the 'heartland of contemporary cultural practice' – and media studies students from all backgrounds need to be taught to understand and appreciate the importance of public service broadcasting for minority groups in particular, as well as the areas in which it needs to improve (as Dyke's 'hideously white' quote attests) (Malik, 2002). In addition, the curriculum should focus on precarity and self-exploitation in creative work, drawing from the experiences of practitioners as well as the growing field of literature on this subject (McRobbie, 2002; Banks, 2007; Brophy and de Peuter, 2007), with an emphasis on how these concerns might affect minority practitioners in particular. Again, the purpose here is not to argue that minority practitioners should only work with a specific type of media organization, but to encourage students to reflect and think more critically about their careers and the choices they make in terms of the types of media companies they would like to work with. This is of course relevant to all students who aspire to work in the cultural industries, but I would argue it is particularly decisive for those belonging to marginalized communities.

Thus, to reiterate, a critical multicultural pedagogy needs to focus aspiring symbol creators onto the conditions of cultural production that can marshal their work into problematic directions. In which case HE plays an absolutely vital role in showing students from minority backgrounds the importance of reflecting continually upon the choices, decisions and strategies that they make throughout the production process.

The potential for cultural transruption, or at least, the avoidance of reductive and racializing forms of commodification is based upon the degree to which the symbol creator can evade the forms of rationalized industrial production techniques that have been imposed throughout the cultural industries (including the subsidized arts sector). It is rationalization through standardized processes that restricts the autonomy of creative managers and prevents them from taking risks on more challenging, less 'commercial' products – and in particular, the narratives of minorities. Such is the saturation of neoliberal economic models in the cultural industries, whether in the form of corporate strategy or state cultural policy (see Hesmondhalgh, 2008), that the reality of being able to totally opt out of rationalized production is impossible. Regardless, the potential for producing challenging forms of cultural production depends on the ability of symbol creators to negotiate these processes in a way that does not compromise their ethical, political and aesthetic ambitions. This is what I believe a critical multicultural pedagogy can bring to HE: exhorting the student to reflect as much on their industrial practice as they do on their craft and the stories they want to tell.

Notes

1. The number of convictions for rioters was unprecedented in English legal history, with 200 jail sentences totalling 604 years handed down, with many believing the length of imprisonments excessive (most of the rioters received four to six year sentences). See Kalra (2002).
2. *Bradford Riots* received ratings of two million – 10 per cent of the market share for 9 pm – which is relatively successful for Channel 4. With regard to critical acclaim, it received outstanding reviews on BBC2's Newsnight Review, and the Radio 4's Front Row, and, somewhat ironically, *The Daily Telegraph* and *The Daily Mail*.
3. *Bradford Riots* actually brought Neil a BAFTA nomination.

References

Alexander, C. (2000) *The Asian Gang: Ethnicity, Identity, Masculinity* (Oxford: Berg).
Archer, L., Hutchings, M. and Ross, A. (2003) *Higher Education and Social Class: Issues of Exclusion and Inclusion* (London and New York: Routledge).
Banks, M. (2007) *The Politics of Cultural Work* (Basingstoke: Palgrave Macmillan).
Bramley, S. (2004) Morris Warns Arts Over Minority Recruitment, *The Stage*, 13 April.
Brophy, E. and de Peuter, G. (2007) Immaterial Labor, Precarity and Recomposition, in McKerchner, C. and Mosco, V. (eds) *Knowledge Workers in the Information Society* (Lanham, MD: Lexington): 177–191.

Campion, M.J. (2005) *Look Who's Talking: Cultural Diversity in Public Service Broadcasting and the National Conversation* (Oxford: Nuffield College Oxford).

Crockett, D. (2008) Marketing Blackness: How Advertisers Use Race to Sell Products, *Journal of Consumer Culture* 8(2): 245–268.

David, M. (2009) (ed.) *Improving Learning by Widening Participation in Higher Education* (Oxon and New York: Routledge).

DCMS (2003) *Communications Act* (London: UK Department for Media, Culture and Sport).

Deans, J. (2002) Connecting With Your Audience, *The Guardian*, 20 May.

Garnham, N. (1990) *Capitalism and Communication: Global Culture and the Economics of Information* (London and Newbury Park and New Delhi: Sage Publications).

Garnham, N. (2000) *Emancipation, the Media, and Modernity: Arguments about the Media and Social Theory* (Oxford: Oxford University Press).

Hall, S. (1996) New Ethnicities, in Morley, D. and Chen, K. (eds) *Stuart Hall: Critical Dialogues in Cultural Studies* (London: Routledge): 442–451.

Havens, T. (2000) 'The Biggest Show in the World': Race and the Global Popularity of The Cosby Show, *Media, Culture and Society* 22(4): 371–391.

Hesmondhalgh, D. (2007) *The Cultural Industries*, 2nd edition (London: Sage).

Hesmondhalgh, D. (2008) Cultural and Creative Industries, in Bennett, T. and Frow, J. (eds) *The Sage Handbook of Cultural Analysis* (London: Sage).

Hesse, B. (2000) Un/Settled Multiculturalisms, in Hesse, B. (ed.) *Un/Settled Multiculturalisms: Diasporas, Entanglements, Transruptions* (London and New York: Zed Books).

Hill, A. (2001) Dyke: BBC is Hideously White, *The Guardian*, 7 January.

hooks, b. (1992) *Black Looks; Race and Representation* (Boston: South End Press).

Hutnyk, J. (2000) *Critique of Exotica* (London: Zed Books).

Kalra, V.S. (2002) Extended View: Riots, Race and Reports: Denham, Cantle, Oldham and Burnley Inquiries, *Sage Race Relations Abstracts* 27(4): 20–30.

Kean, D. (2004) *In Full Colour: Cultural Diversity in Book Publishing Today*, The Bookseller, 12.

Khan, N. (2002) *Towards a Greater Diversity: Results and Legacy of the Arts Council of England's Cultural Diversity Action Plan*, Arts Council England.

Malik, S. (2002) *Representing Black Britain: Black and Asian Images on Television* (London: Sage).

Malik, S. (2008) 'Keeping it Real': The Politics of Channel 4's Multiculturalism, Mainstreaming and Mandates, *Screen* 49(3): 343–353.

McRobbie, A. (2002) Clubs to Companies, Notes on the Decline of Political Culture in Speeded-Up Creative Worlds, *Cultural Studies* 16(4): 516–531.

Negus, K. (1999) *Music Genres and Corporate Cultures* (London: Routledge).

O'Loughlin, B. (2006) The Operationalization of the Concept 'Cultural Diversity' in British Television Policy and Governance, *CRESC Working Paper Series*, Working Paper Number 27.

Ryan, B. (1992) *Making Culture from Capital* (Berlin and New York: Walter de Gruyter).

Saha, A. (2011) Negotiating the Third Space: British Asian Independent Record Labels and the Cultural Politics of Difference, *Popular Music and Society* 34(4): 437–454.

Saha, A. (2012) 'Beards, Scarves, Halal Meat, Terrorists, Forced Marriage': Television Industries and the Production of 'Race', *Media Culture and Society* 34(4): 424–438.

Sharma, S. (2006) *Multicultural Encounters* (Basingstoke: Palgrave Macmillan).

Sharma, S. (2008) Teaching Representations of Cultural Difference through Film, in Pollock, M. (ed.) *Everyday Antiracism: Getting Real About Race in School* (New York: New Press). 186–190.

11

'What Do You Need to Make It as a Woman in This Industry? Balls!': Work Placements, Gender and the Cultural Industries

Kim Allen

Introduction

Higher Education (HE) is an important route into the cultural sector and published figures suggest that there is no shortage of women coming through the HE pipeline: women make up 60 per cent of the student population on HE courses aligned with the cultural sector in the UK (ECU, 2011). However, women represent 38 per cent of the UK cultural industries' workforce (Skillset and Creative and Cultural Skills, 2011), below the UK labour market average of 46 per cent. Female representation varies significantly by sub-sector and occupational group but with markedly significant gender segregation across the sector: for example, in the audio-visual industries, 87 per cent of the workforce in make-up, hair and costume are female, yet women comprise only a very small minority in technical roles (Skillset, 2006). Despite being more highly qualified than their male counterparts, women earn less (Skillset and Creative and Cultural Skills, 2011) and are less likely to be found in top positions (Holden and McCarthy, 2007). Concurrently, workforce diversity agendas within the UK cultural sector have sought to increase female representation and progression.[1]

The discrepancy between the gender composition of HE courses aligned with the sector and the sector workforce itself is intriguing and troubling. While women are clearly attracted to cultural work, many appear to be excluded from forging and sustaining a career in the sector. Thus far, scholarship has mainly focused on the experiences of women who have *already* accessed the sector (see Gill, 2002; Willis and Dex,

232

2003; Marcella et al., 2006; Skillset, 2010a). While this work highlights the difficulties women face reconciling work and family, there remains a compelling case for looking empirically at the experiences of young women who are aspiring to enter the sector: what we may call female 'cultural workers in the making' (Ashton, 2011). Attending to their prior experiences of the cultural workplace can contribute valuable knowledge about gender-based inequalities within the cultural sector and how these are perceived and negotiated. In this chapter, I respond to this gap by drawing on empirical data collected in 2010 for a small-scale qualitative study, commissioned by the Equality Challenge Unit (ECU)[2] into equality issues in HE work placements for the cultural sector (Allen et al., 2010). Specifically, I attend to the accounts of six young women who undertook placements in areas of the cultural sector marked by female under-representation. The analytical focus of this chapter is how female students *subjectively experience* and interpret the cultural sector workplace including gendered working cultures and dominant constructions of 'cultural worker', and how they seek to navigate these. Identifying student work placements as a key site in which young women's choices regarding their future career transitions – their sense of where they belong – are shaped, I argue that female students' experiences of HE work placements warrant serious attention if greater workforce diversity and gender equity within the sector is to be achieved.

I begin by outlining the key contributions of scholarship on gender and cultural work, the field into which my analysis intervenes. Here I introduce work placements as sites of gendered subjectification in which young women find themselves subjected to a range of disciplinary practices and oppressions. I argue that young aspiring female cultural workers are doubly positioned through both neoliberal discourses associated with cultural work *and* post-feminist sensibilities. I then briefly introduce the study. Turning to the empirical data, I identify how the young women experienced, perceived and responded to gender-based inequalities within their work placement experiences. I show how hostile and robustly masculinized working cultures, embedded gender norms and constructions of the 'creative person' as a masculine subject were routinely encountered by young women on their placements. However, I argue that young women are caught within neoliberal and post-feminist discourses and individualistic approaches to equal opportunities that constrain their capacity to challenge existing gender hierarchies. I discuss the difficulties and possibilities for challenging gender-based inequities within the cultural sector and the role of HE in facilitating this.

Gender, cultural work and post-feminism

Critical scholarship on cultural labour has begun to dismantle the utopian and mythologized image of the cultural sector as 'cool creative and egalitarian' (Gill, 2002), illustrating the various 'problems' of cultural work including the presence of entrenched patterns of gender inequality. McRobbie (2002) has argued that despite being deeply attractive to young women as a career pathway – offering the promise of self-actualization and flexible portfolio work to facilitate greater work–life balance – women are more likely to be excluded from careers in the cultural sector. As already noted by Oakley (this volume), industry policy has been increasingly concerned about the 'gender drain' from the cultural sector. Research by UK skills council, Skillset (2010a), suggests that women who choose to have a family face a number of difficulties sustaining a career in the sector, resulting in a withdrawal of women from the industry, particularly those aged 35 years and older (2010a, p. 20). Critical scholarship on cultural work further illustrates how the sectors' informality and dependence on networking as a means of sustaining or finding employment, and the erratic and precarious nature of employment (unsociable and long working hours, short contracts, seasonal employment) make it difficult to reconcile the demands of work with maternity or childcare (Gill, 2002; Willis and Dex, 2003; Marcella et al., 2006; Skillset, 2010a). As Banks and Milestone state, 'the structures of cultural work employment are not conducive to the full participation of women' (2011, p. 84).

Furthermore, as Gill argues in her work on women in new media work, alongside the existence of 'old-fashioned' patterns of gender inequality, *new* forms of gender inequality and sexism exist, 'connected – paradoxically – to many of the features of the work that are valued – informality, autonomy, flexibility and so on' (2002, p. 71), features associated with the freelance, project-based nature of work that characterizes the cultural sector. Thus, it has been argued that the very aspects of cultural work that are seen to liberate women from previous constraints on labour market participation, provide the very means by which gender inequality is reproduced. Adkins' (1999) work on gender and the new economy is particularly relevant here. Adkins questions celebratory claims that there has been a detraditionalization of social relations and a feminization of the labour market. Adkins suggests that there exists an uneven distribution of the 'rewards' of the new economy among men and women. For example, while it is deemed acceptable and achievable for men to perform non-traditional gendered identities in the new economy, women face a great range of difficulties in attempting to perform 'masculine' identities – for example, 'assertiveness', 'ambition' or 'selfishness' – within the workplace. As such, Adkins argues that the barriers that previously excluded women from certain types of work have not been erased but replaced by new, more impenetrable ones.

Applying Adkins' theories to an empirical study of the new media sector, Banks and Milestone (2011) suggest that while female new media workers benefit from a sense of autonomy and pleasure in work, the sector plays host to 'markedly regressive traditional social structures' and enduring features of gender discrimination (2011, p. 73). For example, female employees within 'creative' positions were expected to adopt traditionally female roles, such as taking responsibility for client-facing duties and performing a 'mother-figure' role to disgruntled male colleagues: 'By and large women were only seen as being able to counterbalance male innovation and creativity by taking on supporting roles that befitted their "natural" gender attributes' (2011, p. 81). This positioning of female workers as 'sensitive', 'soft' and 'nurturing' subjects effectively placed them outside of the realm of 'true' creativity.

Similarly, Taylor (2011) argues that dominant constructions of contemporary creative work and creative workers privilege a masculine 'selfishness' which conflicts with gendered positionings of women as other-oriented' and attending to the needs of others. In his work on advertising cultures, Nixon illuminates how the homosocial and 'laddish' working cultures of the creative department and the sector's ritualistic work-based sociality – oriented around drinking and drugtaking – were deeply hostile to female participation, contributing to the sector's gender segregation (Nixon, 2003; see also Nixon and Crewe, 2004). Additionally, gendered constructions of the 'creative person' privilege attributes associated with a model of strident and assertive masculinity – 'hard skin', independence, competition, determination and rationality – operating to exclude women from particular roles in the sector:

> Links between masculinity and creative or cultural sector work and the flourishing of robustly masculine cultures within agency offices and publishing companies formed a considerable block to women's capacity to succeed in these occupations.
>
> (Nixon and Crewe, 2004, p. 146)

Thus as well as the objective, structural disadvantages associated with the bulimic working patterns of cultural work, there exist other, more tacit gender exclusions and conflicts operating at the subjective level.

As Taylor and Littleton discuss (in this volume) these conflicts at the level of creative identification impact unequally on different categories of people and result in diverting some groups away from participation within the sector. These conflicts and forms of exclusion operating at the subjective level are of particular importance when examining the experiences of young female aspiring cultural workers. Whereas policy attention has focussed on the withdrawal of women from the creative labour market at 35 years, connected to decisions to have children, there is worth in looking at younger women who are less likely to have children (as was true for all six women featured here), exploring how they make sense of 'gender' as a factor which might shape their access to the cultural sector.

Another important contribution to this field relates to the way in which individuals understand and negotiate issues of gender inequality. Speaking more generally about the existence of inequalities in the cultural industries – such as low pay or long working hours – Banks and Hesmondhalgh (2009, p. 420) suggest that the highly individualized nature of cultural labour leads to a 'fatalistic' acceptance of inequalities. Indeed, the centrality of neoliberal values and discourses to cultural work – flexibility, autonomy and self-actualization – results in the individualization of risk, with workers tolerating precarity, insecurity and (self-) exploitation for the 'love of the job' (McRobbie, 2002; Banks, 2007). This has particular consequences and unique dynamics when we turn to issues of gender inequality. Gill (2002) writes of the reluctance of new media workers to understand their experience in terms of gender. She identifies the predominance of individualistic and meritocratic discourses which result in an 'unspeakability' of inequalities (see also Gill, 2010; Allen et al., 2012):

> [T]here are clear divergences between men's and women's experiences, and they have no language to make sense of this, except in individualistic terms which inevitably construct women's relative lack of success in terms of individual failure ... Many women buy into this discourse, and individual women can and do succeed. But ultimately its individualism, combined with the 'hip, cool and equal' speak in and about the industry, conceals (and renders difficult to speak of) the serious patterns of inequality that are emerging in this new field.
>
> (Gill, 2002, pp. 85–86)

Gill refers to this 'annihilation' of a vocabulary of inequality as a 'post-feminist problem' (2002, p. 84). Possibilities to critique gender barriers within the cultural sector are curtailed by neoliberal *and* post-feminist discourses of personal autonomy, choice and freedom which frame how individual (female) success can be articulated, performed and understood. In her work on post-feminism, McRobbie (2009) states that young women in late modernity have become reconstituted as 'top girls', positioned as exemplary subjects (2009, p. 72) through an ethos of meritocracy, individualization and competition, achieving in education and the labour market (see also Budgeon, 2001; McRobbie, 2004). However, this capacity is a façade: female 'success' is tightly regulated so as not to challenge the existing gender and (hetero) sexual order. Indeed, McRobbie (2009, p. 82) suggests that the very act of flowing into the labour market as subjects 'with capacity' also provides an occasion for their re-subordination. McRobbie (2009, p. 5) identifies how feminism has been both taken into account and repudiated as no longer necessary or relevant, replaced by an 'aggressive individualism'. This narrow and anodyne language of equality elides broader structural constraints and oppressions, recasting these as individual, private problems to be overcome by hard work, choice and self-determination (see also Walkerdine et al., 2001; Scharff, 2012). I draw on this literature to suggest that the young female aspiring cultural worker is *doubly positioned* by the convergence of post-feminist sensibilities and neoliberal discourses characterizing cultural work more generally (see also Allen, 2008).

Berger, Wardle and Zezulkova (in this volume) identify work placements as an essential aspect of students' preparation for the sector and a 'pedagogically rich' experience. In this chapter and elsewhere (see Allen et al., 2012a) I present an alternative approach to work placements that locates them as a locus of that disciplinary power. I move from a mechanistic view of work placement practices as simply an 'employability practice' to locating work placements as a site of disciplinary practices through which young women are produced and produce themselves as intelligible subjects within a post-feminist and neoliberal climate. I argue that rather than necessarily supporting young women's successful transitions into the cultural economy, HE work placements can be better understood as a realm in which gender (and other) inequalities are (re)produced.

The study

In-depth semi-structured interviews were conducted with HE staff, employers from across the sector, and students from five higher education institutions (HEIs) in England and Wales who had undertaken work placements within the cultural sector. 'Work placements' refer to both placements linked formally to a programme of study to 'extrinsic' placements undertaken in students' 'free' time. In this study these ranged from 'sandwich' placements to internships and placements of several days. Defining cultural occupations is a thorny issue, however this research used the UK government's Department for Culture, Media and Sport's comprehensive definition of the 'creative industries', including sectors ranging from advertising and design through to film and TV (DCMS, 2008).

A total of 26 students participated in the study, enrolled on foundation, under- and postgraduate course within creative arts, media and design disciplines. All belonged to at least one of four key 'equality groups': Black and Minority Ethnic (BME) students, disabled students, working-class students, and students seeking to enter sectors with significant gender imbalance. As discussed above, most sub-sectors of the creative industries have a male majority workforce with the exception of cultural heritage (58% female), visual arts (53%) and designer fashion (50%) (Skillset and Creative and Cultural Skills, 2011). The gender focus of this research was therefore primarily on the experiences of female students who undertook placements in areas of female underrepresentation. In this chapter I focus on the accounts of six female participants (aged between 19 and 25 years old) who undertook placements in 'traditionally' male areas of employment, for example, in creative or technical teams across photography, advertising, film, television and design. Table 11.1 details their biographical information, the sub-sector in which they undertook a work placement and contextual UK labour market data on female representation within this sub-sector and occupational category, where this data is available. To protect the identity of the participating institutions, I have not included the course name on which these participants were enrolled.

Lasting between 45 and 120 minutes, interviews were semi-structured, covering: motivations for undertaking placements; experiences of finding placements and working in the sector; and career plans. Equality issues were approached carefully through probing about specific experiences and questions about potential equality issues using press-cuttings on equality issues within the sector. Some students more readily discussed equality issues than others. Here and elsewhere (Allen et al., 2012a; 2012b.) this hesitancy to identify equality issues is located within the wider context of neoliberal and post-feminist discourses which constrain the possibilities of naming gender (and other) inequalities. Interviews were audio-recorded, transcribed and anonymized.

Table 11.1 Research participants

Name	Demographic information	Placement undertaken	Proportion of women in sub-sector, UK*
Alena	White Eastern European; middle-class	**Photography**: three-week placement with renowned fashion photographer as an assistant with creative team	37% in photo imaging
Amy	White British; middle-class	**Advertising**: two-week placement in creative team of London advertising agency	46% in advertising
Bel	White British; middle-class	**Film**: three-week placement as assistant camera operator with documentary film crew; summer placement on film set with a set design and construction team	42% in film (26% in direction, 5% construction, 9% camera)
Mel	White British; working-class	**Design**: four-week placement at London Design and Advertising agency with creative team	32% in design
Polly	White British; working-class	**TV**: two-month placement as camera assistant on TV production	41% in TV (16% in camera)
Sophia	White mixed heritage; middle-class	**Film**: placements of several weeks as assistant filmmaker on film set; and with the publicity department of international animation company	42% in film (as above)

*Sources: Creative and Cultural Skills (2008); Skillset (2010a); Skillset and Creative and Cultural Skills (2011).

Data were coded and analysed thematically to identify key issues and contextualized using biographical data.

Gender imbalances, infantalization and female 'contamination'

A consistent feature in the young women's accounts was an awareness of gender segregation and hierarchies within their placements and the wider cultural sector. All noted an imbalance in the roles undertaken by men and women and discussed being 'in the minority' within male-dominated teams. For example, Bel, who undertook placements with a set design and construction team on a film set was acutely aware of the male dominance within creative roles and 'top' positions within the film industry:

> Bel: You'll find most women are in make-up or costume. Producer and director – the really important roles – they are *all* male. You see it. And I have heard from successful women who *have* made it, that when they walk on set – they're a producer and an art director – the men will point them to the make-up room! And it's like 'Sorry I am producing this!'

Alena undertook her placement with a 'renowned' fashion photographer, working as an assistant within his small team of creatives:

> Alena: It was very male dominated. Well, in the creative team, where I was, it is men mainly, obviously. His active team in terms of production...all men. I can tell you that in a creative part meaning, working with the camera in broadcast and photographics, anywhere, it's male dominated....The PR team, which means women who communicate, who probably organise him: all female.

There is an interesting rhetorical movement here, with Alena naming the 'obviousness' of the gender segregation, and I return to look critically at this gender awareness later in the chapter. However, what I want to draw attention to here is how the lack of women within 'creative' roles appears to reinforce gendered constructions of the creative person. Thus, Alena's description of the gender split is underlined by a strong binary division between masculine creativity and feminine dispositions for emotion, care and communication.

This construction of the creative person as a masculine subject was not just achieved through the gender divisions in the occupational roles taken up by men and women, but through subtle workplace practices. Mel undertook her placement within a male-dominated creative team at a London design agency and described a privileging of a hard masculinity. Below, Mel described feeling unable to cope with the intensity of the work and sensed that the agency director favoured her male co-workers:

> Mel: The hard work, it's just so committed...there was no talking....I don't know whether that's the difference between male and

female, but I wanted to communicate and bounce ideas but it was just silence.... The guys were quite tough and 'I'm getting on with my work and I don't really want to talk to you'. The men particularly seemed really moody. I think the director preferred boys. I don't know, maybe boys have a stronger personality? Not as emotional? I suppose they think guys are better to deal with the intensity of the work.

Describing her co-workers as moody, silent and utterly committed, Mel's account suggests an equation of ideal creativity with masculine selfishness (Taylor, 2011) which positions feminine emotion and other-directedness as incompatible with creativity and the demands of the sector. For Mel, her desire to communicate with others was experienced as illegitimate, deficit and out of place within the sector's highly individualized working culture. Like others, Mel suggested that women who succeed in the sector must 'act harder' and hide their emotion:

Mel: I do think the women have to act harder. The other woman who worked there, I found her crying once but when I saw her in the office she'd be really intense, cold, robotic... this uber-confident, sleek businesswoman and underneath I saw little bits of doubt, but you have to hide them.

Entering and unsettling these gendered spaces can be risky, inviting suspicion and hostility. Polly, who worked as a camera assistant on a television drama, described her experience as the only woman in the team as a 'fish out of water':

Polly: There were women in the make-up department and wardrobe, but the technical crew like camera, lighting and sound it was all middle-aged men. Then there was little, 19-year-old me. I certainly was a fish out of water.

Polly's description of being a 'fish out of water' is highly evocative of the ways in which young women experience themselves within male-dominated areas of the cultural sector. The term has been used by social theorist Bourdieu to describe the embodied experiences of social class exclusion, for example among working-class students who enter the university – an organizational culture of which they are not a product (Bourdieu and Passerson, 1977). Puwar's more recent work on 'space invaders' (2004) is perhaps more useful in examining the gender exclusions presented in this chapter. Puwar examines what happens when women and ethnic minorities take up privileged positions that have not been reserved for them: in academia, the art world and politics. She suggests that when 'alien' bodies enter spaces in which they have previously been absent they are met with a gaze that 'abnormalises their presence and locates them as belonging elsewhere' (2004, p. 42). These bodies provoke a 'niggling suspicion that they are not quite proper and can't quite cut it' (2004, p. 59). Being the only woman in a male 'space' of the cultural sector not only engendered feelings of alienation and jarring within these young women but also a sense of disorientation among men: the 'natural' inhabitants of that space. Polly, for example, described the questioning looks she received from male colleague as she, like many others, was assumed to have reduced capabilities: 'The camera equipment is usually big and heavy and I felt like sometimes they were looking at me and thinking how can little old me handle it.' Similarly, Bel spoke of male colleagues 'taking pity' on her and taking over, infantilizing practices which put her in her place:

> Bel: There is the attitude of 'we know better, we are men, she doesn't know', of 'ah, let's just sort it out for her, she needs four of them, put them in the box, she doesn't know she needs them yet but we know she does'. So there was that element of construction people taking pity on you and they know best. They just do it.

Interestingly, Bel followed this by pondering whether this attitude of 'we know better' was associated with her being young and a student rather than her gender. In the next section I unpick this hesitancy to name gender discrimination in greater detail.

Discussing the presence of long-established gendered binaries and mind-body dualisms between masculine rationality and feminine emotion which govern entry to professional spheres, Puwar argues that women can be perceived as a threat, representing 'foreign matter that threatens to contaminate the realm of serene, clean thought' (2004, p. 17). This sense of female contamination was present in several participants' accounts, littered with metaphors of war and battle, territories and invasion:

> Alena: Men dominate and it's more difficult for women because once something is male dominated, you have to work really hard... but the infiltration is seen as something that's not that friendly [sic] looked upon.... One woman told me that she went through six

months of hell before she was accepted in the team. They just didn't want her, didn't want a girl there.... I think that there is a little bit of you know, that inner 'ah you're trying to play on a boy's playground, then you're going to play hard' and that's you know. I suppose that's a male nature [laughs]. You just have to go with it because male nature is that once women infiltrate into what is male dominated, men get defensive.

In the rest of this chapter I examine how these young women interpreted and negotiated the gendered culture and practices they encountered. I argue that these responses operate to reinforce rather than challenge gender oppressions and regulatory constraints.

Negotiating gender inequalities: Privatized struggles, 'phallic girls' and mother figures

Participants' responses to the gendered working cultures and hostile practices they encountered within their work placements shared a broad association with post-feminist sensibilities and interpretations that individualize these struggles and result in a retreat from feminist critique. That is to say that while these young women were able to identify particular challenges they faced *as a woman* within a male-dominated space, there were reluctant to name these as discrimination. Rather, they employed a meritocratic discourse of female empowerment and self-determination and were resistant to engage in a critical or politicized analysis of gender within the cultural sector. Bel provides a particularly interesting example of young women's complex negotiation of gender relations within the cultural sector. Earlier we saw how Bel described the clear gender divides within the film industry and the patronizing behaviour of male colleagues who assumed she wasn't up to the job. Later she went on to describe an assignment she wrote comparing women's representation in the film industry in Iran, an Islamic state constructed as oppressive to women, to that within the seemingly more 'progressive' and egalitarian gender regime of America:

> Bel: The last assignment I did was on gender in film. Comparing Iran to Hollywood and it's exactly the same. Who are your crew and who is in charge, there is something like seven per cent women regardless of whether you are in Iran or America.

Despite suggesting an engagement with a critical analysis of gender relations, when asked how she felt about this gender segregation in relation to her own future career trajectory, Bel retreated from any form of critique:

> Interviewer: How do you feel about entering an industry where there is that significant gender imbalance?
> Bel: It doesn't really affect my day-to-day thinking. It doesn't play on my mind or make me think I should join a women's film-making group or something. I don't feel so strongly that I need to shout about it. You just have to get on with it.

Bel was 'gender aware' (Budgeon, 2001), mobilizing a language of feminism and recognizing at some level the differences between men and women's position and power within the industry. Yet, like the participants in Scharff's (2012, p. 51) study of young women's engagements with feminism this gender awareness was relentlessly undone by 'the use of individualistic outlook [that] renders a feminist perspective meaningless'. Caught up in post-feminist and neoliberal discourses of choice and self-determination, Bel disavowed the presence of structural constraints associated with feminist politics or the need for collective struggle in favour of individualized strategies of self-management. Rather than 'shouting about it' she accepted these differences and 'just got on with it', ever more determined to make it in a man's world.

Likewise Polly's account of working in an all-male camera team suggests the presence of laddish working cultures, hostile to female participation. Yet, like Bel, Polly was reluctant to describe these as discriminatory.

> Interviewer: What was it like being amongst middle-aged men?
> Bel: It was a little bit of a shock to the system at first because they're men and some of the jokes they come out with are, you know...
> Interviewer: Did you felt uncomfortable?
> Bel: No. Even though it was a male environment, they'd be joking about but I never felt offended or anything. It was fine.

She went on to suggest that being 'the only girl' can work to her advantage, operating as a 'Unique Selling Point' that will add to her marketability: 'I think the majority of the time it's been an advantage being the only girl because you stand out more'. Through this move, gender as a political category and locus of inequalities is replaced with gender as an individual 'asset' which can be deployed strategically to gain advantage. Structural and systematic gender inequalities are elided, subsumed within individualistic discourses of personal choice and freedom. This became clearer when Polly was asked what could be done to improve female representation within the television industry:

> Polly: I don't think there are enough women in the industry but I don't think it's a case of the industry is being sexist or more diffi-cult for women to get into, I think it's just they don't *think* to go into it...I think it's almost maybe like educating women about all the possibilities that there are...maybe that would change their mind, if they knew more about it.

Thus Polly perceived gender imbalances in the sector not as the outcome of systematic disadvantage but of individual preference and a lack of awareness of these jobs among young women.

These responses illuminate the ways in which wider social forces of neoliberalism and post-feminism, and the normative ideal of the empowered, free and self-determined subject, govern young women's understandings of the significance of gender to shaping access to the cultural sector. As Scharff warns 'if gender ceases to be a category that significantly shapes one's experiences, a critical stance which would involve some recognition of gender – and its intersections with class, race, and sexuality – as a structuring principle becomes difficult to think and articulate' (2012, p. 51). We must, however, also locate these responses within the specific context of the cultural industries where highly individualized working practices and a deep attachment to an image of the industry as liberal, egalitarian and inclusive mean that forms of collective organizing, anti-discriminatory policies or a language of structural inequality are viewed as 'inappropriate hangovers' from the old economy (Banks and Milestone, 2011, p. 79; see also Oakley, Noonan and Lee in this volume for the decreasing power of collective bargaining and the unions).

Post-feminist discourses of female empowerment not only foreclose the possibility of collective political action but also actively reinforce gender hierarchies and oppressions. This can be seen in another set of responses. Participants felt that in order to succeed, both in the work placement and in the sector more generally, women need to be more determined and driven than their male counterparts. However, this had to be carefully managed: participants described a highly enter-prising and strategic performance of femininity as a way of navigating and tempering male hostility. For example, Amy undertook a two-week compulsory placement at a London advertising agency, working within an all-male creative team. For Amy, proving your worth within a male-dominated space demanded self-determination and assertiveness. However, while she felt she had to work harder to be recognized within the creative team, this had to be carefully managed:

> Amy: It's a bloodthirsty, competitive business, you have to be assertive but that's easier for men. Women who are angry get seen as hysterical because it isn't ladylike, whereas for men it's seen as attractive, so it was hard to get my voice heard.

Amy's description of the impossibilities of women enacting anger or aggression within the advertising sector powerfully resonates with Nixon's (2003) work on gender and advertising cultures in which he identifies the perilous landscape in which female advertising creative operate. He argues that female employees' attempts to 'fit in' with their male counterparts by being brash, loud and 'laddish' were complicated by contradictory demands and expectations of normative femininity that deemed such behaviour as inappropriate. He suggests that women within professional 'creative' roles were either constituted as lacking rationality ('eccentric'), or as so hyperbolically masculine (the 'ball-breaker') they pose no threat to the normative ideal. Amy's evocation of the hysterical and eccentric female advertising creative also recalls the 'fearsome models of female authority' – the witch, bitch or school matron – which McDowell (1997, p. 152) identifies in her work on gender identities in the city. To succeed, young women must achieve the fine balance between coming forward as powerful women and maintaining adherence to (heterosexual) gender regimes: 'performing in a male outfit but retaining one's so-called femininity' (Puwar, 2004, p. 148). To be too assertive is to risk being seen as unfeminine and/or a feminist.

Post-feminist sensibilities and articulations of female agency are central to this regulation of femininity within the workplace. Sophia and Alena's accounts of navigating male hostility are particularly illuminating:

> Sophia: What do you need to make it as a woman in this industry? Balls... You have to go with all guns blazing, otherwise men think they know better. But another mistake that women make is they think they need to be aggressive to get what they need. But when a woman's aggressive it scares the shit out of men so it doesn't necessarily work. But not being aggressive doesn't mean being slutty. It means just trying to be on the same par, going on an intellectual

level... So, you choose your battles. If you go in there, really, *really* all guns blazing people, especially women, it won't get anywhere.

Alena: You have to play hard but you also use what you've learned as a woman [about] communication with men... For example, one [male colleague] was very macho, one was a lady's man, so you flatter them, find your way of communicat[ing] with them... For women who want to make it in this sector, I think you do have to turn on 'alpha male' behaviour.

Sophia and Alena's accounts resonate with normative subject positions McRobbie (2009) argues operate as technologies of governance under post-feminism, specifically the 'Phallic Girl' and 'Post-feminist masquerade'. While McRobbie posits these as alternative positions, I argue that Sophia and Alena are carefully alternating between them as they seek to survive within the cultural sector. Thus, in becoming *like* a man – 'needing balls' and turning on 'alpha-male' behaviour – they are enacting the post-feminist 'capacity to become phallus-bearers as a kind of licensed mimicry of their male counterparts' (McRobbie, 2009, p. 83). Yet this enactment of masculine power is a pretence: so as to defuse any threat to masculine hegemony – to come over as too competitive and 'scare the shit out of men' – Sophia and Alena must offset this performance of assertive masculinity with an attractive, desirable and sexually available (but not *too* available) femininity. In these ways they are also enacting the 'post-feminist masquerade' required of young women within the world of work from which they were previously excluded:

> She takes up her place in the labour market and she enjoys her status as a working girl without going too far. She must retain a visible fragility and the displaying of a conventional feminine vulnerability will ensure she remains desirable to men.
>
> (McRobbie, 2009, p. 79)

These enterprising and strategic practices of negotiation represent the very thin tightrope that young women must walk if they are to succeed within the cultural sector. They can be seen as 'compromising acts' (McRobbie, 2009, p. 72) through which the performance of female capacity is always tightly regulated so that existing gender hierarchies remain unchallenged.[3]

A final response articulated by these young women was the identification of informal female mentors within their placements. Each spoke about seeking out and befriending established female workers, women 'survivors' who provided a template for how to progress in a 'man's world'. Some also discussed female academics at their institutions in a similar way. Many suggested that it was easier to confide in these women or ask them for help, than to seek support from men. This reflects other research suggesting that having female 'role models' is a key factor in women's success in the cultural sector (Skillset, 2009). However, while providing inspiration, advice and encouragement, this informal mechanism of supporting aspiring female workers within the cultural sector is itself problematic. In playing the 'unofficial mother figure' (Banks and Milestone, 2011), these female 'mentors' are placed back within the traditional gendered division of labour which militate against the achievement of more gender equal work-based relations. Undertaking this emotional labour ultimately reinforces gendered binaries of the creative person and its Other, thus restabalizing oppressive gender relations within the cultural sector.

Discussion: Breaking the silence – the challenge for higher education

It would be easy for those working in HE to assume that gender inequalities do not exist within the cultural sector: the female majority within the student population on courses aligned with the sector: suggests that these young women are 'Top Girls', set to succeed within the cultural economy. Yet this chapter illustrates the need to look more critically at how gender inequalities play out across the student experience – including preparation for employment – and in subtle forms. HE work placements are significant on a number of levels: not only do they support young people's employability in an overcrowded labour market, these formative experiences powerfully shape students' self-perceptions of where they belong and of what she must do if she is to 'make it' as a cultural worker. It is essential that we take these experiences seriously if we are to achieve a more diverse workforce: while Sophia and Alena were determined to survive these hostile territories, others felt differently. As a result of her experiences, Mel felt she simply 'couldn't hack it': concluding 'I guess I just didn't have tough enough skin'. Mel explained that she was considering a change of career paths.

I have argued that despite being 'gender aware', gender inequalities remain unspeakable for these young women. Reflecting on her own work, Gill (2002) argues that her respondents' reluctance to name gender inequalities presents a dilemma for researchers. She asks, as feminist scholars, 'how can we simultaneously take seriously and accord respect to the respondents' accounts?' (2002, p. 85). As a feminist researcher I too encountered a series of dilemmas, often lived out when interviewing these women, where I wanted to respect their own interpretations while simultaneously creating a space for them to speak the unspeakable – that negative experiences were not simply the result of personal failings but rather rooted in wider systematic inequalities and exclusions.

For female students, indeed all students who are aspiring to carve out a career within the cultural sector, speaking of unsatisfactory or discriminatory experiences can be risky, especially when one's future livelihood is at risk. Furthermore, in the cultural sector where self-exploitation is a badge of honour, speaking of inequalities can provoke accusation of weakness: to break ranks and speak out can be seen as a taboo, a renegade act (Puwar, 2004). Acts of naming need force behind them, they must be 'taken strategically and with the support of advocates who carry weight' (2004, p. 155). HE practitioners have a duty to break the silence and provide a space in which inequalities within the cultural sector – the darker side of its utopian image – can be named. As various chapters in this volume suggest, this critical engagement within the academy must not only address gender inequalities but other forms of exclusion within the sector related to social class, 'race', disability and sexuality. Indeed, as Lee argues, rather than being complicit in the (re)production of wider inequalities, HE must stimulate an 'ethic of cultural work' that challenges the very practices, norms and values that exclude some students from 'making it' in the sector.

Based on the findings of this research, toolkits were produced.[4] These provided practical recommendations for how HEIs could address inequalities in student work placements. These included recommendations to provide clearer guidance on students' legal rights, collecting monitoring data to identify inequalities, and suggestions for how HEIs can create a space for students to share their experiences, for example, by developing a core module on equality and diversity issues in the cultural sector. It may be fruitful for HE practitioners to look outside their own departments for expertise when creating and delivering such a module; for example working with Equality and Diversity staff within the university; or with academic staff working in other disciplines and attending critically to issues of equality, diversity and social justice, such as sociology. Growing discontents with the exploitation of students and graduates across the labour market, including the cultural sector, are being galvanized through the work of a number of campaigning organizations.[5] HEI staff could facilitate students' engagement with such collectivist forms of action so that practices of exploitation, discrimination and inequality within the industry might be challenged.

While these steps can help produce a climate in which the university – and the HE practitioner – can challenge rather than reproduce these inequalities, there are constraints. Addressing systematic inequalities in the cultural sector cannot be achieved by HE alone, but requires the commitment of the industry, a task easier said than done. Further, asking HE staff to transform their practices in the ways I have suggested might conflict with other agendas that they are working with and under within an increasingly market-driven HE system, such as boosting student employability and engaging industry.[6] Relatedly, just as 'speaking out' poses risks for students, it may also create dilemmas for staff charged with this work, who might be accused by employers, colleagues or at an institutional level of being trouble-makers or 'feminist killjoys' (Ahmed, 2010; see also Allen et al., 2012). It is also crucial that such 'equality' work isn't simply taken on by female HE staff. This would not only replicate the gendered binaries and labours discussed above in relation to the cultural sector but also those operating in the academy more generally where female academics are often expected to perform pastoral roles of nurturer, carer and 'mother' (Lester, 2008). Furthermore, Noonan (in this volume) identifies other important challenges: not only may some students be resistant to these critical engagements, finding them unpalatable, HE practitioners also tread a precarious path between delivering critical perspectives about the difficult realities of cultural work, and continuing to nurture students' 'childlike wonder' and enthusiasm for the sector.

That said, gender inequalities within the cultural economy should not be simply accepted or ignored. Borrowing from Butler (1997), McRobbie (2009) writes of the 'illegible rage' as a predominant feature of post-feminism, the interiorization of the female complaint. McRobbie claims that the impossibility for critiquing masculine hegemony has resulted in a variety of discontents and disorders which bubbles beneath the surface of contemporary femininities. I argue that both feminist scholars and HE practitioners have a duty to find ways of making (gender) inequalities legible; to provide a vocabulary and space for students through which they can be identified and critiqued rather than turned back on oneself. I offer this chapter as a contribution to that project.

Author's Note

I would like to thank the ECU, who funded this research, as well as the participants who shared their experiences. I am extremely grateful to Professor Jocey Quinn, Sumi Hollingworth and Dr Anthea Rose who contributed significantly to the research this chapter draws on. I would also like to thank Christina Scharff, Bridget Conor, Tamsyn Dent, Ros Gill and Angela McRobbie for conversations that have informed my thinking on gender and the pains and pleasures of creative labour.

Notes

1. For example, in 2010, Skillset signed up to the UK Resource Centre's (UKRC) Charter to tackle gender imbalance in technology jobs in the sector (Skillset, 2010b). The 'Cultural Leadership' programme sought to support women in reaching high-level positions (see Holden and McCarthy, 2007).
2. ECU works, with financial support from the government, to promote equality and diversity for staff and students in higher education in the UK www.ecu .ac.uk.
3. Elsewhere (Allen et al., 2012a), I identify how the performance of gender within the cultural sector workplace is complicated by class due to the historical positioning of working-class femininity through pathologizing discourses of excessive sexuality. The heteronormative injunctions underlying these post-feminist 'acts' are also a point of exclusion and demand further exploration.
4. See http://www.ecu.ac.uk/publications/diversity-equality-and-access-toolkits
5. Examples include http://carrotworkers.wordpress.com/ and the work of Interns Anonymous and BECTU http://internsanonymous.co.uk/2010/03/13/shooting-yourself-in-the-foot/#more-1214.
6. See Allen et al. 2012b for discussion of HE staff and employer perspectives on equality issues in student work placements.

References

Adkins, L. (1999) Community and Economy: A Retraditionalization of Gender? *Theory, Culture and Society* 16(1): 117–137.

Ahmed, S. (2010) *The Promise of Happiness* (Durham: Duke University Press).

Allen, K. (2008) *Young Women and the Performing Arts: Creative Education, New Labour and the Remaking of the Young Female Self*, Unpublished doctoral thesis (London: Goldsmiths, University of London).

Allen, K., Quinn, J., Hollingworth, S. and Rose, A. (2010) *Work Placements in the Arts and Cultural Sector: Diversity, Equality and Access. A Report for the Equality Challenge Unit* (London: Equality Challenge Unit).

Allen, K., Quinn, J., Hollingworth, S. and Rose, A. (2012a) Becoming Employable Students and 'Ideal' Creative Workers: Exclusion and Inequality in Higher Education Work Placements, *British Journal of Sociology of Education* 34(3): 431–452.

Allen, K., Quinn, J., Hollingworth, S. and Rose, A. (2012b) Doing Diversity and Evading Equality: The Case of Student Work Placements in the Creative Sector, in Taylor, Y. (ed.) *Educational Diversity: The Subject of Difference and Different Subjects* (London: Palgrave Macmillan): 180–200.

Ashton, D. (2011) Media Work and the Creative Industries: Identity Work, Professionalism and Employability, *Education + Training* 53(6): 546–560.

Banks, M. (2007) *The Politics of Cultural Work* (Basingstoke: Palgrave).

Banks, M. and Milestone, K. (2011) Individualization, Gender and Cultural Work, *Gender, Work and Organisation* 18(1): 73–89.

Banks, M. and Hesmondhalgh, D. (2009) Looking for Work in Creative Industries Policy, *International Journal of Cultural Policy* 15(4): 415–430.

Bourdieu, P. and Passeron, J.C. (1977) *Reproduction in Education, Society and Culture* (London: Sage).

Budgeon, S. (2001) Emergent Feminist(?) Identities: Young Women and the Practice of Micropolitics, *The European Journal of Women's Studies* 8(1): 7–28.

Butler, J. (1997) *The Psychic Life of Power: Theories in Subjection* (Stanford: Stanford University Press).

Creative and Cultural Skills (2008) *Creative and Cultural Industry: Impact and Footprints 08–09* (London: Creative & Cultural Skills).

Department for Culture Media and Sport (DCMS) (2008) *Creative Britain: New Talents for a New Economy* (London: Department for Culture, Media and Sport).

Equality Challenge Unit (ECU) (2011) *Equality in Higher Education: Statistical Report 2011* (London: Equality Challenge Unit).

Gill, R. (2002) Cool, Creative and Egalitarian? Exploring Gender in Project-Based New Media Work in Euro, *Information, Communication & Society* 5(1): 70–78.

Gill, R. (2010) 'Life Is a Pitch': Managing the Self in New Media Work, in Deuze, M. (ed.) *Managing Media Work* (London: Sage): 249–262.

Holden, J. and McCarthy, H. (2007) *Women at the Top: A Provocation Piece* (London: City University).

Lester, J. (2008) Performing Gender in the Workplace: Gender Socialization, Power, and Identity Among Women Faculty Members, *Community College Review* 35(4): 277–305.

Marcella, R., Baxter, G. and Illingworth, L. (2006) *Women in the Creative Industries* (London: European Social Fund).

McDowell, L. (1997) *Capital Culture: Gender and Work in the City* (Oxford: Blackwell).

McRobbie, A. (2002) Fashion Culture: Creative Work, Female Individualization, *Feminist Review* 71(1): 52–62.

McRobbie, A. (2004) Post-Feminism and Popular Culture, *Feminist Media Studies* 4(3): 255–264.

McRobbie, A. (2009) *The Aftermath of Feminism: Gender, Culture and Social Change* (London: Sage).

Nixon, S. (2003) *Advertising Cultures: Gender, Commerce and Creativity* (London: Sage).

Nixon, S. and Crewe, B. (2004) Pleasure at Work? Gender, Consumption and Work-based Identities in the Creative Industries, *Consumption Markets & Culture* 7(2): 129–147.

Puwar, N. (2004) *Space Invaders: Race, gender and bodies out of place* (Oxford: Berg).

Scharff, C. (2012). *Repudiating Feminism: Young Women in a Neoliberal World* (Farnham: Ashgate).

Skillset (2006) *Employment Census 2006: The Results of the Sixth Census of the Audio Visual Industries* (London: Skillset).

Skillset (2009) *Why Her? Factors That Have Influenced the Careers of Successful Women in Film and Television* (London: Skillset and Women in Film and Television).

Skillset (2010a) *Women in the Creative Media Industries Report* (London: Skillset).

Skillset (2010b) *Skillset Commits to Tackling Gender Inequality by Signing Charter*, http://www.skillset.org/skillset/press/2010/article_7967_1.asp, date accessed 20 July 2012.

Skillset and Creative and Cultural Skills (2011) *Sector Skills Assessment for the Creative Industries of the UK* (London: Skillset).

Taylor, S.J. (2011) Negotiating Oppositions and Uncertainties: Gendered Conflicts in Creative Identity Work, *Feminism and Psychology* 21(3): 354–371.

Walkerdine, V., Lucey, H. and Melody, J. (2001) *Growing Up Girl: Psychosocial Explorations of Gender and Class* (Basingstoke: Palgrave).

Willis, J. and Dex, S. (2003) Mothers Returning to Television Production in a Changing Environment, in Beck, A. (ed.) *Cultural Work: Understanding the Cultural Industries* (London: Routledge): 121–141.

Afterword: Further and Future Directions for Cultural Work and Higher Education

Daniel Ashton and Caitriona Noonan

Cultural Work and Higher Education aims to explore the intersections between, on the one hand, higher education (HE) policy and practice and, on the other, cultural and creative work. To do this successfully it brings together perspectives from a range of disciplines (including media, psychology, sociology and labour studies) with contributions engaging with student, staff, graduate and practitioner experiences of cultural work. Across the volume, empirical contributions include statistical analysis of creative education and employment experiences and qualitative exchanges with: students at undergraduate and post-graduate levels; HE lecturers with responsibility for work placements; HE lecturers who develop their practice across industry and HE; and industry professionals at various stages of their career. Attending directly to an overlooked area of scholarship on cultural work, this volume explores the kinds of intersections, overlaps and relationships that are now firmly established in the current HE landscape.

To end this volume we are careful not to prescribe rigid solutions for the issues raised here, mainly as these are unlikely to take adequate account of the complexity of the intersections and challenges documented in this volume, or fully acknowledge the difficulty of implementing generic proposals in an education, policy or industry environment. Therefore, the following sections are more modest in their aims, identifying several common themes across the contributions and signposting some of the potentially new agendas for scholarship on cultural work which could productively inform and shape HE, policy-making and employer practice. We hope that by doing this we continue the kind of debate which we invited in the introduction and, with greater urgency, that academic staff, policy-makers and creative prac-titioners will then be able to formulate their own more contextualized interventions.

Critical conversations

It is clear from the various policies and literature discussed in the introduction that HE plays a vital part in the growth and success of the cultural and creative industries. Matheson (2006, p. 62) characterizes this relationship as a 'virtuous cycle' in the way that each reinforces the development of the other. However, while for many these relationships may be desirable and indeed necessary it also raises challenges; how can dialogues about change take place and is there a 'safe' way to have these conversations? Across this volume the various contributors highlight the need for critical conversations to take place. For instance, in the opening chapter Oakley signals forms of critical engagement in relation to internships through the number of campaigning organizations, such as the Carrot Workers Collective, who are raising awareness of working conditions and pay and developing different employment models. Oakley's chapter considers some of the tensions between the individual and cultural work labour markets and brings to the fore how structural challenges and issues of inequalities must be part of HE curriculum from the classroom to the work placement.

Gendered experiences of cultural work and resulting inequalities feature in the contributions from both Taylor and Littleton and Allen. Allen's reference to cross-institution and inter-disciplinary connections for developing course curricula indicates how issues of equality and diversity might be foregrounded. Her closing call to HE practitioners to make inequalities legible firmly connects with the overall commitment of this volume of widening conservations on cultural work and HE. Equally for Saha, teaching within HE is an opportunity to encourage students from minority backgrounds to enter the cultural industries and make their own productions that feature narratives and characters that challenge reductive representations of racial difference. Beyond this encouragement for students to present alternatives, Saha also points to the role of HE as a critical space for addressing the reification of difference within production processes and providing the resources and safe environment for self-reflective work. Saha's suggestions on using extant literature on cultural work and the experiences of industry practitioners as resources for students to explore career choices resonates across this volume, and next steps in this direction could focus on sharing and evaluating curriculum development resources.

While these critical conversations are widely acknowledged as important, and some of the contributions have suggested practical resources (e.g. Allen points to the work placement toolkit with practical recommendations on how HEIs could address inequalities in student work placements), a number of considerations and challenges are also raised by the contributors particularly around whether embedded structural issues of cultural work can be simply eradicated by a process of unmasking and demythologizing. Noonan addresses the positions, priorities and investments of HE students in relation to their creative education and future career and from this she considers how one of the main challenges for researchers and teachers is how to balance this enthusiasm for the future with an understanding of some of the uncomfortable realities of the industry. Again, the issue of subjectivity in student/creative worker identity and experience conditions this engagement. Equally, Ashton's chapter highlights the challenges that industry practitioners may face in communicating workforce issues they have experienced and where they see these fitting within teaching and learning. Moreover, for Lee, the capacity for HE to present a space of critique is undermined by the hegemonic project of neoliberalism and the marketization of HE. Set within his discussion of cultural networks and social mobility, Lee asks whether HE can stimulate an 'ethic of cultural work' that challenges stereotypes of the ideal-type creative worker.

Theory and practice

The vocational tradition in media education has a long history yet it is often considered a poor relation (Durant, 1991). As Durant (1991, p. 415) argues, 'this is the case not only literally (in that it is widely underresourced), it is sometimes also thought to be tainted by its closeness to professional training for the industry, and with the development of instrumental "skills" rather than those of critique'. However, one of the most visible changes in the teaching and curriculum development of creative disciplines has been the involvement of staff and pedagogy which crosses the boundaries of 'theory' and 'practice' (Thornham and O'Sullivan, 2004, p. 733). As a result we see across the chapters a blurring of the 'academic' and the 'vocational' confines, and a fluctuation between 'subject-specific' and 'transferable' (Thornham and O'Sullivan, 2004, p. 734).

While recognizing the critical attention paid to work placements, Berger et al. highlight how the work placement has been an integral part of many media programmes in HE for decades. They argue for it as a valuable learning experience in the creative industries; students make invaluable contacts, gain 'real world' experiences and it can lead to full-time employment. However, for it to be truly successful institutional resources and additional forms of support for reflection are needed. The possibilities of moving from a narrow employer-led, instrumental work placement agenda are outlined here and can be usefully reflected upon in conjunction with questions of identity and equality raised by Lee and Allen.

Naudin's discussion of enterprise is also located as part of a productive merging of theory and practice. In this respect, she considers a comment made by one of her research participants around the risks of cultural work and argues that this can only be truly resolved through reflection on practice. Efforts to connect with the experiences, priorities and goals of aspiring cultural workers find common ground across the volume. The concerns and investments of students are highlighted by Pollard as students reflect on and evaluate their HE experiences in light of their career aims. While this chapter is primarily concerned with individual journeys and the individual dispositions required for successful creative careers, with questions of structure (as raised by Oakley and Lee) covered only indirectly, Pollard also states the importance of reflection on practice as articulated by students themselves.

The merging of reflective theorization and ongoing practice is not confined to students. Ashton suggests that teacher practitioners, in moving from working full-time in the cultural and creative industries to teaching in HE, may be positioned to understand students' career aspirations and to connect critical debates and issues of social justice with these. This concern for exploring how critical debates on cultural work can be made meaningful connects with HE and government priorities on employability. Specifically, Ashton seeks to extend the discussion beyond securing employment to the realities of cultural work. The diverse backgrounds and continued relationships that teacher practitioners have with industry mean that a shared understanding of (academic) critiques on cultural work cannot be assumed and greater connections with industry campaigns may be a way to bridge this gap (Saundry et al., 2006; Bectu, 2013).

Methods and methodologies

We have seen research that engages both inside (Luckman, Berger, Noonan, Naudin, Allen and Saha) and beyond (Pollard, Lee, Taylor and Littleton) the academy, which highlights the range of research sites available and the distinctive insights that may be generated through each of these. The arguments forwarded in this volume are based on a diverse set of methods and methodologies and taken as a whole the volume assembles both statistical and qualitative data.

Pollard's chapter provides the kind of wide-ranging research into student experiences necessary for understanding the complexities of how students might, or might not, 'make their way' as cultural workers. This chapter provides a detailed empirical platform and evidence base through which critical conversations on cultural work and HE may draw. The data Pollard presents was generated through large-scale inquiry, with qualitative research presented elsewhere across the volume employing smaller scale samples. As such, this volume provides a resource for investigating cultural work at a range of different sites and scales. In addressing the meeting points between working in the cultural and creative industries and HE, new methodological possibilities can emerge. This can include facilitating student research into cultural work, as indicated by one of the teacher practitioners Ashton spoke to, and making a shift from students as research participants to research partners (see Jenkins and Healey, 2009).

A commitment to new methodologies for researching worker subjectivities is evident in Taylor and Littleton's chapter and their cross-disciplinary approach to using a qualitative analytic method based on narrative and discursive psychology. Alongside the other methods used across this volume, this chapter helps to foreground how creative identities exist as multifaceted, dynamic and often inconsistent objects of study. Moreover, the diverse voices and stories provided across the volume indicate the need for nuanced accounts of ideology and subjectivity; while some students may be put off by some of the structural issues in the industry, others will not and will welcome them as part of the appeal of creative work.

Competition and co-operation

In connecting cultural work and HE, it is possible to identify contrasting moments of competition and co-operation. In terms of co-operation, Pollard references the industry-valued aptitude for gaining experience of team working through projects and assessments. Addressing co-operation between HEIs and graduates, Taylor and Littleton consider the continuing importance of art colleges in supporting alumni and suggest that such support can extend from those with educational difficulties to social categories under-represented in the wider cultural workforce. Alongside pastoral support in helping to develop confidence, Taylor and Littleton raise the importance of professional networks. These are highlighted less in terms of employment opportunities, and more as a means of moving away from the Romantic image of the individual maker to appreciating the similar interests and difficulties of 'connected creatives' (a view reiterated in Lee's chapter).

A further strand around co-operation comes with Luckman's exploration of classrooms and teams with an international composition, and the enhanced opportunities for students to develop global understanding and potential forms of solidarity. Questions of solidarity and the globalizing trends of creative and cultural industries workforces that Luckman outlines might be considered through Mayer's (2011) examination of television producers and the reliance on the invisible labour of 'non-creatives', such as television set assemblers, and Miller's (2011) examination of the New International Division of Labour. In doing so, a platform may be laid for students to situate their own individual abilities and position within wider cultural workforce labour markets, and appreciate issues of over-supply (Comunian et al., 2011) at a global scale and the hierarchies and inequalities of global cultural production.

In outlining the opportunities of the global classroom, Luckman also notes the networking insights and experiences that may be gained. Taylor and Littleton's comments on support and common difficulties help demonstrate how HE presents transitional spaces in which students and graduates are acutely aware of competing against each other in a labour market characterized by over-supply while also being surrounded by those that most intimately understand shared pressures and anxieties (see also Christopherson, 2009; Lee, this volume). In the rivalry for limited resources, competition becomes a pronounced aspect of the student experience. This can be seen in competition for work placement positions and internships, and how students might be advantaged or disadvantaged through social capital (Lee) and gender norms (Allen).

Future research

The distinctive perspectives of those participating in this volume reveal that any agenda for preparing students to 'work in industry' needs to attend to cultural labour market conditions and cultural workforce issues at various scales (e.g. geographic and industrial) and across the diversity of backgrounds and identity positions occupied by students, teachers and practitioners. It further challenges the homogenous view of cultural industries and creative labour markets, stretching our understanding of the sector and how HE can effectively contribute to that diverse group of industries. While this volume has addressed a range of areas there are still gaps evident in this field which need to be researched through sustained, structured and critical analysis. These include:

- Developing better understanding of the ways in which attitudes towards cultural work are constructed by students and teaching staff in dialogue with established cultural workers. For students making the transition to labour markets, there are a range of contact points including guest speaker talks, project briefs, work placement experiences and increasingly, accreditation of courses from external bodies. These dialogues were widely valued by students in various chapters (see Pollard, Noonan, Berger this volume) but how do these impact on the relationships forged between students, academic staff and industry professionals and does it allow for appropriate critical space to be established?
- As a means of facilitating the critical discussions needed, what experimentations in teaching and learning practices are possible, and indeed necessary. As Berger and McDougall (2012) argue, this will need to take into consideration *what* we teach as the boundaries between various forms of cultural production become blurred, and also *how* we teach perhaps prompting new academic structures and systems which better reflect contemporary cultural production.
- Having identified the relationships and critical discussions between HE and established cultural workers as a research priority, care must be taken to not overlook the ideological positions through which 'critical debate' is understood. For instance, the operation of different academic agendas and ideological positions is illustrated by Hartley et al. (2013) in their outline of a 'pro' versus 'anti' impasse on questions of working conditions. Moving specifically to teaching and learning relationships, Buckingham (1986, p. 93) stresses that critical questioning should not be seen as something that only applies to students, and 'the analysis teachers introduce must be seen, not as neutral tools for the acquisition of knowledge, but as themselves ideological'. In this way, the perspectives from contributors highlighted above and the ongoing discussions that we hope will follow would benefit from explicit reflection on what positions HE practitioners are 'encouraging' students to critically address and why.
- As outlined earlier, this is a crucial moment of change in HE in which the financial burden of education is shifted to the individual.

Providing empirical data on the impact of this structural change and the socio-political reframing of HE is essential, especially in terms of entry routes into the cultural and creative industries. In keeping with the aim of this volume, issues of inequality and exclusion must also be examined in terms of HE's position, for example, in potentially exclusionary admissions procedures (Burke and McManus, 2011) and work placement inequalities (Allen et al., 2012).

- Alongside issues of financial means, critical exploration must remain attentive to other 'silences' and inequalities in the cultural and creative industries. For example, does the emergence of geographically defined creative hubs (Comunian et al., 2011) and associated 'creative cities' (Florida, 2002) exclude or marginalize certain groups and backgrounds?
- The focus of this volume has been predominantly on the British experience of cultural work and HE and it is clear to the editors and contributors that further examination of global contexts is necessary, in particular as policies and modes of intervention become transnational and as models for education and training are taken up elsewhere. A comparison of creative curricula and graduate experiences across different national contexts will provide important creative employment and pedagogic trends.
- One of the most pressing priorities (and one which we attempted to address but which needs much larger-scale attention) relates to the diversity of student pathways. Along with graduates coming from creative degree programmes (see Ball et al., 2010), graduates from business and traditional humanities subjects such as English and history continue to establish careers in the creative industries. What different roles are available, what differences occur in their career trajectories, and what impact will this have on cultural production and the development of different industries such as television, film, journalism and so on?
- Longitudinal studies which are methodologically diverse are surprisingly lacking in this field of scholarship. Furthermore, when the subjects are creative professionals it seems intuitive to apply innovative methods to facilitate a critical discussion of their identity formation and experiences.

Across this volume different interventions are signalled in terms of the policies that might be realized, the teaching and learning environments and practices that can be developed, and the working practices and conditions that may be strived for. The introductory chapter opened by asking 'what is at stake' when cultural work and HE become entwined, and the contributions made across this volume highlight how much is at stake for the development of the cultural and creative industries in stimulating social commentary and artistic experimentation, and ensuring a rich and meaningful working life for its workers. In addressing this, contributors agree that a wider community of educators, workers, students, policy-makers and activists needs to come together to influence this domain. As the first critical examination of the relationship between HE and cultural work, we believe this volume to be a resource for stimulating debate in ways that can inform teaching and learning practices and help in developing new visions, forms of collaboration and agendas for change.

References

Allen, K., Quinn, J., Hollingworth, S. and Rose, A. (2012) Becoming Employable Students and 'Ideal' Creative Workers: Exclusion and Inequality in Higher Education Work Placements, *British Journal of Sociology of Education* 34(3): 431–452.

Ball, L., Pollard, E. and Stanley, N. (2010) *Creative Graduates Creative Futures* (Brighton: Creative Graduates Creative Futures Higher Education Partnership and the Institute for Employment Studies).

BECTU (2013) Campaign Underway in Support of Factual TV Workers, *Say No to Exploitation in TV*, BECTU, http://www.bectu.org.uk/news/1693 date accessed 22 February 2013.

Berger, R. and McDougall, J. (2012) What Is Media Education For? *Media Education Research Journal* 3(1): 5–20.

Buckingham, D. (1986) Against Demystification: A Response to Teaching the Media, *Screen* 27(5): 80–95.

Burke, P.J. and McManus, J. (2011) Art for a Few: Exclusions and Misrecognitions in Higher Education Admissions Practices, *Discourse: Studies in the Cultural Politics of Education* 32(5): 699–712.

Christopherson, S. (2009) Working in the Creative Economy: Risk, Adaptation and the Persistence of Exclusionary Networks, in McKinlay, A. and Smith,C. (eds) *Creative Labour: Working in the Creative Industries* (Basingstoke: Palgrave Macmillan): 72–90.

Comunian, R., Faggian, A. and Jewell, S. (2011) Winning and Losing in the Creative Industries: An Analysis of Creative Graduate's Career Opportunities across Creative Disciplines, *Cultural Trends* 20(3–4): 291–308.

Durant, A. (1991) Noises Offscreen: Could a Crisis of Confidence be Good for Media Studies? *Screen* 32(4): 407–428.

Florida, R. (2002) *The Rise of the Creative Class: And How It's Transforming Work, Leisure, Community and Everyday Life* (New York: BasicBooks).

Hartley, J., Potts, J., Cunningham, S., Flew, T., Keane, M. and Banks, J. (2013) *Key Concepts in Creative Industries* (London: SAGE).

Jenkins, A. and Healey, M. (2009) *Developing Undergraduate Research and Inquiry* (York: Higher Education Academy).

Matheson, B. (2006) A Culture of Creativity: Design Education and the Creative Industries, *Journal of Management Development* 25(1): 55–64.

Mayer, V. (2011) *Below the Line: Producers and Production Studies in the New Television Economy* (London: Duke University Press).

Miller, T. (2011) The New International Division of Cultural Labour, in Deuze, M. (ed.) *Managing Media Work* (Los Angeles, London, New Delhi, Singapore and Washington DC: Sage): 87–99.

Saundry, R., Stuart, M. and Antcliff, V. (2006) 'It's More Than Who You Know' – Networks and Trade Unions in the Audio-Visual Industries, *Human Resource Management Journal* 16(4): 376–392.

Thornham, S. and O'Sullivan, T. (2004) Chasing the Real: 'Employability' and the Media Studies Curriculum, *Media Culture Society* 26(5): 717–736.

Index

Printed and bound by CPI Group (UK) Ltd, Croydon, CR0 4YY